RUSSIA

WHAT EVERYONE NEEDS TO KNOW®

RUSSIA

WHAT EVERYONE NEEDS TO KNOW®

TIMOTHY J. COLTON

OXFORD
UNIVERSITY PRESS

OXFORD
UNIVERSITY PRESS

Oxford University Press is a department of the University of Oxford. It furthers the University's objective of excellence in research, scholarship, and education by publishing worldwide. Oxford is a registered trade mark of Oxford University Press in the UK and certain other countries.

"What Everyone Needs to Know" is a registered trademark of Oxford University Press.

Published in the United States of America by Oxford University Press 198 Madison Avenue, New York, NY 10016, United States of America.

CIP data is on file at the Library of Congress
ISBN 978-0-19-991779-2 (pbk.)—ISBN 978-0-19-991780-8 (hbk.)

3 5 7 9 8 6 4 2
Paperback printed by Webcom Inc., Canada
Hardback printed by Bridgeport National Bindery, Inc.,
United States of America

CONTENTS

LIST OF MAPS

LIST OF MAPS

ACKNOWLEDGMENTS

I am grateful to David McBride of Oxford University Press for commissioning this project and for his guidance throughout. I thank Harvard's Department of Government and its Davis Center for Russian and Eurasian Studies for a rich intellectual environment and steady logistical support. Ideas and inspiration have come, in a sedimentary process, from colleagues I have been lucky enough to engage in a variety of collaborations and dialogues: Vladislav Zubok, Lucan Way, Alexandra Vacroux (who also gets a gold star for organizational sustenance), Daniel Treisman, Kathryn Stoner, Lilia Shevtsova, Richard Sakwa, Thomas Remington, Serhii Plokhy, Nikolai Petrov, Olga Onuch, Andrei Melvil, Michael McFaul, Fyodor Lukyanov, Robert Legvold, Alena Ledeneva, Nadiya Kravets, Mark Kramer, Stephen Kotkin, Oleg Kharkhordin, Huang Jing, Yoshiko Herrera, Henry Hale, Sergei Grigoriev, Leonid Grigoriev, Andrea Graziosi, Leonid Gozman, Vladimir Gelman, Feng Shaolei, Piotr Dutkiewicz, Brenda Connors, Samuel Charap, George Breslauer, Yevgenia Albats, and Rawi Abdelal. Sergei Karaganov, Timofei Bordachev, and Dmitrii Suslov, and the Working Group on the Future of US–Russian Relations they manage on the Russian side, have tutored me on how domestic and foreign policies interconnect. Many of these individuals read and commented on pieces of text. Alexandra Vacroux and Patricia Colton were kind enough to read the manuscript in its entirety with an eagle eye. Hugh Truslow has been unbelievably generous with advice and help in unearthing sources. George Chakvetadze did a fine job of drawing the maps.

RUSSIAN NAMES AND TERMS

The book generally adheres to the Library of Congress trans-
literation table for Romanization of Russian words. Exceptions
are made for proper names for which a different English version
is in common use—as in Nicholas II and not Nikolai II, Alexei
and not Aleksei, and Khodorkovsky and not Khodorkovskii.
The vowels ё, ю, and я are rendered as yo, yu, and ya; e is
rendered as e after a consonant and as ye after a vowel or to
start a word. Diacritics (as in *tsar'* or Yel'tsin) are omitted for
simplicity's sake.

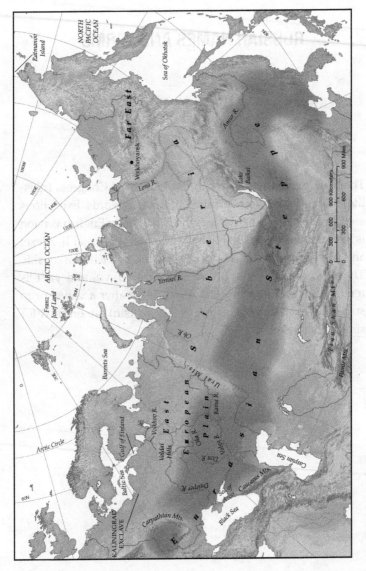

Map 1 The Physical Setting

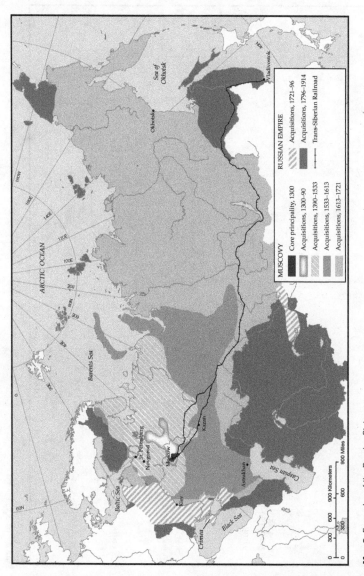

Map 2 Expansion of the Russian State

Legend:

MUSCOVY
- Core principality, 1300
- Acquisitions, 1300–90
- Acquisitions, 1390–1533
- Acquisitions, 1533–1613
- Acquisitions, 1613–1721

RUSSIAN EMPIRE
- Acquisitions, 1721–96
- Acquisitions, 1796–1914
- Trans-Siberian Railroad

ARCTIC OCEAN

Sea of Okhotsk

Barents Sea

Baltic Sea

Black Sea

Caspian Sea

Vladivostok

Okhotsk

St. Petersburg

Novgorod

Moscow

Kiev

Kazan

Astrakhan

Crimea

0   300   600   900 Kilometers
0   300   600   900 Miles

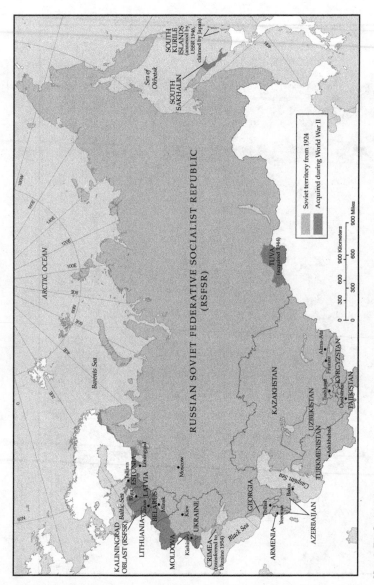

Map 3 The Soviet Union

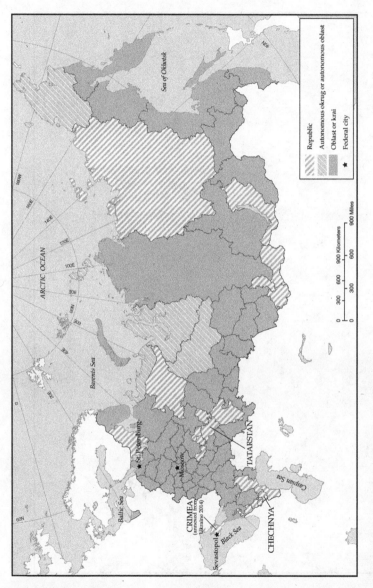

Map 4 Post-Soviet Russia, Regional Boundaries as of 2015

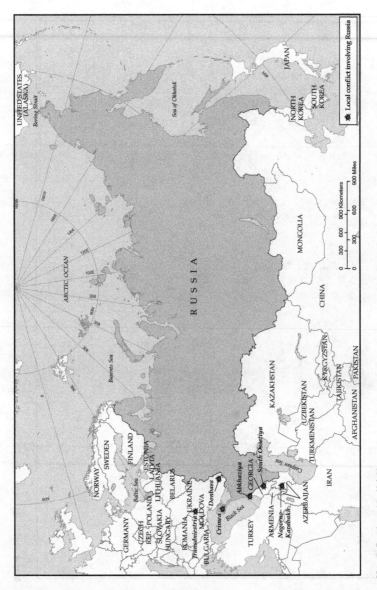

Map 5 Russia and Its Neighbors

RUSSIA

WHAT EVERYONE NEEDS TO KNOW®

1

WHY THE RUSSIAN PHOENIX MATTERS

What is Russia and who are the Russians?

Russia in its current incarnation, known interchangeably as the Russian Federation, came into being in 1991. It is the latest version of what is well and truly a phoenix state, arisen again and again from the ashes.

Russia/the Russian Federation is successor de jure to the Union of Soviet Socialist Republics (USSR), or Soviet Union. The USSR was successor de facto to the Russian Empire of 1721 to 1917 and roughly its equivalent in size. The new or, more accurately, the newest Russia is scaled back from its predecessor, even if its bequest was the heftiest by far of the Soviet Union's constituent units, the Russian Soviet Federative Socialist Republic (RSFSR). Fourteen sister republics, nations half real and half made up—Ukraine, Moldova, Kyrgyzstan, and the rest—peeled off as separate countries.

From the mouths of foreign onlookers, Russia was conflated before 1991 with the Soviet Union, and Russians with the Soviet people. "We are having some difficulty with our public opinion with regard to Russia," Harry Hopkins, Franklin D. Roosevelt's alter ego, advised him apropos Lend-Lease assistance in 1941. "The American people don't take aid to Russia easily." Addressing a joint session of the US Congress after the Yalta Conference of 1945, Roosevelt brought up things Soviet four times but things Russian (the Russian front, Russian forces, and so forth) seventeen times. Harry S. Truman reminisced in his autobiography that when he stepped in for Roosevelt he decided to "get tough with the Russians"; the Soviet dictator, Joseph Stalin, he termed "the Russian premier." In *Dr. Strangelove* (1964), Stanley Kubrick's black-comedic film about a thermonuclear Armageddon, characters in the innards of the Washington White House jabber about Russian radar cover and the Russian doomsday machine, under the gaze of the lantern-jawed "Russian ambassador." "The Russkii," deadpans General Buck Turgidson, "talks big, but frankly, we think he's short of know-how." The Norman Jewison movie *The Russians Are Coming, the Russians Are Coming* (1966) and the bestsellers *The Russians* (1974) by Hedrick Smith, a former Moscow bureau chief of the *New York Times*, and *The Russia House* (1989), a spy fable by John le Carré, bought into the same misnomer.

Terminological confusion is understandable. For the best part of the twentieth century, the USSR was the one and only "Russian" state. "What was the Soviet Union?" Vladimir Putin was to declaim in 2011. "It was Russia, only by another name." The Soviet Union was governed by and large by Russians. Stalin, a Georgian from Imperial Russia's Caucasus holdings, was the glaring exception, rather like the Corsican Napoleon Bonaparte as patriot of France nonpareil. From Lenin to Gorbachev, every senior leader but him was Russian by nationality, although all had non-Russians in the family tree or had lived at length in minority areas, or both. Russians were supreme in the military and industry, in the arts, and among the originators of Soviet know-how, which was more proficient than Hollywood gave it credit for.

That said, the USSR was engineered at the outset by cosmopolitans for whom national boundaries, cultures, and interests were passé. They visualized their handiwork as a supranational contraption with a long reach out into the world they were hell-bent on transforming. Tellingly, Soviet Russia's official anthem from 1918 to 1944 was the battle hymn of the Paris Commune of 1871, "The Internationale," an exhortation to the wretched of the earth to rise up and "unite the human race." Congresses of the ruling party until the very last one in July 1990 concluded with a rousing chorus.

Fast-forward to a quarter-century since the sun set on the USSR and on its nomenclature and aspirational goals. "Russia" (Rossiya, accent on the second syllable) and its cognate adjective "Russian" (*rossiiskii*), as in Russian Federation (Rossiiskaya Federatsiya) or Russian ruble, are disambiguated spatial, political, and civic categories. A *rossiyanin*, from the same root, is a person domiciled in Russia and subject to its laws. *Russkii*, another form of the adjective (rhymes with brewsky, not husky), is an identity category. It doubles as a noun denoting someone of Russian ethnic extraction. The *russkiye* constituted a wafer-thin majority of the Soviet population in 1991. In the 2010s, they are four-fifths of the Russian Federation. The other fifth is non-Russian ethnic groups whose members are nonetheless citizens of Russia, the most substantial being the Tatars, Ukrainians, and Bashkirs. Something like 20 million ethnic Russians live in a diaspora.

There is also a Russian language (*russkii yazyk*) in the East Slavic linguistic subgroup, alongside Ukrainian and Belarusian, with a thirty-three-character Cyrillic alphabet (*кириллица*) based on the Greek ceremonial script. Russian was the "language of interethnic communication" of the USSR, for all intents and purposes the official language. These days it is the state language of the federation (99.4 percent of Russian citizens in the most recent census spoke it) and the mother tongue of 165 million; 110 million or thereabouts can express themselves in it as a second language. Russian is one of six sanctioned languages of the United Nations and the second-ranking content language on the Internet.

Russia is seated foursquare on the East European Plain that sprawls a thousand miles from Poland, the Carpathians, and Romania out to the Ural Mountains. And it has had an ample footprint in Asia for five hundred years. Three-fourths of its landmass and one-fifth of its population in the post-1991 dispensation are in Siberia, where the rivers drain into the Arctic Ocean, and the Russian Far East, past Lake Baikal, where they mostly wend their way into the Pacific. Ergo the references to Russia as center of gravity of a Eurasian space straddling the continental divide.

Why did Soviet Russia so perturb the West?

The Soviet Union had its genesis in the Russian Revolution which burst onto an unsuspecting world in 1917. It proffered a collectivist alternative, rowdy and seductive, to liberal democracy and the market economy. Soviet Russia was a social test kitchen of colossal dimensions—the recipe being the secular creed formulated by the Victorian-era German thinkers Karl Marx and Friedrich Engels and adapted after 1900 by their Russian disciple Vladimir Lenin. The chefs in the kitchen talked big and thought big. They self-identified as destined not only to transfigure Russia per se but to eradicate "capitalism" universally and steer humankind toward "communism," an arcadia of plenty, equality, and "the withering away of the state." From this promised land at the end of history the ascendant Communist Party took its appellation. In the vanguard USSR, in abidance with the Marxist cookbook, the quest was supposed to unfold in a predetermined sequence. On the heels of the first workers' revolution would come an ephemeral "dictatorship of the proletariat"; after that, an interval under "socialism," officiated by a benevolent majoritarian government; and the socialist stage would in turn be the stepping stone to full communism.

The Soviet experiment, a consummate expression of European rationalism, at the same time confounded Western narratives of individualism, constitutionalism, and gradualism, especially once it fell into place that dictatorial governance was one and the same with socialism and was semipermanent, with the stateless communist nirvana nowhere in sight. In the United States, Russia under the Bolsheviks, as it had sometimes been before 1917, was "a screen on which Americans projected their hopes and fears." Martin Malia expresses the point more sweepingly: the Soviet Union hovered as "the great Other in terms of which the world [and not just the United States] was obliged to define itself." On the left, it "represented the socialist antithesis to capitalism, and the future as against the past"; on the center and right, it was a dark twin, "the totalitarian menace to the free world of the West, and the enemy of civilization." Britain and France withheld recognition of the Soviet upstart until 1924 and the United States until 1933. Following World War II and an alliance of convenience against the Axis powers, a Cold War between, coarsely put, a Russian-led East and an American-led West cleaved international politics for two generations.

The totalitarian genus to which midcentury opinion makers relegated the USSR lumped despotisms of the far left in with the ultranationalist despotisms of the far right, as exemplified by Nazi Germany. Under Stalin from the 1920s to the 1950s, the regime bore more than a passing likeness to the ideal type. Granting that its most oppressive attributes were subsequently repudiated or diluted, the USSR to the very end was guided by a monopoly Communist party and by its Marxist-Leninist beliefs.

Western disquiet was reinforced by a fright factor. The Soviet Union was the largest country on the planet. It was third in population to China and India, with 286.7 million people at its last census in 1989, and second economically to the United States. It had upward of 5 million men in uniform, a gargantuan cache of weapons of mass destruction on hair-trigger alert, and the intelligence octopus the chaps in le Carré's Russia House (MI6 central) tracked night and day. The USSR was one of five permanent, veto-wielding members of the UN Security Council. It midwifed a six-nation bloc in Eastern Europe (Bulgaria, Czechoslovakia, East Germany or the German

Democratic Republic, Hungary, Poland, and Romania) and stationed six hundred thousand troops there. As of the late 1980s, Communists also administrated two nonbloc countries in the Balkans (Albania and Yugoslavia), seven in Asia (Afghanistan, Cambodia, China, Laos, Mongolia, North Korea, and Vietnam), two in the Caribbean (Cuba and Nicaragua), and one in the Middle East (South Yemen). Governments laxly on the Soviet template were in power in six African countries (Angola, Benin, Congo-Brazzaville, Ethiopia, Mozambique, and Somalia). Eighty nonruling Communist parties and forty leftist movements and front organizations were more slackly tied to Moscow's apron strings.

The Soviet Union as antagonist was encapsulated in Ronald Reagan's catchphrase "evil empire." The USSR, Reagan said to the National Association of Evangelicals on March 8, 1983, was a rogue among nations. It had compiled a "bizarre chapter" in history. Its grandees "preach the supremacy of the state, declare its omnipotence over individual man, and predict its eventual domination of all peoples on the earth." Soviet Russia had insatiable "aggressive impulses" and had carried out an enormous military buildup. It was "the focus of evil in the modern world."

The specter of a redoubtable foe inhabiting an alternate spiritual universe had hung in the air from the 1940s onward. A famous early instantiation is the "Long Telegram" sent to Secretary of State George C. Marshall from the American embassy in Moscow on February 22, 1946. The author was the deputy chief of mission, George F. Kennan. His top-secret cable prompted the Truman administration to stake out the policy of "containment" of the USSR that President Reagan reaffirmed in the 1980s.

For Kennan, the face-off with the Soviets was "undoubtedly [the] greatest task our diplomacy has ever faced and probably [the] greatest it will ever have to face. . . . We have here a political force committed fanatically to the belief that with [the United States] there can be no permanent modus vivendi."

"This political force," said Kennan, "has complete power of disposition over [the] energies of one of [the] world's greatest peoples and [the] resources of [the] world's richest national territory, and is borne along by deep and powerful currents of Russian nationalism. In addition, it has an elaborate ... apparatus for exertion of its influence in other countries, an apparatus of amazing flexibility and versatility, managed by people whose experience and skill in underground methods are presumably without parallel in history. Finally, it is seemingly inaccessible to considerations of reality in its basic reactions. For it, the vast fund of objective fact about human society is not, as with us, the measure against which [an] outlook is constantly being tested and re-formed, but a grab bag from which individual items are selected arbitrarily and tendentiously to bolster an outlook already preconceived. This is admittedly not a pleasant picture."

Is it worth paying attention to a downsized, post-Soviet Russia?

Soviet Communism has an afterlife through its progeny in the People's Republic of China, the Socialist Republic of Vietnam, the Democratic People's Republic of Korea, the Republic of Cuba, and the Lao People's Democratic Republic, with 1.5 billion people between them—nearly the 1.6 billion who lived under Communism in the 1980s. Marxist-Leninist parties grace the governments of another dozen countries. In its Slavic seedbed, though, the ideology is defunct. The Russia reborn in 1991 is not a beacon for an indivisible and proselytizing philosophy of human affairs. By the usual benchmarks, it is not on a par with the bygone Soviet superpower.

If, however, the Russian phoenix is stacked against other countries in the present and not against the Soviet past, it matters a lot. Shorn of 2 million of the USSR's square miles in 1991, Russia's area of 6,612,000 square miles, counting the Crimean Peninsula annexed from Ukraine in 2014, is even so the largest anyplace (silver medalist Canada has 3,854,000 square miles). West to east, it extends 6,200 miles from its Kaliningrad exclave on the Baltic Sea, a longer flight from Moscow than it is from Munich, to Ratmanov Island on the International Date Line; north to south, 2,800 miles lie between the glacier-covered Franz Josef Land archipelago, above the Arctic Circle, and the subtropical coast of the Caspian Sea. All told, 11 percent of the earth's land surface, 39 percent of Europe, and 29 percent of Asia are Russia. A population of 146.5 million (2.3 million in Crimea) stands at ninth in the world and makes the Russians the most numerous of the European peoples, as many as the Germans and the French or British combined. In gross domestic product (GDP) for 2014, Russia was fifth at purchasing power parity (after the United States, China, India, and Japan) in the accounts of the World Bank; the International Monetary Fund had it sixth, behind Germany. Russia is neck and neck with the United States and Saudi Arabia in the production of oil and second in its export, and second in production and first in export of natural gas. It is a member of the Group of Twenty (G20) economic club— it was disinvited from the upscale G8 in 2014—and of the Brazil–Russia–India–China–South Africa (BRICS) association of emerging nations.

Geopolitically, Russia is a bona fide great power. As before, it bestrides the Eurasian "pivot area," in the still useful idiom of Halford John Mackinder from 1904. With thirteen thousand miles of land borders and twenty-three thousand miles of seashore, it is contiguous with the most regions of importance— eastern and western Europe, the Middle East, South and East Asia, and North America over the Bering Strait. Russia holds the UN Security Council seat in New York once owned by the Soviets. In its mammoth nuclear arsenal are 7,700 strategic and tactical warheads deployed, stockpiled, or retired but functional (2015 estimate of the Arms Control Association); the United States has 7,100, and the other seven nuclear powers about 1,100. Russia is placed second in conventional military strength by firepower.com, noting its "massive modernization and procurement program" since 2008. Russia pays out more on defense than anyone except the United States and China and trails only the United States in sales in the international arms bazaar—think Kalashnikov rifles or Sukhoi fighter jets. It directs GLONASS, one of two global navigation satellite systems (the other is the United States' Global Positioning System, with the Europeans' Galileo in the works); is second in spacecraft in orbit; and in 2014 was responsible for 40 percent of commercial space launches. Hackers at Russian keyboards are as nimble as any at cyber-warfare, and are said by US government officials to be capable of disabling American electric power grids and air-traffic control systems. Russia's navy is evidently busy studying how to employ submarines, unmanned vessels, and seabed systems to eavesdrop on or snip the fiber optic cables that carry 99 percent of transoceanic telephone and digital traffic.

Russia, when all is said and done, impinges on bedrock interests of the United States. It makes its own proud way in regional and world affairs—the "lonely power," in the words of Lilia Shevtsova—while over the years being a partner, an oftentimes exasperating one, in US endeavors. *Forbes* magazine rated President Putin the most influential person on earth in 2015, 2014, and 2013 (followed in 2015 by Angela Merkel of Germany, Barack Obama, and Pope Francis). "Putin continues to prove," *Forbes* editorialized in November 2015, "he's one of the few men in the world powerful enough to do what he wants." Not to be taken lightly is that the nuclear button at Putin's fingertips, should he ever desire to squeeze it, could let loose a calamity more horrific by orders of magnitude than any in American history. One two-stage SS-18 ICBM (intercontinental ballistic missile), with ten independently targeted reentry vehicles in its nosecone, packs an explosive power two to three *thousand* times that of the Little Boy bomb dropped on Hiroshima in 1945. From a silo in the Russian outback, it would take thirty minutes to zip by a transpolar route to ground zero in Miami or Seattle.

The Russian Federation is less potent than the Soviet Union but, arguably, less predictable. Headlines about Crimea and eastern Ukraine in 2014 speak to its disruptive potential. Headlines about Russian warplanes in Syria in 2015–16 speak to a nontrivial capacity and preparedness to project force. Since 2014 relations with Washington and the Euroatlantic alliance have scraped lows unmatched for the post–Cold War period. Ukraine-related sanctions were the most onerous on any major power since the American oil embargo against Imperial Japan in 1940–41. Staggered financially by them and by a plunge in world oil prices, Russia cried foul, flexed its muscles, and groped to even the score.

A second reason to care about Russia is the saga of its exit out of Communism—out of the opera for which Russians composed the libretto, as it were. The harrowing process is still half-finished, and we are still coming to grips with it.

Beginning a critical juncture as fateful as that of 1917, the last Soviet leader, Mikhail Gorbachev, did his utmost to redeem a moribund system, only to have it crumple like a house of cards. A catalyst was his inability to handle the RSFSR hub of the Soviet Union, headed in 1990–91 by his ex-associate and nemesis, Boris Yeltsin. Russia, in its Soviet form having come up short in the Cold War, was not occupied and sanitized by foreign armies, as Germany and Japan were after losing World War II. As first president of the new and still autonomous Russia, Yeltsin kept the place together, built governmental institutions, respected political freedoms, and enacted traumatic economic reforms. But he did not deliver expeditiously on his vow of a better life for all and took a reputational pummeling as a result. Vladimir Putin's passion after Yeltsin has been to fortify the rump Russian state and, entwined with it, a hybrid political regime in which democratic and liberal components have been outstripped by authoritarianism and nationalism. His transition within the transition has carried the day but has not settled where the odyssey will end. The remaking of Russia, gauged against the optimism with which it began, is perforce a cautionary tale—"not a pleasant picture," to plagiarize Kennan from 1946.

Is Russia inscrutable?

West Europeans whose wanderlust took them to Russia early on were perplexed. This was terra incognita, and its denizens wallowed in the difference. Sixteenth-century English travelogues "shared ... both the sense of wonder at the magnificence of the tsar's court and the distaste for a way of life that seemed to them crude, inhuman, and uncomfortable." Russian idiosyncrasy remained in vogue in the nineteenth century. The widely read *La Russie en 1839*, by the French aristocrat Marquis de Custine, typified Russia as "the most singular state now to be seen." A contemporary from Germany, Johann Kohl, did Custine one better: "So remarkable and peculiar a people have never before appeared in the pages of history." Exceptionalism was a staple of domestic thought as well. The editor Vissarion Belinskii popularized the phrase "the Russian soul" (*russkaya dusha*) in the 1840s. "Russia cannot be understood through the mind alone," the poet Fyodor Tyutchev memorably opined in 1866; "in Russia one can only believe." Novelist Ivan Turgenev wrote a prose poem in 1878 about the unsung peasant (*muzhik*) of the empire's hinterland as the "All-Russian Sphinx," voiceless and unfathomable.

The brave new world of Communism after 1917 changed the basis of Russia's exoticism but not the degree. Witness the celebrated adage of Winston Churchill, made on BBC radio in October 1939, about deciphering "a riddle wrapped in a mystery inside an enigma." William Randolph Hearst Jr., who won a Pulitzer Prize for dispatches on meetings with Soviet VIPs in 1955, conveyed in one of them the relish with which Western ambassadors debriefed his team: "Shreds of information are so hard to come by in Moscow that they studied our every move as a possible beam of light on Russia's inscrutable plans."

In certain regards, Russia has been and is inimitable. A tenet of this book is that this inimitability, and how to weigh it against other variables, are topics for empirical discovery and not for assumption a priori. Russia has a way of obeying stereotypes, of upending them, and just as surely of begetting new ones. Inscrutability in its past was in no small part an artifact of the muffling and skewing of data by the Russian government, as Hearst beheld in the 1950s. In our day the information flows more profusely and more verifiably. Turning it to good use, what everyone needs to know about Russia can be gleaned through level-headed inquiry and laid out in straightforward fashion.

2

FOUNDATIONS

How did geography influence Russia's development?

To make sense of Russia, start with geographic endowment. Any atlas will draw the eye to its salient features: a gigantic physiognomy, northerly and easterly location vis-à-vis Europe, and, for most of its extent, topographic uniformity.

States and protostates have come and gone on the East European Plain for a thousand-plus years. Russia's antediluvian ancestor—and the etymological wellspring of all things Russian—was Rus, a conglomerate of East Slavic principalities with continuously shifting boundaries. It was centered at first on Novgorod, on the Volkhov River in the northwest of present-day European Russia, and shortly thereafter on Kiev, on the Dnieper River in what is now post-Soviet Ukraine. By testimony of the East Slavs' spotty "primary chronicle," Rus was established in 862 by a Norse adventurer, Rurik, plying the waterways between the Baltic and the Black Sea. Its consanguineous rulers and population were converted to Christianity in the tenth century. When it was overrun in 1237–40 by Mongol horsemen out of Asia, some Rurikid offshoots to the north and east, in the basin of the Volga River, were spared occupation and let off with payment of an annual levy. A lineage may be traced unbroken from the picayune Grand Duchy of Muscovy (Moskoviya), tax collector for the Tatar sidekicks of the Golden Horde, to the twenty-first-century federation. Moscow (Moskva), founded in 1147, five hundred miles from

Kiev as the crow flies, was the Muscovite capital. Its imposing triangular bastion (*kreml* or Kremlin) is on the Moskva River, which feeds the Oka, a tributary of the Volga. Grand Prince Ivan III discontinued the tariff to the Tatars in 1476. In 1480 the warriors of Akhmat Khan turned tail before Ivan's host on the Ugra River, making Muscovy the regional overlord.

From under 15,000 square miles in 1300, the grand duchy exploded by force of arms, purchase, and marriage to 150,000 square miles in the mid-1400s and 1 million at the coronation in 1533 of Ivan IV (the Terrible), the prince who decreed himself *tsar* (tsar, Caesar) or absolute monarch. By 1600 the Kremlin's writ ran over 2 million square miles and by the 1720s over 5.7 million square miles. That was when Peter I (the Great) rebranded Muscovy the Russian Empire and made St. Petersburg, the ornate window on the West he had built on the Gulf of Finland, its capital. At its zenith in 1866, Russia's imperium was 8,803,000 square miles. Only the Mongols and the British ever exceeded it.

Russia overtook France as the most populous European nation about 1760. It tripled its numbers by the time a first census in 1897 recorded 126 million people under its suzerainty—66 million in the bounds of the federation of 1991. On an oversize canvas they were thin on the ground, as Custine remarked with some embellishment: "There is nothing but distance in Russia, nothing but empty plains extending farther than the eye can reach." The empire had fifteen persons per square mile in 1897, one-tenth of the French figure and one-eighteenth of the German. This low density perseveres. Of eighty-four countries with a population of over 10 million in 2016, eighty have more people per square mile than Russia's twenty-one and only three have fewer: Kazakhstan (a former Soviet republic) with sixteen, Canada with ten, and Australia with eight. In Siberia and the Far East, population density per square mile is the same minuscule eight as Australia's.

Latitude and longitude have framed Russian life no less than magnitude. Novgorod is situated at 58°54′N, Moscow at 55°45′N, and St. Petersburg (Petrograd from 1914 to 1924 and Leningrad from 1924 to 1991) at 59°56′N. This far north of the equator, the growing season is limited to four or five months, icy winds gust in from the Arctic and North Atlantic, and winter is lengthy and harsh. In Eurasia, isotherms (the lines climatologists draw to link points of equal temperature at a given time) slant from northwest to southeast, so that the more you go due east the chillier it gets. The "North Pole of Cold," the most frigid spot in the hemisphere, is near the secluded town of Verkhoyansk in the Sakha republic of the Far East. About 60 percent of Russia's terrain (30 percent in European Russia) is sheathed in *taiga*, a coniferous forest rooted in acidic, nutrient-poor soil; permafrost lies beneath 50 to 55 percent; precipitation is irregular and droughts are recurrent.

It summed to an inhospitable habitat for agriculture, suited to spring plantings and hardy, early-maturing crops, and with distance barriers that inhibited growers from harvesting more than they could eat or trade locally. The reticence and risk aversion integral to such an ecosystem were part and parcel of Russia's society and of its political culture. An agrarian surplus to underwrite economic accumulation thus came at a snail's pace. Urbanization, industry, and the finer things in life lagged. Russian backwardness (*otstalost*) was an idée fixe for the leadership. For peasants, the national drink, *vodka* ("little water"), said to have been introduced by Genoese traders in the fourteenth century, offered some release at feast days and solace during the snowbound months.

Russia was and is the easternmost as well as the northernmost country in Europe (by the 1600s it would be the same in Asia), and ipso facto remote from the bustling trade lanes round Europe's heartland. Its river artery west of the Urals, the Volga, runs south into the Caspian—a saltwater but land-locked sea. There was no shipping from the Caspian to the Sea of Azov and Black Sea, and the world's oceans beyond, until the opening of a canal from the lower course of the Volga westward to the Don River, excavated by Soviet convict laborers, in 1952.

Owing to its whereabouts, Russia was buffeted by cultural crosscurrents from Scandinavia, the Balkans, the Middle East, and the Asian Silk Road. The baptism of the Kievan grand prince, Vladimir I, in 988 was at his request by priests from Byzantine Constantinople; his emissaries were captivated by the splendor of their services, onion-domed temples, and icons when on a religious shopping voyage in 987. The metropolitan of Kiev was to move his see to Moscow in 1325. Constantinople's split from Rome in the schism of 1054, and its fall to the Turks in 1453, accentuated Russian isolation from the European mainstream. Eastern Orthodoxy and its clergy are configured in autocephalous national branches. Primates are not answerable to a Catholic pope in the Vatican and lack the autonomy from government of the average Protestant denomination. In Russia, the church looked askance at foreigners and worshiped in recondite Old Church Slavonic, cut off from the vernacular. Russia slept through Europe's Reformation and Renaissance humanism. When Western Europe changed over to the Gregorian calendar in 1582, it stayed on the Julian calendar, which by 1900 had it thirteen days behind.

Why did Russia get so huge?

The first outward heave, in the fourteenth and fifteenth centuries, immersed the East Slavic statelets within several hundred miles of the palaces and churches of the Moscow Kremlin. A wave to the east after 1582 took the tsar's coat of arms, with its two-headed Byzantine eagle, across the Urals and the three mighty south–north rivers of Siberia (the Ob, Yenisei, and Lena), making use of river branches and portages. Semimilitary Cossacks reached the Pacific at Okhotsk in 1637 and put up a Muscovite fort in 1649. Their keels laid there, Russian ships sailed to Alaska, a possession from 1733 until the United States bought it for pennies in 1867, and to California and Hawaii.

Enlargement to the south, from the Oka River to the Black Sea, and to the west took until the early 1800s. The finale, in the nineteenth century, was expansion to the southwest, into the alpine Caucasus region between the Black and Caspian seas, and to the southeast, into the deserts and valleys of Central Asia, or Turkestan (*stan* is the Persian suffix for "land" or "place"), and the Amur watershed fronting the Sea of Japan.

Why this phenomenal aggrandizement? Orthodox missionaries provided some yeast, typically following and not preceding the flag. The tsars had a cultural affinity for "ingathering" pieces of the extinct Kievan Rus. The first trophy was Novgorod, which seceded from Rus in 1132 and had a Hanseatic League trading post and frontage on the Baltic and Barents seas. Ivan III conquered it in 1478, scotching its republican constitution. The East Slavic lands on the left bank of the Dnieper were brought under control of Moscow in 1654; the mother city of Kiev was wrested from the West Slavic Poles in 1667.

Initially the gist of Russian expansionism was security. The "empty" East European Plain, whose geometric center Moscow is close to, is worn down by erosion and denudation, and devoid of internal obstacles to movement and of natural frontiers. The maximum elevation of its highpoint, the Valdai Hills near Novgorod and the headwaters of the Volga and Dnieper, is 1,140 feet. Muscovy's short and northerly coastline (it had none until acquiring Novgorod) made it impervious to maritime predation but not to terrestrial. The low-slung Urals (average height 3,500 feet) were more a speed bump than a rampart. To the south, the East European Plain overlaps with the Eurasian Steppe, five thousand miles of treeless grasslands from Manchuria to the Danube delta. "A calf born at the foot of the Great Chinese Wall," discerned the German sojourner Kohl, "might graze his way along till he arrived a well-fattened ox on the banks of the Dniester" (in post-USSR Ukraine and Moldova). This prairieland was roamed not only by animals but by the pastoralists who tended to them and by well-armed raiders. Its northern fringe only a few days hard ride from Moscow, the steppe was the Mongol and Tatar cavalry's thoroughfare into Europe. It was only sensible for Russia to seek out outposts and to extend its security perimeter in the direction of marine and mountain limits, such as they were, and in the middle of Asia to sedentary populations that could be colonized and serve as buffers. Russian Cossack communities, armed but not remunerated by the crown, policed many segments of the frontier zone.

As time passed, Russia gravitated from a protective to a forward posture. Geographic depth, the quelling of the Tatars, and then Peter the Great's standing army—conscripted for life until the term was reduced to twenty-five years in 1793—freed it to scout out opportunities at every point of the compass. To the east and northeast, it amassed land at the expense of outgunned aborigines; to the west and southwest, of the Ukrainian Cossack Hetmanate, Poland, the Ottoman Empire and its Crimean Tatar vassals, Denmark, and Sweden; to the south and southeast, of Safavid Persia, the nomads and semi-nomads of the Eurasian Steppe, the upland peoples of the Caucasus, Tien Shan, and Pamir ranges, and Manchu China.

Trade and warm-water ports had always figured in Russia's growth. Coalfields and mineral deposits lured it into the Urals. In the explorers' dash from there to the Pacific, the bait was fish, salt, and the furs of Siberian fox, ermine, and sable. By the eighteenth century, agricultural settlement on the rim, to satisfy land hunger by peasants in overpopulated areas, was another factor.

The western vector, into Europe, grew out of Peter the Great's landmark victory over Sweden in the Great Northern War of 1700–21. Russia was now in the ensemble of continental powers, as good as equal to France, England, Austria, and Prussia/Germany. Jousting with the French culminated in the Russian foray by Napoleon's Grande Armée, Borodino, and the incineration of Moscow in 1812, immortalized in Leo Tolstoy's *War and Peace*. Russia searched for safety in final conquests in

Europe (Finland in 1809 and Romanian-populated Bessarabia out to the Prut River in 1812). After the Congress of Vienna of 1815, it was an avid participant in the conservative Concert of Europe. Loss of the Crimean War of 1853–56 to Britain, France, and the Muslim Ottomans was a humiliation. The Russian Black Sea Fleet was disbanded under the peace treaty, and restored only in 1871. The League of the Three Emperors of 1873 to 1887 was a high-water mark in Russia's post-Crimea cooperation with Germany and Austria-Hungary. When St. Petersburg and Vienna fell out over the Balkans, the empire moved away from the Germanic powers and into an alliance with France in 1892. In 1907 it signed an Anglo-Russian Convention and put aside the "Great Game," the geostrategic rivalry with Britain over the caravan routes and mountain passes between Turkestan and India.

What was the import of being an empire?

Sheer size made policing, taxation, census taking, and the nitty-gritty of government grueling. Kohl, sightseeing from St. Petersburg to the Black Sea, was astounded by "the amount of health continually sacrificed on these endless Russian roads" by adjutants and couriers. "These travelers often arrive at the [coach] stations so numbed with cold and so exhausted and worn out, for want of sleep, that it is necessary to lift them from their carriages." To top it all off, Russia was not a homogeneous nation-state but an empire of heterogeneous populations. The predominant group was the ethnic Russians, taken with no great precision to be subjects of the tsar who were Russophone and Eastern Orthodox.

In law, Peter made Russia an empire in 1721 and subdivided it into provinces or governorships (*guberniya*s) under civilian governors and military governors-general. In fact, Russia had assumed an imperial form one-and-a-half centuries before. Finnic and Baltic tribes comingled with the Russians on the edges of Muscovy. Ivan the Terrible upped the ante by taking the strongest Tatar khanates left—at Astrakhan, where the Volga meets the Caspian, in 1556, and at Kazan, at the confluence of the Volga and the Kama River from the Urals, in 1562. The Tatars spoke a Turkic language, were Sunni Muslims, and were much larger than previously subjected groups. The peoples of Russian Eurasia were henceforth absorbed into what was more and more a multiethnic, multilingual, and multiconfessional crazy quilt.

Linguistic propinquity, Orthodoxy, and historical path gave East Slavs a unique place in the imperial order. The incorporation in the seventeenth and eighteenth centuries of people who in this day and age would be Ukrainians and Belarusians raised questions about ethnonyms and the signification of "Russian." In the government's taxonomy, Little Russians (*malorossy*, today's Ukrainians), White Russians (*belorossy*, today's Belarusians), and Great Russians (*velikorossy*, today's Russians) were limbs on a "common Russian" (*obshcherusskii*) trunk, communicating in dialects of one language. The Tatars and non-European minorities were bracketed as "aliens" or "people of different birth" (*inorodtsy*).

Most if not all of the time, imperial governance was down-to-earth and bendable. In the 1860s, 23 percent of the army officer corps was non-Orthodox, the main subset Lutheran Germans from the former Swedish domains on the Baltic; there were many Germans and Finns, Tatars, and Poles at court and in the civil service. The epitome of Russian multiculturalism was Karl Nesselrode, chief diplomat of the empire from the Napoleonic to the Crimean wars. "Born in Lisbon as the son of a German Catholic father and Jewish Protestant mother, and baptized in the Church of England, he was for more than four decades Russian foreign minister, without in the process having learnt to speak Russian properly."

At the grassroots, the formula hinged on indirect rule through notables, who were usually welcomed into the Russian nobility, and acceptance of preexisting social relations and folkways. For the Russians, one might say, nation and empire were joined at the hip. In their overland empire, the psychological distance between the regnant nationality and the others was less than in the overseas empires of the West Europeans. "The Russian Empire grew by settlement," notes Orlando Figes, "and the Russians who moved out into the frontier zones, some to trade or farm, others to escape from tsarist rule, were just as likely to adopt the native culture as they were to impose [Russian ways] on the local tribes.... One of the consequences of this encounter was a cultural sympathy towards the colonies that was rarely to be found in colonizers from the European states."

Pleasing and horizon-stretching as imperialism was for the Russian ego, it bred problems. The Great Russians had been 95 percent of the population in the mid-1600s; in the 1897 headcount, they were 44 percent, using the language marker (the census takers asked about native language and religion but not nationality). Little and White Russians stood at 22 percent, Tatars and other speakers of Turkic languages at 11 percent, the Poles at 6 percent, and Jews (Yiddish speakers) at 4 percent. Eighty-five percent of Great Russians lived within the borders of the Muscovy of 1650. Eight of the empire's ten most heavily populated cities (all except St. Petersburg and Moscow) were in minority-dominated areas. Great Russians were not overtly favored in economic and social policy and in 1900 lagged behind Latvians, Estonians, Lithuanians, Jews, Poles, Tatars, and Bashkirs in life expectancy. The result was head-scratching over "impoverishment of the core" (*oskudeniye tsentra*) of the imperial construct.

Added to the demographics and economics, by 1900 a national awakening, and organized advocacy for self-determination, was infecting the borderlands. The ferment was most perceptible in the northwest, where the indigenes—the Poles, Balts, and Finns—were Roman Catholics or Lutherans and were ahead of the Russians economically and socially. There was a backlash among Russian conservatives and precautionary moves to suppress the languages and cultures of the Poles but also the Ukrainians and Belarusians. For Russians who pondered opening the system up, the fear was that democratization, by conferring rights on minorities where preferences for autonomy were rife, would be the slippery slope to loss of empire.

What was distinctive about the Russian autocracy?

Until not so long ago, most people the world over were governed undemocratically. Muscovy's and Imperial Russia's autocracy (*samoderzhaviye*) shared political DNA with other such regimes. A hereditary monarch was legitimized by the divine right of kings and by a "patrimonial" ethos, as Max Weber termed it, equating him with the paterfamilias of a household. Economy and society were under pervasive state regulation. The plebeian majority was excluded from political activity.

But Russian kingship did overstep the autocratic norm. The tsar's claims to the full plenitude of power—*vlast*, a redolent and untranslatable Russian word—were outlandish by any measure. There was a humdrum corporatist politics in which the potentate mediated between courtly cliques and business clans. On the grand politics of setting the country's itinerary, all petty considerations were stifled for the sake of preservation and extension of the realm in an unfeeling international milieu.

Royal prerogatives were unscathed by the Time of Troubles, an intermezzo of tumult and incursions by Poles and Swedes after the death of the last Rurikid tsar, heirless, in 1598. The Romanov dynasty enthroned in 1613 was every bit as overbearing. Peter the Great a century later folded into the state's mission the technological and economic Europeanization of the empire—surgically, without unraveling the entitlements of the tsar. From the 1760s to the 1790s Catherine II (the Great), a transplanted Prussian princess who ascended to the throne by overthrowing her mentally unstable husband, Peter III, set geopolitical "glory" as a prime goal of the system and affirmed that no regime other than absolutism could keep Russia, with its elephantine girth, intact. The sovereign must be unobstructed, she made it known in her "Instruction" of 1767, for "no authority other than one centered on his [or her] sole person can take actions commensurate with the extent of so vast a dominion." "Every other form of government whatsoever would not only be prejudicial to Russia but would bring its ruination." As a specimen of the havoc wreaked by weak-kneed institutions, and in a smaller country, Russian autocrats could point to the Polish–Lithuanian Commonwealth, with its assembly of the nobility where every deputy had the "free veto" to block laws. Between 1772 and 1795, the commonwealth was partitioned between Russia, Prussia, and the Habsburgs and expunged from the map of Europe; Russia got 66 percent of it.

The institutional checks and balances, territorial councils, and participatory bodies found in most European monarchies since medieval times were a long time coming in Russia. It never did have feudalism, with its thicket of contractual relationships. It took until Nicholas II's October Manifesto in 1905 to obtain a nonbinding constitutional document and until 1906 for Russia to get a parliamentary assembly, elected on a property suffrage. (The Muscovite Council of *Boyars* [Princes] and the grandly named Governing Senate of the empire were strictly consultative.) A federal system, which would have divided authority between a central government and strong regional authorities closer to the population, was proposed in the nineteenth century by St. Petersburg and Moscow liberals such as Alexander Herzen and Nikolai Ogarev, by Siberian regionalists, and by Ukrainian intellectuals. It found no takers in the emperor's Winter Palace.

The great majority of Russians made their peace with the ancien regime. "In Russia," as Johann Kohl put it, "where there are few persons who feel the vanity of this world very deeply, and where independence of character is not very general ... [people] will adapt ... with wonderful suppleness to the prevailing mode." "The energy of the upper classes is directed to the same end—to labor in the state machine in the capital, and in the several [provincial] governments," and "very few live apart as independent citizens."

Social interests that were able to act as brakes on government in western Europe were punier here, partly because the costs of collective action and representation were exorbitant in a physical space of this breadth. Russia's territory was put to penal use, as criminals and political delinquents were banished to the wilds of Siberia and the Far East; they tramped there on foot, in leg irons, in prodigious quantity—1.2 million between 1754 and 1917. The government expurgated the press, limited foreign travel, and ordered males to shear their beards. The Russian Orthodox Church was manacled to the state chancery in the eighteenth century, its patriarch (metropolitan) taken away and its monastic lands nationalized; an Old Believers sect that spurned liturgical changes was persecuted. Russia's hereditary nobility and gentry were a service caste until 1762, many of them receiving land as an appanage, and at the mercy of the emperor after that. Chattel serfdom was on the way out in western Europe when the legal code of 1649 toughened it in European Russia, making fugitives out of farmhands fleeing their landlords. Serfdom was gotten rid of only in 1861, and in such a manner as to leave a great many peasants hogtied by redemption payments and by communal procedures for apportioning arable land and pasture. The urban bourgeoisie could go unheeded so long as Russia was a kingdom of villages. In 1910 only 14 percent of Russians lived in towns of five thousand or more, a drop in the bucket compared with the 39 percent in France, 49 percent in Germany, and 69 percent in Britain.

The autocracy and the autocrat were not all-powerful. The chasm dividing them from the populace fostered distrust and a disinclination to pitch in for the common good. The ramshackle state machine itself was undermanned, undereducated, and venal. Tsars from Peter forward bemoaned the hurdles to getting their orders discharged. Bureaucrats tyrannized lowly subjects as they dug out payments to supplement meager salaries and competed through make-work for the goodwill of superiors. To quote Custine, "In Russian administration, minuteness does not exclude disorder. Much trouble is taken to attain unimportant ends, and those employed believe they can never do enough to show their zeal. The result of this emulation among clerks and commissioners is that the having passed through one formality does not secure the stranger from another. It is like a pillage, in which, after the unfortunate [creature] has escaped from the first troop, he may yet fall into the hands of a second and a third."

Was society in the old order smothered by the state?

If it may not have had much say over political issues, Russian society was neither passive nor stationary. Kept in check by the state, it was never smothered by it, and it changed willy-nilly.

Law grouped the population into four "estates": nobility, clergy, townspeople, and peasantry. But the boundaries were spongy. Emancipation of the serfs and the growth of industry and cities made them spongier still and germinated new occupational groupings.

A constituency that cut across the habitual categories was the *intelligentsia*—Russia's intellectuals, artists, and bohemians, who often were the sons of the gentry or clergy. In the 1830s two schools of thought arose: Westernizers were for change in accord with individual strivings; Slavophiles were for Russian singularity and "togetherness" (*sobornost*). Russian ideas and learning never congealed in either mold. An Imperial Academy of Sciences, formed in 1724, employed European and Russian cognoscenti and organized scientific expeditions. Universities trained a million engineers, technicians, doctors, and educators by 1914. Chemist Dmitrii Mendeleev (inventor of the periodic table), mathematician Nikolai Lobachevskii (inventor of non-Euclidian geometry), physiologist and psychologist Ivan Pavlov, earth scientist Vladimir Vernadskii, and economist Nikolai Kondratiev were all international trendsetters in their disciplines.

The Romantic bard Alexander Pushkin débuted a modern Russian literature in the 1820s and gave it a place of honor in the national imagination, enshrining the writer as sage, teacher, and healer. After his untimely death in a pistol duel in 1837, novels, plays, and poetry of note sprang from the pens of Nikolai Gogol, Ivan Turgenev, Fyodor Dostoevsky, Leo Tolstoy, Anton Chekhov, and the versifiers of the fin-de-siècle Silver Age. Western critics, remarks Martin Malia, "were prepared to acclaim the Russian novelists as the masters of the foremost school of fiction in Europe."

Composers Nikolai Rimsky-Korsakov, Modest Mussorgsky, Alexander Scriabin, and Peter Tchaikovsky mated European melodies to native musical traditions, making the Russians, in Malia's words, "a prime source, second only to [Richard] Wagner, of musical modernism throughout Europe." Painting and sculpture took up naturalist and socially progressive aesthetics, paid for by moneyed collectors. By the early nineteen hundreds Russia had avant-garde architectural ateliers, a film industry, and a vibrant dance scene centering on the stages of the Mariinskii Theater in St. Petersburg (the Kirov from 1934 to 1991) and the Bolshoi in Moscow. The impresario Sergei Diaghilev's peripatetic Ballets Russes electrified European audiences in 1909; three of its most scintillating scores in the coming years (for *The Firebird*, *Petrushka*, and *The Rite of Spring*) were by Igor Stravinsky. In the most illustrious ballet, the levitating Firebird, making the characters dance madly until they fall asleep, "was transformed into the symbol of a phoenix-like, resurgent peasant Russia, the embodiment of an elemental freedom and beauty."

Economic producers had a tenuous status in Russian society. The dynamics of capital accumulation in Europe depended on the timing of the industrial takeoff, as the historiography has pinpointed. In Britain and the Low Countries, small and family companies were the driving force; in Germany, it was the big banks; in the latecomer Russia, development was boot-strapped by government, playing catch-up with the frontrun-ner states and their armies. The state promoted mines, metal workshops, and trade fairs. When ex-serfs were made available for factory labor, it bankrolled new industries and hastened to develop canals, ports, and, with loans and technical sup-port from Third Republic France, the world's longest railway system; the Trans-Siberian Railroad, opened in 1916, ran six thousand miles from Moscow to its terminus in Vladivostok. But the role of entrepreneurs was in flux. A new business class was crystallizing. The petroleum fields at Baku, on the Caspian, were auctioned off to nonstate firms in 1872, and non-nationals (the Nobels, Rothschilds, and others) were allowed to invest in them; privately owned Russian rigs in 1900 produced half of the world's crude oil. Financiers, manufacturers, and the "rail-way kings" in transportation bore responsibilities earlier held by government and chafed at maltreatment by administrators.

Late-imperial Russian cities were decked out with electric power, streetcars, and department stores. In the environs, ur-banism met the village at the *dacha*, the summer home where members of the upper and middle classes could unwind, away from work and from the political police and their informants. And a civil society was stirring. An undergrowth of voluntary associations and philanthropists pursued joint interests and good causes. Liberal and conservative savants pushed the idea of *obshcheniye*, mutuality and intercommunication among indi-viduals and groups.

Why did Imperial Russia go for revolution and not reform?

The Russian Revolution was so earthshattering that it is tempt-ing to read the imperial past as a mere prelude. But all roads did not lead to 1917. Revolution might have been averted had the tsars been more resolute about evolutionary change and had they forsworn international entanglements that overtaxed their powers.

The Great Reforms of Alexander II, 1855 to 1881, were the one time an emperor took a staunchly ameliorative line. They were catalyzed by defeat in Crimea, which clarified the inferiority of the old regime's institutions, army, and technology. Besides manumission of the serfs, Alexander rearmed and revamped the military (shortening conscript service to six years), set up elected municipal governments, and liberalized Russian courts. The tsar-liberator was assassinated in his royal carriage in March 1881, at which point the pendulum swung to obscurantism under his son and namesake Alexander III.

After Alexander III's death in 1894, Nicholas II, the last of the Romanovs, was almost as dyed-in-the-wool. Only under duress did he edge toward piecemeal change. Russia's thrashing in a Pacific war with Japan—a non-European, nonwhite parvenu—kindled urban strikes and rural upheaval in 1904–5. Nicholas sent 2,500 to the gallows while also instituting a bicameral parliament, a ministerial cabinet, and political parties; Pyotr Stolypin, his prime minister and interior minister, pushed to make propertied yeomen out of decommunalized peasants and settle them on the Siberian frontier. To the bitter end, the tsar jealously defended his right to veto legislation and appoint cabinet members. He twice sent the Imperial State Duma, the lower house of the legislature, packing when it defied him, and rewrote the electoral code to advantage monarchist parties.

The counterpart to rigidity in the state was a revolutionary movement against the state. Student hotheads from the People's Will society threw the bombs that killed Alexander II (six previous attempts on his life were spoilt by gendarmes); anarchists and leftists later cut down governors, judges, and in September 1911 Premier Stolypin. The Russo-Japanese War incited an undertow of extremism on the right. The Union of the Russian People, rabidly anticapitalist and anti-Semitic, was a precursor to European fascism, organizing pogroms against Jews and reformist members of the intelligentsia.

The possibility of the Eurasian empire with feet of clay muddling through was foreclosed in August 1914, when in its third foreign mishap since 1850 it sleepwalked into the Great War, later to be known as World War I. Out of a misplaced sense of honor, and in league with its Balkans friend, Serbia, and allies France and Britain, Russia took on Germany and the Austro-Hungarian Empire in an eastern theater bigger and more fluid than the western. It had to transport troops into action from a much larger rear than Germany and Austria, and along a third as many railway tracks. No sooner had Russians in their greatcoats arrived in force than Turkey entered the fray in October 1914. Nicholas's war aims were extravagant—Habsburg Galicia and Bukovina, Istanbul (Constantinople) and the Turkish Straits between the Black Sea and the Mediterranean, and those districts of Anatolia populated by the Oriental Orthodox Armenians.

Hours before his army's mobilization, Nicholas had a premonition of "a monstrous slaughter" if war came. It was so very true. Preliminary Russian successes were negated by territorial losses and mutinies. Two million servicemen and a half-million noncombatants died in military action and 4 million soldiers fell prisoner. Inflation, interruptions in provisions, and restriction of vodka sales to restaurants only gnawed at support on the home front. Relations between the Great and Little Russians were inflamed. Bread riots in Petrograd in February 1917 led to an uprising when peasant draftees balked at orders to fire on the crowd. On March 2 (March 15 under the Gregorian calendar Russia was to accept in February 1918), Nicholas abdicated to his younger brother, Grand Duke Mikhail Romanov, regent for the adolescent and hemophiliac *tsarevich* (heir-presumptive), Alexei. Mikhail turned down the scepter until a government in concordance with "the will of the people" could tender it.

A middle-of-the-road Provisional Government vested by the State Duma pronounced Russia a republic on September 1 (14), 1917, and called an election for a Constituent Assembly which would draft a democratic constitution. Hanging on to the tsar's objectives, it refused to pull out of the Great War; an insane offensive in July against the Austro-Hungarians and Germans in Galicia miscarried in fifteen days. Come autumn, Russia was in a condition of diarchy, as Prime Minister Alexander Kerensky cohabited with the "soviets" (*sovets*)— councils elected at raucous meetings of factory workers, soldiers, and peasants. The soviets flocked to socialistic groups and in case after case to the most ascetic and confrontational of Russia's Marxist parties, the Bolsheviks. The Petrograd Soviet, its heady slogans "All Power to the Soviets" and "Peace, Bread, and Land," was the bellwether. On October 25 (November 7), 1917, pro-Bolshevik Red Guards swarmed into the Winter Palace and overthrew Kerensky and his government. The day after, the All-Russian Congress of Soviets appointed the Bolshevik leader, Lenin, as head of the Council of People's Commissars, the first Soviet government.

3

COMMUNISM

Who were Lenin and the Bolsheviks?

"Revolutions," ruminates the protagonist in *Doctor Zhivago*, Boris Pasternak's tour de force about a physician-poet who outlasts the Russian Revolution, "are made by fanatical men of action with one-track minds, geniuses at confining themselves to a limited field." Yurii Zhivago taps into the same vein as Kennan's reference to the Soviet leadership in the 1940s being "committed fanatically" to its animus against the West.

In 1917 and right through Russia's protracted revolution, the man with the most one-track mind of all was Lenin (b. 1870). Lenin hatched Bolshevism in 1903 as the militant wing of the five-year-old Russian Social Democratic Labor Party, the Russian affiliate of the Socialist International. "Bolshevik" was a reference to the majority (*bolshinstvo*) his group won in a handful of votes at the Social Democrats' 1903 congress. Its lodestar was revolution without delay, and revolution presided over by professional revolutionaries from the intelligentsia and not by unskilled workers or trade unionists. In 1912, at a conference in Prague, Lenin severed the group from the "Mensheviks" (minority) into a Russian Social Democratic Labor Party (Bolsheviks). Two more infelicitous names, with parentheses, were to follow: All-Russian Communist Party (Bolsheviks) from 1918 until 1925, and All-Union Communist Party (Bolsheviks) from 1925 to 1952. From 1952 to 1991, the organization was the Communist Party of the Soviet Union, or CPSU.

Lenin (an alias—he was baptized Vladimir Ilyich Ulyanov in Simbirsk, on the lower Volga) studied law at university and clerked in an attorney's office, but joined the revolutionary underground in the 1890s and spent two years in prison and three in the Siberian boondocks. His modus operandi was sectarian and conspiratorial. This did not change when political parties were legalized in 1905 and Bolsheviks were elected to the Duma in 1907. The party was banned in 1914 for its antiwar position.

Lenin left Russia in 1907 for Western Europe, where he had lived the émigré's life from 1900 to 1905, and once again churned out pamphlets and did party business from afar. After August 1914, he agitated to fracture the Socialist International, whose signatories had voted for credits for the "imperialist war," and to open the sluicegates to "class war" and revolution. He returned only in April 1917, in a sealed train from Geneva courtesy of the German government. Six months after his party came out of hiding with the grand total of twenty-four thousand members, it took power—"vlast"—with not an iota of experience at governing.

"The Internationale" bade men and women of the left to demolish present society "down to its foundations," and on the carcass to build "our new world," where "those who have nothing will become everything." Axiomatic for the Bolsheviks was that socialist revolution in the empire of the Romanovs alone would be in vain: its forces of production were just moving out of the agrarian into the industrial, capitalist phase. Socialism, Marxist scripture taught, could be introduced only in a mature capitalist society, on the shoulders of a majority of the downtrodden. The most to be hoped for in Russia was that a rebellion would set alight a more expansive conflagration, emboldening socialists to grab power in Berlin or Paris and then ride to the rescue of their Slavic comrades. To this end, the Bolsheviks worked from day one to institute a Comintern, or Communist International, to displace the timorous Socialist International. Delegates from thirty-four far-left national parties pledged at a Comintern congress in March 1919 to foment revolution in unison, to which end each was to create "iron military order in its ranks."

Why did the Bolsheviks prevail in the Russian Revolution?

The coup d'état of October/November 1917 paralyzed the state and flung out centrifugal forces. Patches of the former empire took to governing themselves or to out-and-out chaos. Feckless Kerensky made off to France and would die a natural death in New York fifty-three years later. The Romanovs, held under house arrest, had no such luck. King George V denied Nicholas II, his first cousin (and spitting image), asylum in Britain, against the advice of Prime Minister Lloyd George. Grand Duke Mikhail was murdered in a wood near Perm in June 1918. In July Nicholas, the German-born Empress Alexandra, Alexei, and their daughters Anastasia, Maria, Olga, and Tatyana were shot and bayoneted in the cellar of a merchant's mansion in Yekaterinburg, over the ridge of the Urals from Perm. Reds (Bolsheviks and pro-Bolsheviks), Whites (anti-Bolsheviks), and Greens (peasant guerrillas) went at one another in a Russian Civil War that lasted until 1921.

The Reds were on their own, without the longed-for lifeline from the international proletariat. On behalf of a radiant future, they perpetrated misery, and suffered it, in flabbergasting amounts. The precept of "democratic centralism" forced the party's footsoldiers to do as they were told in central directives, categorically and under pain of expulsion. Despite almost dying from an assassin's bullet in 1918, from which he never fully mended, Lenin was able to squelch internal squabbles and in 1921 to get the party's congress to outlaw formal factions within it. The Bolsheviks' cells in the soviets—the elected bodies that were their ticket to victory in 1917—drafted bills and resolutions, shepherded them through the legislative process, and had councilors do the bidding of the soviets' executive arms, most headed by party members. The Whites, by contrast, had no organizational core and were a patchwork—monarchists, republicans, constitutional democrats, free-wheeling Cossacks, Russian jingoists—commanded by politically obtuse military officers. The underarmed Greens had no set ideology, fought mostly in central Russia, and were often led by illiterates.

It helped the Bolsheviks' cause that they were alert to cultivating a mass base. A truce in December 1917 was a gesture to war-weary soldiers. Germany held out in peace negotiations for Ukrainian, Belarusian, Baltic, and Crimean Tatar territories housing one-quarter of the population. Lenin gritted his teeth and went along with the capitulatory Brest-Litovsk Treaty of March 1918. Party propaganda made hay with antiforeignism when Britain, France, the United States, and Japan invaded coastal areas and openly supported the Whites. In a barrage of edicts, factories were nationalized, foodstuffs and housing redistributed to manual workers, and gentry estates abolished.

Debate had simmered in the Socialist International about how to respond to Europe's cultural and linguistic diversity. The Austrian Marxists Karl Renner and Otto Bauer propounded "extraterritorial autonomy," affording rights to the members of minority groups as individuals, regardless of location. The alternative was the territorialized solution, federalism, which Lenin came to espouse by 1914. Foreseeing political profit with the minorities, he cast a socialist Russia as a "union of regions" with every right to separate after a referendum. As a first stab at the problem, the Congress of Soviets resolved in January 1918 to redo the empire as a "federation of Soviet national republics." It would be left to workers and peasants in each republic "to decide independently . . . whether they wish to participate in the federal government . . . and on what terms."

There was more to the Bolsheviks' victory than zealousness, esprit de corps, and programmatic content. They never shied away from the mailed fist. By the time of the slaying of the royals, they had dispersed the Constituent Assembly, where the village-based Socialist Revolutionaries had a plurality of the delegates and only 23 percent were Bolsheviks. In brisk order the party instituted a secret police force, the Cheka—the Extraordinary Commission for the Struggle against Counterrevolution and Sabotage, headed by Felix Dzerzhinsky—and retooled the paramilitary Red Guards into a conscript Workers' and Peasants' Red Army, with ex–tsarist officers in many command posts. Lenin's snap decision in February 1918 to reposition the seat of government from Petrograd to the ancient capital, Moscow, made to escape the then-advancing Germans and never reversed, gave the Reds the central nodes of railroad and telegraph. Operating on the interior line out of old Muscovy, the Red Army and allied militias were able to pick off the strongholds of the Whites one at a time, at far ends of Russia—from the Caucasus to Crimea and central Ukraine and Belarus (which the Germans left after armistice), the Urals, and the Pacific. Mopping up Green detachments was left to the later stages of the conflict. Lenin masterminded the war from a Kremlin study in the palace of the imperial Governing Senate, looking out over Red Square and St. Basil's Cathedral.

Collateral damage rippled out from the battleground. War Communism, the rough-and-ready policy paradigm of 1918–21, drew on World War I mobilization and the Bolsheviks' unabashedly hard-left convictions. An incipient civil society was straitjacketed; those associations that got through the meat grinder of the war were bent to the party's will. Government posses requisitioned peasants' grain for urban Russia and the army, provoking a drop in the harvest, rural banditry, and degeneration into barter. Cities emptied out pell-mell as industrial production, now under government dictate, nosedived. Disaffection spilled over to the army and climaxed in a sailors' revolt at the Kronstadt naval base, the headquarters of the Baltic Fleet, in March 1921.

Mortality was the worst in any civil conflict to date, bar none, with 950,000 military deaths and 8 or 9 million civilians expiring from combat, captivity, epidemic disease, or starvation. The grimmest of the famine was in the breadbasket provinces of the Volga valley. Peasants were reduced to eating pets, acorns, tree bark, and roof thatch. Herbert Hoover's American Relief Administration (ARA) and the International Committee of the Red Cross fed 10 to 12 million Russians a day in 1922. The ARA workers who stopped by a shelter near Samara found the floor "littered with bundles of dirty, stinking rags, concealing the cadaverous bodies of young children with such old, shriveled faces that they look like mummies." Orphans and juvenile castoffs slept and panhandled on the streets of Soviet cities until the 1930s.

The Bolshevik faithful read the outcome of revolution and civil war as giddy vindication of their common denominator since 1917: that in politics the end absolves the means, come what may. For Russia, the time was a crucible for methods righteous, arbitrary, and vengeful—censorship more suffocating than under the tsar, confiscation of property, arrests by social type, hostage taking, and summary executions by the Cheka.

To those familiar with the old Russia, the shell-shocked society that emerged from the maelstrom was all but unintelligible. Three million Russians took flight from their motherland between 1917 and 1929. In Paris, Berlin, Belgrade, and elsewhere, they "made up a shadow nation ... the remnants of a vanished world." Intellectual and artistic luminaries like Marc Chagall, Sergei Diaghilev, Vladimir Nabokov, Igor Sikorsky, and Igor Stravinsky were but the cream of the cream.

When and how did the Communist regime gel?

The Bolsheviks/Communists threw up legal scaffolding in the July 1918 constitution for the RSFSR, that is, for the empire minus its then breakaway or enemy-occupied extremities. The title stood for the Russian Socialist Federative Soviet Republic; abstrusely, the second and fourth terms in the title were to switch places in 1936. The fledgling republic, so said the constitution, was "a free union of free nations," dedicated to "the obliteration of exploitation of man by man, elimination of the division of society into classes, pitiless repression of the exploiters, the socialist organization of society, and the triumph of socialism in every country." Authority was vested nominally in the bottom-up soviets, even as top-down executive organs were asserting primacy over them. Beginning with the Turkic Bashkirs of the Urals in March 1919, homelands were designated for the larger of the minority ethnicities. The four-fifths of the RSFSR's citizens who were ethnic (Great) Russians were unaffected.

On December 30, 1922, the RSFSR and three Red Army–domesticated socialist republics to its west and southwest—Belarus, Ukraine, and Transcaucasia—initialed a union treaty of twenty-six articles. A constitution for a federal USSR, or Soviet Union, came into force on January 31, 1924. The Soviet hammer-and-sickle waved over 97 percent of what had been the Russian Empire, 8,144,000 square miles. The eastern stretches of a restored Polish state, Finland, Bessarabia (into Romania), and the Baltic provinces of Livonia, Courland, and Vilna (now reconstituted as interbellum Estonia, Latvia, and Lithuania) were the major losses.

The new union was a quasi-empire whose format "cloaked nonconsensual control in the language of self-determination and sovereignty to blur the line between domination and consent." But the change in modality had immense aftereffects. Tethering administrative–territorial anatomy to ascriptive identity, ethnofederalism was to reify ethnicity where it had previously been weedy or nonexistent. It would be all the more so when the Soviet census, starting in 1926, asked the individual to state her or his ethnic affiliation or nationality (*nationalnost*); when demographers and cartographers painstakingly drew political and administrative boundaries to correspond with community boundaries; and when identity papers introduced in the 1930s ("internal passports") contained a line recording the national-Ity of the bearer, not to be removed until the post-Soviet 1990s. These arrangements helped make the Soviet Union a Eurasian mosaic of nationalities and not a melting pot.

Some ranking Bolsheviks, including Dzerzhinsky and the party's new chief functionary ("general secretary"), Joseph Stalin, had intended for the national minorities to be given only subaltern precincts, embedded as islands in a sea of Russianness, in one Russian socialist republic where the common waters had no ethnic coloration at all. At the behest of Lenin, the "union" (*soyuznaya*) republics of the USSR were made coequal—as he said, the Soviet Union was to be "a federation of republics possessing equal rights," among them the right to secede. The RSFSR itself had the very same right, on paper, fine print that came back to haunt the Soviet state in its late-century time of troubles. The RSFSR, moreover, was Russian in the civic sense only, and not named after or consecrated to the interests of the ethnically Russian. The Russians, as Terry Martin writes, were "the Soviet Union's awkward nationality, too large to ignore but likewise too formidable to [be given] the same institutional status as the ... other major nationalities."

Between 1924 and 1936, five national republics in Turkestan were carved out of the RSFSR (Kazakhstan, Kyrgyzstan, Tajikistan, Turkmenistan, and Uzbekistan) and Transcaucasia was trisected (into the South Caucasus republics of Armenia, Azerbaijan, and Georgia). Eponymous "titular" or "entitled" (*titulnaya*) nationalities had prearranged linguistic and cultural rights. The East Slavic Little Russians were now a normal nationality, Ukrainian, with a language and not a dialect, and not part of an overarching Russian people; the White Russians or Belarusians, too, had their linguistic cranny and republic. Fifty languages that were in oral form only were transcribed by Soviet specialists, in Latin script in the 1920s and after

1930 in Cyrillic. The Great Russians were great no more, just Russians ("russkiye"); the imperial designator remained in casual use. An indigenization (*korenizatsiya*) policy trained cadres from the titular groups and seated them in positions of authority in their republics; the Russians, exalted as "elder brothers," predominated at the Soviet center. Russian was the lingua franca and Cyrillic the common alphabet (except for the Hebrew script for Yiddish, the sui generis Armenian and Georgian alphabets, and after World War II Latin orthography for Estonian, Latvian, and Lithuanian). The union republics would in time settle at fifteen. Nine subsumed cookie-cutter provinces—*oblasts*—which had no ethnic identity and were more or less the size of the tsarist guberniyas. Nested within six of the union republics were lesser nationality units, the "autonomous Soviet socialist republics" or ASSRs. Sixteen out of twenty-two ASSRs in 1939 were located in the RSFSR.

The 1924 constitution touted Marxist ideals anew: the union would be "a step towards unifying the toilers of all countries into a World Socialist Soviet Republic." The Moscow Soviet held a juried contest for a futuristic Palace of Labor where the world soviet was to meet. But the fiery talk about revolution tomorrow was ringing hollow. A Comintern-backed Bavarian Soviet Republic lasted only three weeks in April–May 1919; Romanian troops that August squashed a Hungarian Soviet Republic under Béla Kun, after four and one-half months of decree making and scuffling with all in the vicinity; a Red Army march on Warsaw to export revolution to Poland and Germany, commanded by the swashbuckling Mikhail Tukhachevskii, failed in July–August 1920; and short-lived republics went up in smoke in Alsace, Upper Saxony, Slovakia, and the Persian province of Gilan. The first pro-Soviet regime to last was in Outer Mongolia, sandwiched between eastern Siberia and China. The Mongolian People's Republic came about in July 1921, when Mongol Communists teamed up with Soviet platoons in hot pursuit of a renegade White general. A month later a people's republic was declared in the mountainous region of Tuva, on Mongolia's northwestern flank, largely barren of human habitation. A Russian satellite since 1914, Tuva was to be annexed outright by the Soviet Union (as an ASSR within the RSFSR) in 1944.

In a concession to cruel reality, the end goal of a worldwide firestorm of revolution with its epicenter in Russia was put on hold, though in no way forsaken. The government, uninvited to the Paris Peace Conference of 1919, broke out of its solitude with the Anglo-Soviet Trade Agreement of March 1921. The Treaty of Rapallo with Weimar Germany, concluded in April 1922, paved the way for diplomatic and economic cooperation with Russia's World War I enemy. Until the Nazi takeover of 1933, Germany trained pilots and military engineers in the Soviet Union and sold Moscow equipment for its armaments industry; joint projects included work on advanced aviation and armor systems and chemical weapons.

How to cope with the domestic blowback from the postponement of utopia was a conundrum for the regime. Lenin, desperate for postwar recovery, scuttled War Communism in March 1921 and embarked on his New Economic Policy (NEP). Leaving the "commanding heights" of heavy industry, banking, and the rail network with the state, the NEP prescribed private ownership and markets in agriculture, light industry, and some trade. Peasants were relieved of grain requisitioning and allowed to pay a tax in kind (a cash tax after 1924) and to sell their surplus at the going price. The NEP's mixed economy was a roaring success. Pre-1914 production was equaled by 1926, and urban growth resumed.

Liberalization in economics had no political counterpart. Elections to the soviets were put on an ever tighter leash. The Mensheviks, who had controlled the republic of Georgia during the Civil War, were erased in 1921, and the last oppositionist party, the Socialist Revolutionaries, in 1922 after a show trial. Soviet officialese held that the USSR was a dictatorship of the proletariat, and more virtuous than the "bourgeois democracy" of capitalist countries because of its bond with industrial workers. But the legislative soviets, now noncompetitively elected, had been transmuted into a façade for the executive branch, and the executive into a façade for the party apparatus. What masqueraded as a dictatorship of the proletariat was a party-state dictatorship *over* the proletariat and everybody else.

What were "socialism in one country" and "the revolution from above"?

Lenin thought he was putting up the NEP for ten or twenty years. This is not how it panned out. Even before his early death in January 1924, at the age of fifty-three, officials and party members recoiled against coddling "counterrevolutionaries" and "profiteers" such as the peasants working rural parcels and the "NEPmen" (small-time manufacturers, carters, shopkeepers, and service providers) of the cities. Looking forward, the regime's chosen formula was "socialism in one country." Concocted by the theoretician Nikolai Bukharin, it was appropriated in 1924 by General Secretary Stalin and cunningly attributed to the departed Lenin. Socialism in one country was about self-sufficiency. The precocious revolution the Russians had made, in the wrong place developmentally, was now solid on its feet. The "capitalist encirclement" of the USSR by ideological opponents could not be allowed to hold it back. "Building socialism" at home, ex nihilo, would bring modernity and in the fullness of time Marx and Engels's full-grown communism—and its export.

In 1928–29, after a half-decade of polemics and bruising power struggles, the party operationalized socialism in one country as a seismic, post-NEP "revolution from above." This latest spasm of revolutionary energy was as totalizing as that of 1917 to 1921. "There are no fortresses Bolsheviks can't storm" was the refrain that captured the Promethean temper of the times.

The cornerstone of the revolution from above was breakneck collectivization and industrialization. On the receiving end, prosperous peasants (*kulaks*) were expropriated and 1.8 million of them sent to concentration camps or exile. Farmworkers and the nomads of the Eurasian Steppe and Arctic were corralled into collective farms (*kolkhozes*). They were to meet mandatory production quotas but also be outfitted with seed grain, tractors, fertilizer, and electric power at government expense. In protest, as during the Civil War, villagers burned and hid crops and butchered livestock. Famine supervened in Ukraine, the RSFSR, and Kazakhstan, and with no international food aid upcoming. In the towns, the NEPmen were taken off the street and private shops closed. Mines and factories, all now the property of the state, were put under governmental commissariats and given one- and five-year output plans by Gosplan, the State Planning Committee. Flagships like the Magnitogorsk Iron and Steel Works in the Urals, the Dnieper Hydroelectric Station in southern Ukraine, and the Moscow subway set the tone. "Shock workers" vied to overshoot production shares. Alexei Stakhanov, a miner in eastern Ukraine, set a record for jackhammering and shoveling 227 metric tons of coal in one day in 1935, during the second five-year plan. He was pictured on the front cover of *Time* magazine and in 1938 elected a deputy of the USSR Supreme Soviet, the new rubberstamp parliament.

In the same groundswell, Russian culture was chastised and drilled in the new ways. The regime tore into organized religion as a relic of superstition, cashiering Christmas trees (known hereafter as New Year's trees) and Easter eggs. Most houses of worship were closed, recycled as warehouses or jails, and church bells were melted down for industrial use. By 1940 only about five hundred Russian Orthodox parishes were still holding services, where there had been fifty thousand in 1914; mosques for Central Asian Muslims dwindled from twenty thousand to one hundred. Writers, the most admired members of the intelligentsia, were enjoined to be "engineers of human souls." They, architects, painters, sculptors, cinematographers, and composers were all to produce in the genre of "socialist realism," associated with the proletarian scribe Maxim Gorky. It glorified functionality, the collective, and service to socialism.

Who was Stalin and what was his role?

Once Lenin's embalmed body was put on exhibit in a ziggurat mausoleum on Red Square in 1924, Stalin reigned supreme in the Soviet Union until 1953, or 40 percent of the Communist period.

Joseph Stalin (b. Iosif Vissarionovich Jugashvili in 1878 or 1879), expelled from an Orthodox theological seminary in Georgia as a youth, was on the run as a clandestine Bolshevik operative in the Caucasus after 1903 and stuck it out for seven years in Siberia. In the Civil War he answered for nationalities policy in the Council of People's Commissars and was a political officer and troubleshooter in the army. He counted enough for Lenin to nominate him to the party's policy-making Central Committee right after the Prague conference of 1912 and to be one of five on its first executive Politburo (Political Bureau) in 1919.

Lenin, though troubled by Stalin's uncouthness, put him forward for the new general secretaryship in April 1922, the month before he took to his bed with a crippling stroke. Lenin later had second thoughts. In a "Testament" laboriously composed with his wife, Nadezhda Krupskaya, the following winter, he asked the party congress to "think about a way to remove Stalin and appoint another man in his stead who [would be] more tolerant, more loyal, more polite and more considerate to the comrades, less capricious." But the reproof was kept under wraps, Stalin promised to be less obnoxious, and he retained his job. Had Lenin not been wheelchair-bound and suicidal, Stalin might not have gotten off scot-free.

Lenin had led by virtue of personal charisma and status as a forefather. He was head of government but held no position in the party other than seats in the Politburo and its parent Central Committee. Stalin came across as a drudge and a nondescript aficionado of the Bolshevik line when placed beside Lenin or firebrands like Leon Trotsky (chairman of the Petrograd Soviet in 1917 and organizer of the Red Army), Grigorii Zinoviev (party secretary in Petrograd/Leningrad and emcee of the Comintern), and Bukharin. But Stalin turned the tables on the naysayers. The superficially menial post of general secretary, or head of the Central Committee Secretariat, was critical in the infighting before and after the death of Lenin. Lenin's missive set down in 1922–23 that Stalin had even then "concentrated boundless power in his hands."

As gatekeeper of the Communist Party, Stalin standardized its bookkeeping and finances and took charge of its burgeoning workforce of *apparatchik*s. A post–Civil War shakeout of the state service let him hire and fire personnel in all branches through *nomenklatura*—the noun for both a list of slots under party tutelage and the occupants. From his office on Old Square and, after 1930, in the Kremlin's Senate building, Stalin packed the committees that sent delegates to a party congress that now resembled a pep rally more than a deliberative body. He and his confrères had supplanted the party's electorate, its mass membership, with a compact selectorate that without interference from below handpicked the inner cadre of Central Committee, Politburo, Secretariat, and general secretary. Patronage and protection, conjoined in a "circular flow of power," let Stalin reward supporters and flush out Trotsky, Zinoviev, Bukharin, and other wayward Old Bolsheviks. In the regions, the party first secretaries ran auxiliary political machines as prefects of the new regime.

In December 1929, with the Soviet Union in the throes of its revolution from above, festivities for Stalin's fiftieth birthday were the coming out of a slavish personality cult. One strand was patrimonialism, a reprise of the tsar as a stern but caring father. But "comrade Stalin," lauded for perspicacity on everything from military science and town planning to linguistics, far outshone the emperor of old. Stalingrad (in the RSFSR), Stalino (in Ukraine), and Stalinabad (in Tajikistan) bore his name; flowerbeds were done in the shape of his mustachioed visage; placards of gratitude to him "for our happy childhood" hung over the entrances to daycare centers and schools. The USSR constitution of 1936 was presented as "the Stalin constitution."

With tragic implications, the man Soviet Russia put on a pedestal had a sociopathic streak. His psyche, as Stephen Kotkin says in his magisterial *Stalin: Paradoxes of Power*, was shaped by a "supremacy-insecurity dyad." The leader's makeup meshed with the broader deportment of the regime. "Both the revolution ... and Stalin's personal dictatorship within it found themselves locked in a kind of inbuilt, structural paranoia, triumphant yet enveloped by ill-wishers and enemies."

To lose Stalin's good graces in the 1920s could spell disgrace and superannuation. In the 1930s it could spell extermination. Fifty-six percent of the delegates to the 1934 party congress, and 71 percent of the Central Committee selected there, were arrested, interrogated, and executed as turncoats by 1939. In the venomous Great Purge of 1936 to 1938, ex-Politburo members, in their number Bukharin and Zinoviev, were put on trial and shot; Trotsky, cast out from the USSR in 1929, was felled by a Soviet agent in Mexico in 1940, with a mountaineer's ice axe. The judiciary, regional bigwigs, industrialists, the intelligentsia, and the officer corps were ensnared—Mikhail Tukhachevskii, the marshal who led the jaunt into Poland in 1920 and crushed the Kronstadt seamen in 1921, was shot in June 1937, as were his spouse and two brothers. Béla Kun of the Hungarian Soviet Republic of 1919, later a Comintern worker, was among the hundreds of foreign Communists disposed of. The head of the secret police, Nikolai Yezhov, having obeyed orders to the letter, was incarcerated in 1938 and met his end in 1940. In the union republics, the ranks of those overly attached to the titular nationality were decimated. The dead were unpersons, their names stricken from books and the encyclopedias and their faces airbrushed out of photographs.

A new constitution in 1936 retold the fairytale that power was exercised by the soviets but recast the USSR as "a socialist state of workers and peasants," no longer, formulaically, as a dictatorship of the proletariat. It blended in a reference to the Communist Party's directorial role, as "the leadership nucleus of all organizations of the working people." Even the party made a mockery of the niceties. The Central Committee and Politburo seldom met, as extemporaneous commissions were more to Stalin's taste, and not one congress was convened between March 1939 and October 1952. In 1941 he was made chairman of the governmental Council of People's Commissars (the Council of Ministers after 1946) concurrently with general secretary. It scarcely mattered: comrade Stalin's word was law.

Was Stalin's Soviet Union totalitarian?

The enunciated goals of Soviet Communism collided with those of the right-wing dictatorships of interwar Europe, and the two were on opposite sides in World War II. Still, it dawned on some that Stalin's Russia, Adolf Hitler's Third Reich, and Benito Mussolini's Fascist Italy were birds of a feather and constituted a discrete and virulent type. From the hoary authoritarianism of years past, totalitarianism was differentiated by the ambition and means to achieve total penetration of, and hegemony over, society. Mussolini's 1923 dictum—"Everything within the state, nothing outside the state, nothing against the state"—gave the totalitarian mystique in a nutshell. Aphorisms to this effect came from pioneers of dystopian fiction like Aldous Huxley, George Orwell, and the Russian Yevgenii Zamyatin, whose 1921 *We* was a blistering preview of police-state practices.

In their much-cited *Totalitarian Dictatorship and Autocracy*, Carl J. Friedrich and Zbigniew Brzezinski in the 1950s gave a checklist of the gears of totalitarian orders of the left and the right: (1) an ideology, "consisting of an official body of doctrine covering all vital aspects of man's existence to which everyone ... is supposed to adhere" and making "a chiliastic claim, based upon a radical rejection of the existing society and conquest of the world for the new one"; (2) a single mass party, vertically organized and led by one man, "the 'dictator'"; (3) "terroristic police control, supporting but also supervising the party for its leaders" and employing an up-to-date toolbox for surveillance and punishment; (4) a "near-monopoly of control, in the hands of the party and its subservient cadres, of all means of effective mass communication"; (5) regime control of the instruments for armed combat; and (6) "central control and direction of the entire economy through ... bureaucratic coordination."

The USSR in its heyday had (1) the archetypal messianic credo in Marxism-Leninism; (2) the CPSU as mass party, and its general secretary as Orwellian Big Brother; (3) wanton terror; (4) state- and party-run media (from the Central Committee tribune *Pravda* to the factory newsletter), secrecy cloaking the government and party, and ubiquitous thought police charged with forging "the new Soviet man"; (5) a disarmed society; and (6) an economy owned and managed entirely by government.

If any one of the six pillars is to be underlined, it is the third, terror. Its scope and impact cannot be overstated. It was meted out by retributory agencies following in the footsteps of the Cheka—the OGPU (United State Political Directorate, formed in 1922), NKVD (People's Commissariat of Internal Affairs, 1934), MVD (Ministry of Internal Affairs, 1946), MGB (Ministry of State Security, 1946)—all ensconced in the Lubyanka, the squat insurance-company head office Dzerzhinsky hijacked in 1918. The internal passports issued in 1932 let the police track urban residents aged sixteen and over nationwide (until 1969, peasants got papers only when leaving for work in the city). In the Great Terror, the paroxysm of violence extending the Great Purge of the nomenklatura into society, 1,548,000 persons were taken under arrest in 1937 and 1938 and charged with political wrongdoing; 682,000 were shot. Three to 4 million, if not more, died in the famine after agricultural collectivization, and 1.5 million in the deportations of untouchables such as priests and former nobles, White officers, kulaks, and NEPmen. Gulag, the Chief Directorate of Corrective Labor Camps and Colonies, was a state within a state. Eighteen or 19 million prisoners, political and nonpolitical, passed through it between 1930 and 1953; another 6 to 7 million were resettled to desolate northern and eastern tracts of the RSFSR. Who can say how many innocents, like Yurii Zhivago's Lara, were "forgotten as a nameless number on a list that afterwards got mislaid"? *Gulag Archipelago,* the magnum opus of the former prisoner Alexander Solzhenitsyn, remains the best guide.

One omission in overviews like Friedrich and Brzezinski's is the Soviet phobia about subversion from without. The borders were compulsively patrolled. Cross-border travel was admissible only for official delegates; the nonconvertibility of the USSR ruble limited even them on the outside. Foreign books and newspapers were perused in closed libraries. International mail was intercepted, and correspondence even with family members could be seditious. Radio receivers were hardwired for four national channels. The spurious arraignments from the show trials of the 1930s all charged the defendants with being Western stooges.

Another facet not to be missed had to do with civil society. Any new freestanding association was beyond the pale. Those few older ones the Kremlin put up with—the Russian Orthodox Church being the classic example—were infiltrated by informers. The party-state ginned up its own mass activities and transmission belts and made participation in them de rigueur. Elections to the pyramid of soviets were a travesty with a lone name on the ballot—the candidate of "The Bloc of Communists and Non–Party People"—but stated turnout closed in on 100 percent. A flotilla of regimented organizations permeated social groups central to political socialization. Boys and girls were streamed into the Little Octobrists at the age of seven, the Young Pioneers at ten, and the Komsomol (Communist Youth League) at fourteen. Workers were members of the official labor unions. Women, writers, and even beekeepers and philatelists had special-purpose organizations.

Compliance with instructions is never total in a totalitarian system, and ingenuity is never zeroed out. Decision makers in Stalin's time had to be artful dodgers so as to endure in body and mind and do their allotted duties. Scientists, engineers, and artists worked wonders off-the-cuff. Andrei Tupolev and Vladimir Petlyakov inked plans for the USSR's best bomber planes in a *sharashka* (hush-hush NKVD laboratory) from 1937 to 1941; in a related lab, Sergei Korolyov and Valentin Glushko were the brains of the Soviet missile program. Osip Mandelstam wrote luminous verse as an outcast in Voronezh; he died in transit to a labor camp in 1938. Mikhail Bulgakov, blacklisted for publication, gave salon readings of his cryptic masterpiece *Master and Margarita* in 1939; the novel did not come out in print until 1966, twenty-six years after he passed away. Sergei Prokofiev and Dmitrii Shostakovich, two of the virtuoso music makers of the century, composed superb symphonies under fire for "formalism" and "antidemocratic" thoughts. The young Solzhenitsyn was arrested as an army captain for making jokes about Stalin in letters to a friend. He drafted twenty-eight poems and prose texts in jails and camps between 1945 and 1956—jotting them down, memorizing them, and shredding the slips of paper.

How did World War II affect Soviet Communism?

High Stalinism was driven as much by the laws of the geopolitical jungle as by dogma and power lust. With Hitler rising in Europe and a militarist Japan on the prowl in Asia, the international context could not have been uglier. In a talk to industrial executives in 1931, Stalin signposted up-tempo, state-led development as the one means of keeping the USSR afloat. The union had better be forewarned by the history of Muscovite and Imperial Russia, which were beset time after time. "Those who fall behind get beaten," Stalin fulminated. Unless Soviet Russia caught up with the leading nations in ten years, "we shall go under."

The development gap had not been shut when Germany rumbled into the USSR on June 22, 1941, but the Soviets did not go under, either. Stalin had been lulled into complacency by the Molotov–Ribbentrop Pact of August 23, 1939 (named after the foreign ministers Vyacheslav Molotov and Joachim von Ribbentrop), and by its furtive protocols extinguishing Poland and ceding him a cordon sanitaire in the west. Hitler expected a short war. "We have only to kick in the door," he crowed to his generals, "and the whole rotten structure will come crashing down." With the enemy at the gates of Moscow and Leningrad and 45 percent of the population under the German yoke, the Red Army had its back to the wall. The tide turned with victory in the epic battle for Stalingrad, a steppe city six hundred miles southeast of Moscow, in February 1943. The USSR took Germany's unconditional surrender with its allies on May 8–9, 1945. In August it marched into Japanese-occupied Manchuria, the southern half of Sakhalin Island, and the four islands in the Kurile chain just north of Hokkaido—redress for 1904–5 and in Manchuria a beachhead for Mao Zedong's Chinese Communist forces. Soviet annexation of the four islands in 1946 was never to be accepted by Tokyo.

World War I did in the Russian monarchy. World War II gave the Communist dictatorship a new lease on life. Its organs of repression were not idle: failed commanders were shot, deserters and shirkers sent to penal battalions, and whole nationalities deported for purportedly collaborating with the Germans. But Soviet power was also able to pose as the defender of society writ large, against an assailant for whom the peoples of the USSR were subhuman. Six million soldiers and .officers took out party cards at the front (4 million Communists died there). The "all-people's war" was to define the Soviet state almost as conclusively as the nativity story of class war and revolution. A victory parade on June 24, 1945, recapped the new mythology. Forty thousand soldiers traipsed through Red Square. They hurled German regimental banners onto a bonfire and held aloft the Soviet flag flown over the Reichstag in Berlin on April 30, the day Hitler took cyanide in his Führerbunker.

The embattled Kremlin soft-pedaled revolution: it closed down the Comintern in 1943, sacrificing it on the altar of realpolitik, and superseded "The Internationale" with a "USSR State Anthem" in 1944. In the rarefied air of Teheran, Yalta, and Potsdam, there was Stalin in his collarless tunic, puffing on a long-stemmed pipe and posing for photographs with his compeers in the anti-Axis Grand Alliance. The USSR was given occupation quadrants in Germany and Austria and reparations in the form of forced laborers and industrial plant. At San Francisco in June 1945, it was made a charter member of the United Nations (the Soviets had stayed out of the League of Nations until 1934). It had veto power in the Security Council and three votes in the General Assembly: for the central government, Ukraine, and Belarus.

To galvanize the effort, the Soviet government invoked the ghosts of the past and beamed the propaganda spotlight on love of country. The war was labeled the Great Patriotic War, the original Patriotic War having been the repelling of Napoleonic France in 1812. The clarion cry coming out of the trenches was "For the Motherland, for Stalin!" (*Za Rodinu, za Stalina!*). The wartime line was Russocentric, as Stalin saluted "the valiant image of our great forebears" and the 1944 anthem serenaded an "unbreakable union" of republics, "eternally united by Great Russia." In 1943 Stalin made overtures to Russian Orthodoxy, allowing the bishops to meet and select a patriarch. Fifteen thousand churches were reopened by war's end, and the League of Militant Atheists, which had been in the van of church closings, was given the boot. At a Kremlin banquet for military leaders in May 1945, Stalin, the Georgian who spoke thickly-accented Russian, lifted his glass "first of all to the health of the [ethnic] Russian people, because it is the most outstanding nation of all the nations forming the Soviet Union." He singled out the Russians' "clear mind, hardy character, and patience."

Thirty-four million men were conscripted for the Soviet war machine, and 13 million were under arms in 1945; hundreds of thousands more fought as partisans. In the rear, planners evacuated factories to the east and funneled 75 percent of production to provisioning the army. The unemployed and underemployed were pressed into the labor force, workdays were lengthened, and there was a return, temporarily, to food rationing. The USSR surpassed Germany and in some categories the United States in cranking out ordnance like tanks and howitzers (105,000), artillery pieces (516,000), and airplanes (143,000).

The scars left by the war were horrendous. A quarter of the Soviet capital stock lay in rubble in 1945, sown acreage was down by one-third, and there was famine in grain-growing areas. The gruesome human arithmetic is inexact, what with intangibles like boundary changes, migration, POWs, and the Holocaust of the Jews. Russian historians guesstimate that 8.7 million Soviet soldiers died as cannon fodder or in captivity, and there were some 18 million civilian deaths (in the USSR's postwar borders), for a net hemorrhage of 26 to 27 million people; 13.6 million were from the RSFSR. Eleven or 12 million fewer babies were born than would have been in peacetime. The war dead were disproportionately young and male, leading to cockeyed sex ratios (10 million fewer men than women in their twenties and thirties in 1946), a falloff in fertility, and more abortions and households headed by war widows and unwed mothers. The effects were only partially offset by pronatalist medals and stipends.

Territorially, the USSR was on the winning end. It gobbled up a half-million square miles—three states on the Baltic littoral, once provinces of the empire (now Estonia, Latvia, and Lithuania), and slabs of land from abutting European countries

(Finland, Germany, Poland, Czechoslovakia, and Romania) and Japan. The constitutive union republics grew from eleven in 1939 to sixteen, to be pared to fifteen when Karelia, ceded by Finland after the Winter War of 1939–40, was reduced in rank to a subsidiary of the RSFSR in 1956. All the subject territories were Sovietized through kolkhozes, forced-draft industrialization, purges, and deportations.

Ex-post the annexation spree was not the unalloyed blessing it had seemed ex-ante. Little love was lost here for Russia, the Soviet Union, or Communism. NKVD/MVD records show that a half-million Ukrainians, Lithuanians, Latvians, Estonians, and Belarusians fought the Soviets in rural areas until brought to heel after 1950. In the nastiest years, 1944 through 1946, government forces killed 134,000 guerrillas and arrested 195,000. Eighty-five percent of the dead and 67 percent of the arrestees were members of the Ukrainian Insurgent Army and affiliated organizations in Galicia and Volhynia (western Ukraine), whose population was Greek Catholic and had never before lived under the Russians. Lithuania, where the majority confession was Roman Catholic and a "forest brothers" group was strong, produced 11 percent of the combat dead and 22 percent of those arrested. There would come a time, when the Communist Party untied political controls in the 1980s, that the Baltic trio, the western oblasts of Ukraine, and also Moldova (predominantly Bessarabia, taken from Romania) were to be cauldrons of anti-Soviet ethnonationalism. Karelia and Kaliningrad province (formerly East Prussia, capital Königsberg), would probably have been, too, were their native populations not have been largely banished.

A Stalin speech at the Bolshoi Theater in February 1946 dashed hopes that when the guns fell silent there would be a reprieve from terror and conventional Soviet agitprop and resources would be reallocated to consumption. The war, he said, had been "in the nature of an examination of our Soviet system," and the system had "passed the test of fire."

Marxism-Leninism was back, political practices were not to be touched, and heavy industry would be the alpha and omega for a minimum of three more five-year plans. A State Department query about the obdurate Bolshoi homily occasioned George Kennan's Long Telegram.

What was the Cold War, and was there any connection with the internal system of rule?

Prior to World War II the Soviet Union's one client state was Mongolia (ignoring the hermetic microcountry of Tuva, with its population of eighty-one thousand, ingested by the USSR in October 1944). This changed when the war gave the Soviets mastery in Eastern Europe. Intracapitalist contradictions, after a generation's wait, had broken Moscow's way.

Stalin was sure, as he confided to the Yugoslav Communist Milovan Djilas in the spring of 1945, that, in the political void opened up by the war, "Everyone imposes his own system as far as his army can reach. It cannot be otherwise." Communization under the aegis of the Soviet Army (as the Red Army was restyled), the secret services, and their Communist brethren and satraps was at full blast when Winston Churchill in March 1946 made his classic comments at Fulton, Missouri, about an "Iron Curtain" sundering Europe down the middle. A Communist coup in Czechoslovakia in February 1948, Stalin's refusal to let the copycat people's republics participate in the Marshall Plan, and the Soviet blockade of Berlin in 1948–49 spurred Harry Truman to make containment of the USSR official American policy, as recommended by Kennan and others in the national-security elite. In 1949 the United States took the lead in setting up the North Atlantic Treaty Organization (NATO), an anti-Soviet defense pact. The Soviets instated a Council for Mutual Economic Assistance (Comecon), for suturing the economies of Eastern Europe to the USSR, in 1949, and a Warsaw Pact for the bloc armies in 1955.

Theoretical revisions accompanied these empirical vicissitudes. For interwar capitalist encirclement and wartime cooperation with the Western democracies, ideologist Andrei Zhdanov in 1947 swapped a dichotomous world pitting a rapacious "imperialist camp," marshaled by the United States, against an upstanding "anti-imperialist democratic camp," marshaled by the Soviet Union. Without missing a beat, the USSR went from the "hot" war against the racialist Nazis to a "cold" war against the liberal West. Belief that the breeze was in its sails was braced by the coming to power of Communist parties in Asia—in Soviet-occupied North Korea in 1948, hewing to the East European pattern, and in China in 1949 and North Vietnam and Laos in 1954, after rural insurgencies against non-Communist governments and foreign occupiers. Although the quixotic World Socialist Soviet Republic had been excised from the 1936 constitution, the USSR was now the megastar in a solar system of real countries living out Marxism-Leninism. Beyond the bloc, decolonization of the empires of the West Europeans was a godsend to Communists and to Moscow-sympathetic "national liberation movements."

It was the exception for Russians and Americans to trade shots directly in the Cold War. Incomplete records show that fifteen US and perhaps three Soviet planes were shot down in incidents between 1950 and 1970; most were doing reconnaissance. There was larger-scale fighting only once, during the Korean War. From 1951 to 1953, under a shroud of secrecy, Soviet air-defense batteries and airplanes based in Manchuria, painted with North Korean or Chinese markings, engaged UN forces. Dogfights of swept-wing MiG-15s against American F-86 Sabres were the first ever aerial combat between jet-propelled aircraft. During the Vietnam War, while local air-defense operators were being trained in 1965–66, Soviet military advisers operated some radars and antiaircraft artillery against American bombers.

The rule in the Cold War was that direct hostilities were abjured, as the superpowers grappled indirectly through allies, proxies, and covert networks. If there was reason for Moscow to be sanguine about the "correlation of forces" at the onset, the spores for future crises had been strewn. The USSR's stepchildren in Eastern Europe, wobbly in legitimacy, auditioned unlicensed reforms of the Soviet model and catered to nationalist feelings. Josip Broz Tito and the Yugoslav League of Communists spoke out contemptuously against Stalin in 1948 and were written out of the bloc; Stalin mulled over invasion and thought better of it. The Soviets were to send tanks to East Germany in 1953 and Hungary in 1956, and come close in Poland in 1956. Frictions developed with China, whose homegrown Maoist regime was appalled by de-Stalinization (see below) and by Russian condescension.

Nerves were further frayed in the sphere foremost for Soviet policy makers—military power. The USSR demobilized after V-E Day, drawing forces down to 4 million by 1948 (about 2.5 million more than the Americans). Troop strength was back to 6 million by 1953, then skidded to 3.6 million by 1960 (1.1 million more than the United States). Detonation of a Soviet A-bomb at a test site at Semipalatinsk, Kazakhstan, in August 1949, aided by secrets purloined from Los Alamos, was evidence of an ability to vie with the West qualitatively. Hydrogen bombs, ICBMs, and reactor-powered submarines came in the 1950s, and prewar biological and chemical weapons programs were redoubled.

The USSR was compelled to stay abreast of an adversary with far deeper pockets. Its planned economy in 1950 was at most 35 percent the size of the free-enterprise economy of the United States; it crested at about 60 percent in the 1970s. The Soviet Union was a superpower, yes, but by dint of herculean effort, stretching every sinew, that robbed the population of the fruits of growth.

Frail allies and an encumbered economic base were consonant with a brittle worldview. The Cold War excused the centralization of power and vigilance against contamination by non-Communists and foreign powers. In its own way, the regime was mimicking the age-old Russian nexus between external insecurity and internal unfreedom.

Who was Khrushchev and what was "the thaw"?

As the years crept up on him, Stalin left the prosaic work of state to administrative committees and to technocrats he enlisted after the Great Purge. In the wings, he intrigued against one and all. In 1949–50 a "Leningrad Affair" with a Russian-versus-Soviet angle rocked the USSR's second city. The victims, clients of the recently deceased ideology chief Zhdanov, were said in closeted trials to have indulged Russian particularism by planning to make Leningrad the capital of the RSFSR, leaving Moscow as USSR capital, and to create an RSFSR branch of the Communist Party with its own first secretary. A score of functionaries were shot, two hundred imprisoned, and two thousand Leningraders and alumni of its nomenklatura exiled. Among those put to death were the prime minister of the RSFSR, Mikhail Rodionov, and the chairman of Gosplan. In 1952 Stalin prepared a housecleaning of the central organs of power for which a fictive "Doctors Plot," about physicians with Jewish surnames conniving to poison politicos and generals, was to be a pretext. Only his death of a cerebral hemorrhage on March 5, 1953, forestalled it.

The earthy apparatchik who won out in the internecine tug of war that ensued was Nikita Sergeyevich Khrushchev (b. 1894 to peasants in Kursk province of the future RSFSR). Khrushchev became a Communist in 1918 and logged thirty years in the party apparatus. He befriended Stalin's second wife, Nadezhda Alliluyeva, in Moscow before her suicide in 1932, but his network was densest in Ukraine, where he was a protégé of Stalin henchman Lazar Kaganovich and worked from 1938 to 1949 as party secretary, wartime commissar, and premier. Stalin minions who misjudged Khrushchev selected him as CPSU first secretary (this was the general secretary's title from 1952 to 1966) in September 1953. Like Stalin, he got traction from the Secretariat, its two thousand in-the-loop employees, and its patronage mill. He got the better of challengers in the Presidium (as the Politburo was known from 1952 to 1966) by June 1957, when the Central Committee excommunicated a resistant "antiparty group." In March 1958 Khrushchev supplemented his party job with chairmanship of the Council of Ministers.

The epithet for the post-Stalin interlude was taken from the novella "The Thaw," put out in a literary monthly by Ilya Ehrenburg in May 1954. The Soviet hierarchs agreed the political climate would have to mellow—or else the cycle of personal dictatorship would repeat itself, with all that entailed for their safety of life and limb. A straw in the wind was an amnesty in late March of 1953 that disgorged more than 1 million inmates from Gulag. Another was the disavowal in April of the Doctors Plot. In June Lavrentii Beria, the overseer of the police organs since 1938, was arrested. According to Khrushchev, Beria was "getting his knives ready for us," but there was more to it than that: Beria had been pressing for faster reforms than the Presidium majority wanted. For his pains, he faced a military tribunal and was executed on December 23, 1953, said to have plotted to trade territory for peace treaties with Germany, Finland, Romania, and Japan. Beria was the last member of the Soviet top echelon to be shot. The principals in the vanquished antiparty group in 1957 were merely tossed down the chute to humble positions—Kaganovich to a potash mill in the Urals, former premier Georgii Malenkov to a power station in Kazakhstan, and Vyacheslav Molotov to the Soviet embassy in Mongolia.

As part of the rectification, the security police were put in ironclad subordination to the party in 1953–54 and enfolded into a unified Committee for State Security (KGB), still based in Moscow's Lubyanka. Four million prisoners altogether were amnestied, a move that did not sit well in cities inundated with common criminals. Political offenders in labor camps and penitentiaries decreased from five hundred thousand to a remainder of ten thousand, and Gulag as such was to be disestablished in 1960.

On February 25, 1956, Khrushchev delivered a searing, five-hour-long report "On the Cult of Personality and Its Consequences" to a nocturnal session of the Twentieth Congress of the CPSU. The "Secret Speech" was not secret; the contents were read out to party cells that week and taken up by the world media. It piled scorn on the veneration of Stalin and indicted him for his misanthropy and narcissism, policy blunders, and violations of "collective leadership." De-Stalinization came to a crescendo in 1961, when the Twenty-Second CPSU Congress ordered the sarcophagus holding Stalin's body extruded from the Lenin sepulcher on Red Square and the wartime hero-city of Stalingrad was retitled Volgograd. A modulation of censorship let editors print politically heterodox fiction and memoirs. *One Day in the Life of Ivan Denisovich*, Solzhenitsyn's novel about the rounds of a Gulag inmate, Shukhov, sent out shock waves; it came out in the magazine *Novyi mir* in November 1962. Much of his *Gulag Archipelago* was based on letters mailed to him after the publication of *One Day*.

The thaw's chief contribution was a quantum discount in gratuitous violence through the cessation of terror. With three exemptions—Soviet Germans, the Tatars of Crimea, and the Meskhetian Turks from Georgia—the ethnic communities exorcized in World War II were repatriated after the Secret Speech. Blunt repression, as it is known in the scholarly literature, gave way to stratagems of deterrence, co-optation, and divide-and-rule. Defetishization of the leader and the letup in fear eroded the party's air of infallibility and opened up space for rational argumentation. "In the absence of terror, institutionally linked groupings increasingly asserted a self-awareness of themselves as [having] interests that were somewhat at variance with those of the party." The proscription on contact with outsiders was warily unwound: in July–August 1957 the USSR hosted the Sixth World Festival of Youth and Students; Muscovites mingled with forty thousand international guests and discovered the joys of blue jeans and American chewing gum. Registering openness to the forlorn Soviet consumer, Khrushchev and his administration redirected billions of rubles to agriculture and foods, everyday wares, and a housing program to move urbanites into single-family apartments from barracks and communal flats filled to the gills.

Real as these changes were, no reformation in-depth of the party-state was forthcoming. The regime was now posttotalitarian, yet kept an authoritarian lynchpin. Khrushchev had no across-the-board refit in mind and was under little compulsion to do one: opinion in the establishment, outside oases of intelligentsia liberalism, was no more congenial to it than he was. "We were afraid," he was to unburden himself later, "the thaw might unleash a flood, which we wouldn't be able to control and which could drown us."

Nikita Khrushchev was the quintessential true believer, although with a conscience. At the 1961 CPSU congress he rammed through a Panglossian party program saying the Soviet Union would overtake the United States in per capita production by 1970 and attain the "majestic edifice" of full-fledged *kommunizm* by 1980. His critique of Stalin and Stalinism, on close examination, was halfhearted, skipping over single-party rule, the extirpation of intraparty factions, and collectivization. Complicity in past sins—Khrushchev himself was "up to the elbows in blood," as he said in retirement—cooled his ardor for truth-telling.

Khrushchev's cultural defrost was diffident and had no room for artists whose fare strayed too far from socialist realism. The 1958 Nobel Prize in literature was bestowed on Boris Pasternak for *Doctor Zhivago*, which was in print in the West (in foreign languages and in Russian, with support from the US Central Intelligence Agency) but not in the USSR. Khrushchev, who never read the book, directed a campaign of vilification that resulted in Pasternak refusing the prize, having suicidal thoughts, and being driven out of the Union of Writers. In 1961 the KGB searched the apartment of Vasilii Grossman, once a popular war correspondent and now a disillusioned storywriter, and confiscated the manuscript of his novel *War and Fate,* which likens Stalinism to Hitlerism. Khrushchev received a letter from Grossman and ordered Mikhail Suslov, the party's ideological vicar after Andrei Zhdanov, to reconnoiter. Suslov read only annotations on the text by aides, but that was enough for him to fume in a meeting with Grossman that the volume could not see the light of day in Russia for ... two or three hundred years. "Why should we add your book to the atomic bombs that our enemies are preparing to launch against us? ... Why should we publish your book and begin a public discussion as to whether anyone needs the Soviet Union or not?" Khrushchev left it at that.

In the area of identity politics, Khrushchev overturned the concordat with Russian Orthodoxy and in 1959 commenced a campaign for "scientific atheism," shuttering two-thirds of the church's properties and levying punishments on Islam and other confessions. With the nationalities, Khrushchev nativized republic cadres but on other counts was a centralizer, working toward a "merger of nations" in the USSR into one Soviet people. The party apparatus and government were purged in 1959 in the two union republics, Azerbaijan and Latvia, which had resisted a proposal to reduce teaching of the titular language to a discretionary program. The Central Committee in 1960 issued a directive against "idealization of the past and manifestations of national narrow-mindedness."

In international relations, Khrushchev discarded the Stalinist thesis of "the fatalistic inevitability of war" between camps and dusted off "peaceful coexistence," a turn of phrase from the 1920s connoting a weary recognition of the enemy's strength. The Soviet Union pruned active-duty troop levels by eight hundred thousand in 1960–61 and in 1963 was party to the Partial Test Ban Treaty (post-Soviet Russia signed the Comprehensive

Test Ban Treaty in 1996). Against this has to be put Khrushchev's Manichean thinking, modified to add a "nonaligned" group in the Third World for which the two Cold War alliances would compete. He whipped up the Cuban Missile Crisis of October 1962, which ended in him backpedaling, and rescinded Soviet manpower cuts after it. He also stood by the division of Europe, dousing a national revolt in Hungary in 1956 and in 1961 erecting the Berlin Wall between the two Germanys, with its watchtowers, barbwire, and landmines.

Policy gaffes leeched away at support for the first secretary. The late Khrushchev was enamored of pet projects, boorish outbursts, and fitful reorganizations. To compensate for an economic slowdown, he had labor discipline tautened and, on June 1, 1962, prices for meat and butter raised, so as to dampen demand. The changes backfired. A wildcat strike hit an electrolocomotive factory in Novocherkassk, in the south of European Russia; army troops fired at workers with machine guns, killing twenty-nine and injuring eighty-four. Seven protesters were shot for "banditry" following trial in a courtroom packed with party members, and others given long prison sentences. Novocherkassk, to borrow from the Russian social historian Vladimir Kozlov, was "the visible tip of the iceberg—the unseen part was the pent-up grumbling and various 'anti-Soviet phenomena' that were occurring all over the country. . . . Marginalized persons carried out a . . . wave of 'hooligan resistance,' producing [an] unprecedented outbreak of uprisings and mass resistance."

The circular flow of power had its shortcomings once animal fear of the leader and his hatchet men was gone. Khrushchev's seventieth birthday in April 1964 smacked of the sycophancy he had deprecated for the Stalin period. On October 14, 1964, the party Presidium and Central Committee relieved him of his posts on account of age and health. Disenchanted acolytes had been conspiring against him for six months, under his nose, and had looked into having him killed in an airplane crash. *Pravda* pilloried Khrushchev for "harebrained schemes, half-baked conclusions, rash decisions and actions divorced from reality, bragging, and bluster." He was packed off to a dacha near Moscow and died in 1971. The memoirs he taped there were printed in translation in the United States and Western Europe in 1970 but in Russia not until 1988.

Who was Brezhnev and what was "the epoch of stagnation"?

The new CPSU first secretary (the title of general secretary was resurrected in 1966) was Leonid Ilyich Brezhnev, one of the ringleaders against Khrushchev. Brezhnev (b. 1906) had been a Communist since 1929 and was by education a land surveyor and metallurgist. A wartime commissar and a mainstay of Khrushchev's Ukrainian machine, his base was the industrial Dnepropetrovsk oblast in the southeast—he was made a Presidium member in June 1957 and second secretary to Khrushchev in June 1963.

The unoriginal thinking and plodding decision style that were soon apparent in Brezhnev reflected his temperament and a willful policy of dissociating himself from the antics of Khrushchev. They also reflected a consensus on the Soviet Olympus about the exercise of power. A classified motion passed at the October 1964 plenum of the Central Committee resolved that from this day forward dual tenancy of the two uppermost offices was impermissible. The choice for prime minister was the astute industrial technocrat and former chairman of Gosplan, Alexei Kosygin. At the polished table of the Politburo (as the Presidium was rechristened in 1966) sat Brezhnev cronies, hardcore ideologues, and ministers who lobbied tirelessly for their agencies.

The Communist Party had been paying lip service to collegial decision-making since the Secret Speech. There was now some meat on the bones. In a memorandum to US President Gerald Ford before talks with the Russians in Vladivostok in 1974, Secretary of State Henry Kissinger, who had met Brezhnev singly and with Richard M. Nixon, noted that Brezhnev "seems to operate fairly comfortably within the constraints of collective leadership, although he has not hesitated to advance his own interests at the expense of his colleagues." "He appears to prefer the human interaction of a closely-knit working group to the more complex and abstract rewards of the solitary leader. . . . [He] gives the impression of being highly sensitive to the needs of the collective, constantly reassuring himself that his colleagues can have no conceivable grounds for complaint or soliciting their compliments." Brezhnev had his eccentricities, Ford heard from Secretary Kissinger: "You will find his hands perpetually in motion, twirling his gold watch chain, flicking ashes from his ever-present cigarette, clanging his cigarette holder against an ashtray. From time to time, he may stand up behind his chair or walk about. He is likely to interrupt himself or you by offering food and drink. His colleagues obviously humor him in his nervous habits."

To citizens who were not offered food and drink, a minicult of Brezhnev in his second Kremlin decade altered the equation. A ghost-written memoir trilogy was printed in a run of 15 million in 1978 and awarded the Lenin Prize for literature in 1980. But the cult was more inane than dignifying, and it extolled Brezhnev as a team player and a paragon of Communist rectitude and humility, not a superman.

A corollary of groupism was "respect for cadres." Where the nomenklatura had Khrushchev to thank for security of the person, it had Brezhnev to thank for what verged on security of tenure. In the CPSU Politburo, the mean age of full voting members tiptoed from fifty-eight after the 1966 party congress to sixty-one after the 1971 congress, sixty-six in 1976, and seventy in 1981. In 1980 a dying Kosygin was replaced as prime minister by Nikolai Tikhonov, a lackluster steelmaker whose claim to fame was having had a desk near Brezhnev's in 1940s Dnepropetrovsk; he was seventy-five, one year younger than Kosygin. The Twenty-Sixth CPSU Congress in 1981 was the first since 1923 at which no change was made in the Politburo and Secretariat lineup.

A quiescent attitude toward government and society complemented the immobility of personnel. The central object was unambiguous: self-preservation of the elite and reproduction in society of the existing state of affairs. The talk segued from leapfrogging to communism to "developed socialism" or "real socialism," which is to say socialism as found in the contemporaneous Soviet Union. The pejorative "the epoch of stagnation" (*epokha zastoya*) was pasted to the period only after Brezhnev's death in 1982.

Khrushchev's erratic reorganizations were scratched in 1964–65. There was no straight-out re-Stalinization, and no reversion to indiscriminate arrests and killings, but the regime stopped washing its dirty linen in public and partway rehabilitated Stalin's reputation. Stricter internal passport regulations, "prophylactic measures" (education and conversations with KGB officers), and a 1966 decree criminalizing "dissemination of ideas that discredit the Soviet political and social order" tamped down hooliganism. Commemoration of victory in World War II was puffed up into a pageant every May 9, and "military-patriotic education" saturated classrooms, the media, and youth organizations. In the bloc, the Czechoslovak Prague Spring, and its "socialism with a human face," was heresy to the Kremlin, which was also uneasy about Slovak nationalism tainting next-door Ukraine; five hundred thousand Warsaw Pact soldiers snuffed it out in August 1968. The defection of Svetlana Alliluyeva, Stalin's daughter, to the United States just the year before did not augur any better for the ideology the Politburo was trying to freeze in the teeth of time.

Brezhnev at a fête on turning seventy in 1976 toasted "the great things accomplished . . . under the guidance of the party" since 1964 and the Soviet Union's international cachet: "Never before in our history has the country had such authority and influence." A fourth Soviet-era constitution in 1977 heralded the USSR as "a socialist state of the whole people," that is, of white-collar employees as much as of workers and peasants. Article 6 on the monopoly of the CPSU (repeated verbatim in a constitution for the RSFSR in 1978) was in line with the 1936 Stalin constitution in everything except the boilerplate: "The Communist Party, armed with Marxist-Leninist teachings, determines the general outline of the development of society ... leads the Soviet people in their creative labors, and scientifically plans their struggle for the victory of communism."

The gerontocracy was not monolithic and did not snub change in all its forms. In foreign policy, détente with the West resulted in the US–Soviet Strategic Arms Limitation Treaty (SALT) and the Anti-Ballistic Missile (ABM) Treaty arrived at with President Nixon in 1972, the Biological and Toxin Weapons Convention (BTWC) of 1972 (whose terms the Soviets cheated on), the Ostpolitik agreements with Chancellor Willy Brandt of West Germany, and the Helsinki Final Act on European security of 1975.

The 1964 communiqué on Khrushchev had chided him for "unwillingness to take into account what science and practical experience have worked out." After his ouster, Soviet experts could investigate an abundance of particular issues and give them an airing. The Ukrainian agronomist Trofim Lysenko, who had lorded over Soviet biology since the 1940s with pseudoscience about the inheritance of acquired characteristics, was defrocked. The party hierarchy was now open to suggestions of marginal improvement in a variety of domains, so much the better if they were couched as tryouts. In literature, Chingiz Aitmatov, Fazil Iskander, and Yurii Trifonov wrestled with generational change, societal memory, and morality. Soviet science fiction was able to parody aspects of developed socialism. Filmmakers like Andrei Konchalovskii and Sergei Paradzhanov traversed the same imaginative landscape, as did vocalists like Bulat Okudzhava and the iconic folk singer Vladimir Vysotskii, who introduced criminal and street jargon into their music.

Outweighing the ginger steps forward was a dogged conservatism. The military buildup to which Ronald Reagan adverted in his evil empire speech was indeed the biggest ever in peacetime. It carried Soviet forces to 5.3 million men in 1981, about 3 million more than the United States, and achieved nuclear parity. In the Third World, the Soviet Union supplied North Vietnam with matériel and three thousand military advisers for its war with the Americans, airlifted Cuban forces to Angola, Mozambique, and Ethiopia, and aided other left-wing regimes. In 1984 it had access to naval and air force installations in eight countries and military assistance agreements with thirty-four.

In-country, the political freeze had an unanticipated side effect: a subculture of dissent intent on defending individuals and demanding changes to the Soviet political system. The die was cast at the trial of writers Andrei Sinyavskii and Yulii Daniel in February 1966 and their sentencing to labor camp, for making "anti-Soviet agitation and propaganda" and publishing it in Europe and the United States under pseudonyms. Their work was distributed through an innovation of the late 1950s, *samizdat*—typed manuscripts and photostats handed from reader to reader. The Moscow Helsinki Group, a Committee on Human Rights, and a USSR branch of Amnesty International kept their heads above water; Helsinki monitoring groups were formed in Ukraine, Lithuania, Georgia, and Armenia. The atomic physicist and civil libertarian Andrei Sakharov was put under home confinement in Gorky (Nizhnii Novgorod) in 1980 but did not stay quiet. Foreign exile, voluntary or involuntary, was the path trod by others. Three hundred thousand Soviet Jews emigrated in the aftermath of the Arab–Israeli war of 1967. Cultural figures by the dozen took the road west—Sinyavskii, Solzhenitsyn, and Joseph Brodsky (writers), Andrei Amalrik (historian), Ernst Neizvestny (sculptor), Mstislav Rostropovich (cellist), Alexander Galich (songster), and Natalya Makarova and Mikhail Baryshnikov (Kirov Theater dance partners), to name a few.

The rank-and-file cared little about the dissidents and samizdat, or about the oppositionist leaflets and graffiti now and again seen in public spaces, but they jawed in their kitchens and dachas about incompetence and injustice. Unauthorized political speech in the private sphere—gossip, yarns, jibes, innuendo—took root. The KGB and its informers listened to it, and taped it, yet could not stamp it out. As Amalrik put it in his prophetic *Will the Soviet Union Survive until 1984?*, the police "devote enormous effort to keep everyone from talking and then waste further effort to learn what people are talking about and what they want." Street protest was not unheard of but was kept under an information lid. Russian data ferreted out by Mark R. Beissinger fix 264 peaceful demonstrations and 50 outbreaks of mass violence in the USSR between 1965 and 1986, with a threshold of 100 participants. Two thousand four hundred and twenty-four persons were convicted for anti-Soviet activity. The busiest times were the middle 1960s and the early 1980s. "Acts of contention remained isolated and were rarely repeated, primarily because of the expectation of repression." More common recourses were melancholy and drunkenness: per capita consumption of alcohol (sold in the state stores and home-distilled) rose by 40 percent between 1960 and 1980.

The party owned up to one-off blemishes and setbacks, but that was all. The bemedaled septuagenarian at the rudder was fatigued, could not sleep without sedatives, and reportedly booked sessions with a Caucasus astrologist and faith healer. "Brezhnev's inability to function," Anatolii Chernyayev, a sharp-eyed Central Committee apparatchik, jotted in his diary in September 1975, "is becoming ever more noticeable. He returned from vacation on August 29 and hasn't made any appearances, and there is no sign of him at the [Secretariat]. All matters of any significance are dependent on him, so nothing is getting done."

What were the pluses and minuses of the Soviet development model?

The Soviet development model had fortés but also inborn disabilities. They were more disconcerting over time, as they chipped away at the party-state's capacity and support base.

The model was predicated on ABCs of economic organization incompatible with those of the marketplace. Pretty well all the means of production were state-owned. The pedals and knobs were worked by Gosplan and more than twenty bureaucratic helpers, such as Goskomtsen (the State Committee on Prices) and Gossnab (the State Committee on Material-Technical Supply), the custodian of the state's mind-bending lattice of "material–technical balances." Going far beyond gross output quotas, they intruded in minute detail into inputs, scheduling, and pricing. Heavy industry—energy, mining, metals, chemicals, machine tools, transport stock—was prioritized in investment. In final output, guns won out over butter, as 25 to 30 percent was allocated to the gluttonous military–industrial complex. Autarky was preferred over foreign trade, except with socialist countries.

USSR Inc. was moored in a bottomless faith in big government and comprehensive rationality. The system performed best when locked in on large, well-bounded, and urgent tasks. The giant construction sites of the 1930s and arms production in World War II would be vivid examples. Another was the space program superintended by the previously jailed Chief Designer Sergei Korolyov (the Soviets' Wernher von Braun), with the aid of German rocket scientists captured at Peenemünde. Soviets reveled then, and Russians still do, in the prowess of the first manmade earth satellite (Sputnik-1 in October 1957), the first animal in space (the female dog Laika on Sputnik-2, wearing a canine space suit, in November 1957), the first human spaceflight (Yurii Gagarin aboard Vostok-1 in April 1961), the first woman and also the first civilian astronaut (Valentina Tereshkova in 1963 on Vostok-6), the first multiperson crew in space (Voskhod-1 in 1964), the first spacewalk (by Alexei Leonov, from Voskhod-2 in 1965), and, after Korolyov's death in 1966, the first rover on a celestial body (Lunokhod 1, on the moon in 1970) and the first space station (Mir in 1986).

Brezhnev kept the megaprojects tradition going with the 2,300-mile Baikal–Amur Mainline Railroad, tracking north of the Trans-Siberian through the resource-rich Russian Far East, and safely north of the Chinese border; 1 percent of Soviet GDP per year was expended on it from 1974 to 1984. In a similar mold were extension of Comecon's Friendship pipeline grid to fetch oil and gas to capitalist European markets and, on a lighter note, staging of the 1980 Summer Olympics in Moscow. When the Olympic torch was carried into Lenin Stadium in July, the Salyut-6 astronauts appeared on the scoreboard and greeted athletes over the public address system. The Soviet sport program itself might be categorized as a long-term megaproject. The USSR first took part in the Olympic Games in 1952. In Summer Olympics from 1952 to 1988, it stood first in the medal count in six appearances and second in three; in the Winter Olympics, it finished first seven times and second twice.

From 1920 to 1939, the USSR's socialist economy outper-formed the Western countries; it kept pace after 1945, post-ing the strongest rates of any industrial nation in the 1950s. Soviet GDP climbed from 49 percent of the US total in 1960 to 57 percent in 1975, as tabulated by the CIA. The companions of industrialization were urbanization and social modernization. Sixty-nine percent of the Soviet population lived in towns and cities by 1979 (17 percent had in 1926) and literacy was over 99 percent (versus 57 percent in 1926).

At the best of times, the model had its defects. With a pre-dilection for investment and heavy industry, the USSR led the world in making commodities like steel, fertilizer, and oil; per capita consumption was mired at one-third of the American level. Cradle-to-grave "welfare authoritarianism," as Westerners sometimes called it, provided full employ-ment, education and healthcare gratis, a cheap roof over one's head, and a pension; the government skimped on costs and services were a shambles. Drabness plagued Soviet construc-tion, as unforgettably sent up in Eldar Ryazanov's 1976 televi-sion film *The Irony of Fate* (where a Muscovite overimbibes on New Year's Eve, takes a plane to Leningrad, and falls asleep in an identical apartment, in an identical multistory building, at an identical address on an identically named street). In manufacturing, the assortment of retail goods dovetailed badly with demand, breeding queues while supply of unwanted products kept on growing. The Ministry of Agriculture's kolkhozes and *sovkhozes* (its larger "state farms"), disappointing the hopes of the collectivizers, were monuments to inefficiency and sloth. Tiny auxiliary plots attached to peasant farmsteads produced more than 25 percent of Soviet food on 3 percent of the tillable land, and about half of city dwellers grew compensatory potatoes and vegetables at their dachas.

Faults like these might have been ignored had the economy been vigorous enough to let the government meet its make-or-break commitments. But the five-year plan of 1976–81 (the Soviet Union's tenth) slowed growth to a crawl, and a world petroleum glut after 1980 depressed hard-currency income by 60 percent. The economy of the USSR expanded in the late 1970s by an anemic 3 percent annually, says the CIA, or by 2 percent per capita. Retrospective studies by Russian statisticians hold that the CIA minimized the deceleration and that the USSR was only a smidgen above zero growth.

The crux of the matter was a failure to refocus from extensive to intensive development. Extensive growth springs from the accretion of land, labor, and capital inputs. The Soviet model, unreformed, was extensive, which was workable when factor inputs were unutilized or underutilized. As time went by, cheap inputs into the planned economy were exhausted— most good land was under cultivation; almost all working-age men and women were in the workforce and population growth was slowing; raw materials and energy were coming from more remote (and colder) areas; and new technologies were increasingly capital-intensive. At this point, the USSR ought to have banked on intensive growth, motored by gains to productivity of resource use. Leaders and economists talked about making such a switch. It did not happen, and output per worker plateaued at 40 percent of the American level. Premier

Kosygin made no better than a start in 1965 on a rationalization of economic planning; it bogged down in the bureaucracy and was gutted on Brezhnev's say-so by 1970.

The corpus of activities the Politburo and its central planners now synchronized was far more intricate than the barebones industrial economy of Alexei Stakhanov and the early five-year plans. The coordinative processes at their disposal were still, in the political economist Charles E. Lindblom's pithy figure of speech, "all thumbs, no fingers": the stout thumbs of coercive resource allocation but not the supple fingers that come from profits, price signals, and intersupplier competition. Micromanagement sidetracked the planners from macroissues and gave producers perverse incentives. Gosplan staff above ratcheted up the plan; line officials below camouflaged capacity and wastefully stocked up on materials. The grafting of computers and programming models onto aspects of planning and inventory control, through a "statewide automated system of management," was a dud; it engendered a hierarchical surveillance system as opposed to a distributed electronic network. The CPSU apparatus and its branch economic departments were forced more than ever before to intercede to clear bottlenecks.

Central planning was egregiously handicapped regarding innovation, the sine qua non of intensive growth. Planning "from the achieved level"—fixing success indicators at last year's number plus an increment—had a conservative bias, as it discouraged managers from making outsized gains in output which would be woven into the next year's assignments. Basic research was the preserve of the USSR Academy of Sciences (Peter the Great's academy renamed), in near-seclusion from the universities, production, and international peers. All manner of discoveries—in rocket propulsion, semiconductors, lasers (two of the three scientists to win the Nobel Prize in physics in 1964 for inventing the laser were Soviets), genetics, and hydraulic fracturing (fracking) for oil and gas—were gestated in the academy's institutes and in Soviet industrial laboratories. But they languished by reason of secrecy and the unfeasibility of commercializing them. The West led by miles in computers, robotics, bioengineering, miniaturization, and most applications of technology to economic processes. First in space in 1957, the Soviet Union was beaten to the moon by Apollo-11 and the United States in 1969. In May 1974 the Politburo axed plans for manned lunar landings, after launch failures of the behemoth N-1 booster rocket. The Buran reusable orbiter, the USSR's answer to the US Space Shuttle, managed but one flight, in 1988; the one machine built was to be destroyed in 2002 during a hangar collapse at the Baikonur spaceport in Kazakhstan.

The travails of central planning had as their byproduct circumvention of the approved channels. An unofficial "shadow" or "gray" economy—of face-to-face relationships and give-and-take (*blat* in Russian slang, corresponding to *guanxi* in Chinese)—nestled in the interstices of the official economy. One in fifteen Soviet émigrés to the United States, surveyed in the 1980s, said they had used blat or *protektsiya* (personal protection) if they got a first job before World War II; in the late Brezhnev years, one in two had. The first cousin to blat and protektsiya was corruption, or payments for leniency, deal sweeteners, and bribery to procure goods in short supply. Corruption expressed and nourished a moral disequilibrium. The musty ideology before which the party genuflected gave no satisfactory cure. Even in athletics, the sizable Olympics medal haul in the 1970s and 1980s was not done without the aid of blood doping and performance-enhancing drugs.

Faced with a restive population, "authorities ... carried out continual and often economically unfounded increases in wages, pumped money into the consumer sector, permitted the growth of the black market, and redistributed resources to the benefit of national border areas.... Through such measures, the state for some time succeeded in distracting people from spontaneous protests and anti-Soviet political activism." The people were distracted but not assuaged. As Valerie Bunce observes, the social homogenization wrought by the leadership, and its nontransparent decision style, led to groupthink in which Soviet citizens, like East Europeans in the bloc, "assume[d] that bad and seemingly unfair outcomes were produced in quite deliberate fashion by the party."

Did factors other than economics undermine the regime?

Not all the headwinds encountered were in economics. A farrago of systemic problems prefigured turbulence ahead.

One seminal problem was imperial overreach. By the second half of the 1970s, Communist regimes in Eastern Europe were teetering. To finance export-led growth, they went into debt to international banks and lending agencies, then beseeched Moscow to bail them out. In 1980 a Solidarity labor movement with 10 million members threw down the gauntlet to the Polish United Workers' Party, fired up by shipyard electrician Lech Wałęsa and by the example of a new Polish pope, John Paul II. The Soviet Union prodded a military government under Wojciech Jaruzelski to bring in martial law in September 1981.

Nor was all well with the congeries of "states of socialist orientation" in the Third World, such as Ethiopia under the Derg, Nicaragua under the Sandinistas, Angola under the People's Movement for the Liberation of Angola, and Benin under the Military Council of the Revolution. Coupled to Moscow by friendship and assistance treaties, all were underdeveloped and had economic problems which Soviet handouts did little to counter. Most faced Western-backed insurgencies.

By the time General Jaruzelski lowered the boom in Poland, the Soviets had stumbled into trouble on another flank. The tsars had contended with the British for Afghanistan, Asia's "graveyard of empires" and one of the world's poorest and most illegible countries, and the USSR ran the costliest assistance program there. The pro-Soviet People's Democratic Party toppled the monarchy in 1973, but the villages rose up against disrespect for Islam and Afghan tradition. A Marxist evangelist, Hafizullah Amin, taking power in 1979, further antagonized believers. On December 27, 1979, Soviet airborne troops parachuted into Kabul, killed Amin, and foisted a more pliable leader. The Politburo's plan was to pacify the towns, train security forces, and get out.

Afghanistan did not go according to plan. The Soviet Army was sucked into an intractable civil conflict. The war was the death knell for East–West and Soviet–American détente. The United States boycotted the 1980 Moscow Olympics, and the USSR and its allies repaid the favor for the 1984 summer games in Los Angeles. The CIA's Operation Cyclone shipped Stinger antiaircraft missiles and dollars to the mujahideen. Six hundred thousand soldiers fought in the Soviet Union's Vietnam; about fifteen thousand were flown home in zinc coffins and sixty-five thousand were wounded.

Inside the USSR, the regime faced restlessness over the nationality issue. Brezhnev related in October 1977 that he had overruled "some comrades" who wanted to scrap ethnofederalism and shut down the union republics. The party's sworn aim after 1964 was acculturation and antiseptic "drawing together" of the Soviet nations, not Khrushchev's fusion of them. The hands-on recommendations were the strengthening of Russian-language training and partiality toward titular cadres in their home regions.

In the republics, as the economy misfired, some CPSU officials made discreet appeals to the population's sense of self, which was bound up with interpretations of the past, local customs, and religion. This was not sufficient to keep anticolonial and nationalist sentiment from effervescing. The largest public demonstration on this basis, in Yerevan, Armenia, in April 1965, turned out one hundred thousand protesters to demand that Moscow authorize a monument to the victims of the Armenian genocide of 1915. The peaceful event was not anti-Russian (the death marches in 1915 were in Ottoman Turkey) and produced an amicable result, an official memorial that opened in 1967. But the self-immolation on Khreshchatyk, the central boulevard of Kiev, of former freedom fighter Vasyl Makukh in November 1968 (yelling "Rid Ukraine of the colonizers!") was an omen with a different message. A nineteen-year-old student named Romas Kalanta committed suicide by fire in Kaunas, Lithuania, in May 1972, leaving behind a note pointing a finger at the Soviet regime; mourners from his funeral procession attacked a police station and CPSU offices; thirteen of Kalanta's conationals followed his example that same year. Rioters jammed the streets of Tbilisi, the Georgian capital, in April 1978 when a draft constitution (summarily retracted) equalized the status of the Russian and Georgian languages; of Dushanbe, Tajikistan, in May of 1978, after a Russian mugged a Tajik man in a park; of Tallinn, Estonia, in October 1980, to protest against Russification and bare food shelves; and of Ordzhonikidze, in the North Ossetiya republic of the RSFSR, in October 1981, over police corruption and ethnic discrimination.

Anti-Russianism was not unknown in the corridors of power. As early as 1972, Anatolii Chernyayev was overhearing in the Central Committee Secretariat that in the non-Russian republics "the dislike and even hatred of Russians is growing on the basis of a spreading belief (which is, by the way, widely introduced by the local Party and government apparatus—as an alibi for themselves) that everything is going badly because the Russians are holding everything at the top, and they are incompetent and stupid."

National consciousness was also, ominously, on the upswing among the Russians of the RSFSR and Eurasia. Their majority was jeopardized by aftershocks from World War II and disparities in procreation rates. Ethnic Russians were 58 percent of the Soviet population in the 1939 census; this fell to 55 percent in the 1959 census, 53 percent in 1970, and 52 percent in 1979. In the final Soviet census, in 1989, their share was a shade below 51 percent. Russians contributed 45 percent of Soviet population growth during the 1959–70 intercensus period, non-Russian Slavs 14 percent, nationalities that were

Muslim by tradition 32 percent, and others 9 percent; during the 1979–89 intercensus period, Russians contributed 33 percent, other Slavs 10 percent, Muslim groups 50 percent, and others 8 percent.

The inkling that Russian interests were being slighted touched not so much on demographics as on government and culture. The "Russian" (Rossiiskaya) republic—the RSFSR— was obsessively controlled from on high and had less institutional closure than other federal units. No subdivision of the Communist Party was given over to it, leaving it without the authoritative coordinators and power brokers found in Tbilisi or Tallinn—a point said to have been made by those purged in the Leningrad Affair of 1949–50. The governmental Council of Ministers of the RSFSR, in the recollection of Nikita Khrushchev, had the final word over "a few third-priority issues." Its premier, the republic's ranking representative, was by custom only a candidate (nonvoting) member of the Politburo, outranked by the party first secretaries of several union republics and of the Russian metropolises of Moscow and Leningrad. The last thing General Secretary Brezhnev wanted, like Stalin and Khrushchev, was a Russian viceroy who would answer for 60 percent of the party membership. Khrushchev instituted an unproductive Central Committee Bureau for RSFSR Affairs in 1956 (Stalin had similar units in the 1920s and 1930s) and chaired it himself. Brezhnev wound the bureau up in 1966. An RSFSR daily newspaper, *Sovetskaya Rossiya*, went into circulation in 1956 but was tightly censored.

Among the literati, a Russophile voice made itself felt— tremors of things to come. Extremist associations, and there was a spate of them, were dispensed with by the KGB. An All-Russian Social-Christian League for the Liberation of the People planned in all seriousness to unseat the Soviet government in November 1967, on the fiftieth anniversary of the Bolshevik takeover; all seventy members were detained, and twenty were imprisoned or exiled. A self-described "Russian nationalist journal," *Veche*, typed out in samizdat from 1971 to 1974, leveled broadsides at "the zoological hatred of Russians" in the borderlands and the "falsely internationalist propaganda" of the CPSU. The KGB reported to the Central Committee in March 1981 about growing numbers of *rusists* ("Rusites," an antiquarian term for the inhabitants of Kievan Rus) among the intelligentsia. The Rusites, said the KGB, were fond of "empty talk about the need to preserve Russian culture and relics for 'the salvation of the Russian nation,'" and some were flirting with "enemies of the Soviet system."

Most Russophiles kept clear of antiregime agitation. In the arts and letters, some exponents bandied about anti-Westernism, a flashback to the nineteenth-century Slavophiles, and had fans in high places. Others took umbrage at specific Soviet policies—for the "village prose" group in belles lettres, unbridled industrialization and the neglect of the countryside. Folklorists in the once debarred school of Yevgenii Gippius studied the evolution in the Russian interior of polyphonic music, oral legends, and doggerels. Painter Ilya Glazunov and movie directors Andrei Tarkovskii and Andrei Mikhalkov-Konchalovskii explored religious motifs and romanticized pre-1917 Russian life. Ecology was another leitmotif. The pollution of pristine Lake Baikal near Mongolia, the world's most voluminous body of fresh water, was a cause célèbre, attracting many a petition and letter to the editor, as was a ministerial plan to reroute water from the Yenisei and Ob rivers in Siberia into the Amu Darya of Central Asia and irrigation canals for the cotton plantations there.

Soviet society in its sundown years was not the atomized and dumb herd it may have seemed from a distance. The sticking point was more that the political system, set in its ways as post-totalitarian but still undemocratic, was so static.

What were the consequences of the death of Brezhnev?

Brezhnev had two coronaries in the 1950s and suffered from several chronic conditions. He toyed with retirement in

1976–77, when medical readouts took a turn for the worse. Exchanges with Politburo elders were fruitless: keeping him in the Kremlin was as convenient to them as to him. Respect for cadres let him run on autopilot until his death on November 10, 1982.

Brezhnev did not groom an heir or nominate a lieutenant who might backstab him the way he did Khrushchev in 1964. His departure ushered in an interregnum framed by offstage machinations. The vacancy was filled, momentarily, by Yurii Vladimirovich Andropov (b. 1914), the Soviet Union's spymaster and enforcer-in-chief as KGB chairman from 1967 to 1982. Before the Lubyanka he had been ambassador to Budapest during the Soviet suppression of the Hungarian rebellion in 1956 but, as a Central Committee official from 1957 to 1967, was seen as broad-minded and consulted experts from the Academy of Sciences. As CPSU general secretary, Andropov was a stickler for ramrod discipline in officialdom, the workplace, and the intelligentsia. He did also inject some introspection into Soviet discourse, as he decried lethargy in public policy and called for "major decisions" to get the USSR "onto the rails of intensive development."

Andropov could hypothetically have led the Soviet Union down the reform trail blazed in China by Deng Xiaoping, inculcating the marketplace in economics and retaining Leninism in politics, or, from a different starting gate, by Third World developmental dictatorships like those of Park Chung-hee in South Korea and Augusto Pinochet in Chile. But he was a diabetic on kidney dialysis and sightless in one eye—no match for the chain-smoking, maotai-quaffing Deng, who was ten years older and outlived him by thirteen. Andropov dropped from sight in September 1983 and breathed his last on February 9, 1984. He had almost no time in which to act, and a war scare cast a pall over domestic reformism throughout his tenure. Operation Able, a NATO nuclear-weapons command exercise held in November 1983, won some in the party apparatus, military, and KGB over to the view that an American nuclear attack on the Soviet Union was pending. The fear dissipated after Andropov's death.

The new caretaker was Konstantin Ustinovich Chernenko (b. 1911), the mumbling Brezhnev understudy (their paths crossed in Moldova in 1950) who had come off second best to Andropov in 1982. The choice of somebody utterly unqualified to lead a nuclear-armed titan was the last gasp of the epoch of stagnation. Chernenko got through a sickly year as general secretary, much of it indisposed at sanatoriums or the Kremlin hospital, and succumbed to emphysema on March 10, 1985.

The ignominy of three snowy-haired leaders in twenty-eight months being laid in the ground behind the Lenin mausoleum, to the strains of Frédéric Chopin's "Funeral March," put the onus on the selectorate to find a hale and hearty successor. On March 11, 1985, it passed the mantle to Mikhail Sergeyevich Gorbachev, the Politburo's youngest and most recent inductee.

Who was Gorbachev and what was perestroika?

The accession of Gorbachev (b. 1931) betokened a turnover of generations and not just of personages. He was reared on a wheat-farming kolkhoz in the Stavropol region of south Russia and majored in law at university. Clambering up the party's promotions ladder, he made it to Stavropol first secretary in 1970. He was summoned to Moscow as Central Committee secretary for agriculture in 1978 and admitted to the Politburo inner sanctum as a candidate member in 1979 and a voting member in 1980. Gorbachev's rise was abetted by Andropov and by Mikhail Suslov, both of whom had Stavropol pedigrees.

The setting into which Gorbachev rode was fraught with pressures, from all sides, for waking the Soviet Union out of its torpor. By his telling, he did not need to have his arm twisted. He writes in his memoir Life and Reforms that the night before the Politburo and Central Committee voted him in he said to his wife, Raisa, that he had no choice but to be a change agent: "I came here [in 1978] in the hope and belief that

I could get something done, but so far there has been very little to show for it.... We can't go on living like this." His chosen "something" was to be calculated on the fly.

It took no time for Gorbachev, with the powers of the Secretariat, to steal a march on the Communist Party old guard by rejuvenating the Politburo and the Central Committee staff. His archrival, Grigorii Romanov, the Leningrader who minded the defense industry in the Secretariat—and a possible spearhead for an economics-first Chinese course—was pensioned off in July 1985. In a matter of months there were newcomers as foreign minister (Eduard Shevardnadze, replacing the elderly Andrei Gromyko, who had been at Stalin's side at Yalta), prime minister (Nikolai Ryzhkov, replacing the eighty-year-old Tikhonov), and party ideologist (Alexander Yakovlev). In policy, the early Gorbachev was confined to Andropov-like sermonizing and a drive to reduce alcohol intake, which thirty years anon he admitted had been a misguided "axe thump over the head."

When he found his stride in 1986, Gorbachev made *perestroika*—"rebuilding" or "restructuring"—his masthead. This term of art bespoke an effort for weighty, but within-system, improvements to the regime. The aim was to shake up and shape up Communism, not break it up. "We were talking about making the system better," says Gorbachev plaintively, "and not about revolution. We thought then that this was doable." He was opening a Pandora's box.

Perestroika would not replay the Chinese variant of reform. Gorbachev tackled the "economic mechanism" first in his oratory and alluded to Lenin's New Economic Policy, which Deng Xiaoping had witnessed as a student in Moscow in the 1920s. But he left the reference hanging and dithered on changes to the minutiae of the command economy. Those fixes he did make were tinkering and were draped in red tape. Soviet peasants got some elbow room in the five-year plan to sell surplus produce for a profit. A 1988 law endorsed small "cooperatives" in retail services and inside state factories and ministries.

It all paled before rural decollectivization and the freeing up of urban enterprise in China, and Deng's cheeky slogan, "To get rich is glorious." Gorbachev put more energy into retarding the effects of economic reform than into fostering it.

With economics on the back burner, Gorbachev, in even sharper juxtaposition to Deng Xiaoping in Beijing, took a shine to reform of governance and politics. The showpiece was a word that took its place in the lexicon beside perestroika—namely, *glasnost*, which translates as "openness," "sincerity," or in its most catholic reading "freedom of expression." Gorbachev endorsed glasnost tentatively at the Twenty-Seventh CPSU Congress in February 1986 and with more fervor after the reactor meltdown at Chernobyl, Ukraine, that April. In one passage of *Life and Reforms,* he imputes it to the need to unclog information conduits and obviate future Chernobyls. In another, he talks of jolting the people out of their apathy and bringing them into the agora: "I got to sense that the impulses coming from above were getting stuck in the vertical structures of the party apparatus and the organs of government. Glasnost would make it possible to make contact with people directly, over the heads of the apparatchiks, and to fan their activism and win support." So it was that political reform, impelled by idealism and expediency, became the locomotive of change. Oddly enough, as Gorbachev says, the counterforce was the apparatchiks who answered to him as party chief.

Astonishingly, glasnost morphed into a "Moscow Spring," a wholesale liberalization akin to the Prague Spring flattened by Soviet tanks in 1968. In December 1986 Gorbachev ordered Andrei Sakharov liberated from internal exile, a volte-face on human rights. Small discussion clubs and "informals," unlicensed organizations to press this cause or that, made waves starting in 1987. An easing of censorship put the Khrushchev thaw to shame. The media brimmed with debate on one taboo subject after the other. Glavlit, the government's expurgator of the press, was to be dissolved in 1990. Esteemed authors were let out of the Soviet memory hole, some such as Zamyatin,

Pasternak, and Grossman posthumously (*We, Doctor Zhivago,* and *War and Fate* all went into print in 1988). Disclosures gushed out about Stalin, Gulag, and Leonid Brezhnev's family. Tengiz Abuladze's *Repentance* (1987), an allegory of totalitarianism, was one of a host of revisionist films about the Soviet past, but the most devastating movies were about antiheroes in the present. In documentaries and feature films, "alienated youth with their protest rock, drugs, punk dress, and hairstyles offered a critique of the now apparently meaningless sacrifices of the older generation: these conformist parents could not let go of the Soviet myths instilled in them, despite the fact that their difficult lives clearly belied those myths."

Alexander Dubček in Czechoslovakia had expounded a ten-year timeline for getting to "democratic socialism" with multiparty elections, reserving a role for a revived Communist Party. Gorbachev headed off in this direction in 1987 with a new buzzword—*demokratizatsiya,* "democratization." Democratization Gorbachev-style hearkened to the Russian Revolution by breathing life back into the soviets, the councils which lent the Soviet Union its name. The fulcrum was the electoral system, redone to sanction multiple candidates—not yet multiple political parties. An extraordinary conference of the CPSU went along in July 1988; a banner hung in the hall read "All Power to the Soviets," the Bolshevik motto from 1917. On March 25, 1989, a USSR Congress of People's Deputies was chosen under the amended procedures, in the country's first semifree election since the election of the Constituent Assembly in 1917. With a sprinkling of nay votes, Gorbachev on May 25 was chosen chairman of the Congress and of the Supreme Soviet, the working parliament selected from its ranks.

Most mesmerizing for world opinion was the dovish about-face in Soviet foreign policy. To rein in military spending, defang the Reagan administration's Strategic Defense Initiative (Star Wars), and enhance reform prospects, Gorbachev and Foreign Minister Shevardnadze resuscitated East–West détente and took in "new political thinking." New thinking broke the ice for arms-control agreements with the United States: the Intermediate-Range Nuclear Forces (INF) treaty of 1987, ridding Europe of an entire class of nuclear weapons, and the Strategic Arms Reduction Treaty (START) of 1991. Gorbachev repealed the "Brezhnev doctrine" that claimed the right to use force to save fraternal regimes. He wearied of the morass in Afghanistan and withdrew the Soviet Army. The final column of troops crossed the Amu Darya into Tajikistan on February 15, 1989.

Gorbachev, as his congress gathered on live Soviet television in May of 1989, seemed to perch on the political mountaintop. Unbeknownst to all, the beginning of the end for him—and for Soviet Communism, Soviet Russia, and the bipolar world—had transpired. As the president of an abruptly post-Communist Czechoslovakia, the playwright and ex-dissident Václav Havel, was to tell the US Congress only nine months down the road, change was coming on at warp speed, at such a clip "that none of the familiar political speedometers is adequate" to clock it.

4

A NEW RUSSIA

What went wrong with the attempt to reform Communism?

Mikhail Gorbachev in 1990 was the only Russian statesman ever awarded the Nobel Peace Prize (the scientist and rights advocate Sakharov won it in 1975). The committee, and justifiably, commended him for his "leading role in the peace process." In summitry with the West, Gorbachev punched holes in the Iron Curtain and curbed the Cold War and the arms race. When domestic politics is factored in, his peacemaking was a double-edged sword. It deprived him of the foreign bogeyman with which Russian and Soviet rulers have customarily validated their power.

More detrimental than the East–West dialectic was contagion from the Soviet bloc. Gorbachev sought to lighten the burdens of empire and gambled that he could nudge Moscow clients into doing efficacious national perestroikas. Left to swim or sink, they all floundered in 1989. Non-Communists buoyed up by the refashioned Solidarity took possession of the Polish government on September 12; the Berlin Wall was breached on November 9; the Romanian dictator, Nicolae Ceaușescu, was the last to be dethroned, and (singing "The Internationale") faced a firing squad on December 24. By 1991, when the Warsaw Pact and Comecon self-liquidated, Germany was reunified, the out-of-bloc Communist regimes in Albania and Yugoslavia were taken down, and to the east the Mongolian People's Revolutionary Party shared power with democrats after multiparty elections. Evaporation of its community of faith sowed skepticism about the shelf life of the Soviet prototype. Reversals and retreats buttressed the feeling that Gorbachev lacked the killer instinct and would be shoved aside.

To ride the tiger of reform, Gorbachev would have had to piece together a stable reformist coalition. In Czechoslovakia, Dubček had garnered support from anti-Stalinist intellectuals, trade unions, and Slovak nationalists. Deng Xiaoping's alliance in China befitted his business-first reforms: with entrepreneurs and officials, governmental and party, who stood to be enriched by marketization. Gorbachev did not take a leaf out of Dubček's or Deng's book and was never comfortable wooing social audiences.

The precondition of a durable reform pact was a lucid vision of some conjoint future. Gorbachev articulated none. "No one is able to say in detail what perestroika will finally produce," he mused in his Nobel Lecture in Oslo in June 1991. "It would be delusional to think it will be a 'copy' of anything else." Gorbachev went mute as the house of Communism was taken apart brick by brick. His endpoint was as chimerical as the over-the-rainbow communist paradise of the 1961 CPSU platform. In memoirs in 1995, Gorbachev could still not fasten a sobriquet, referring only to "a smooth transition from one political system to a different one." At the plenum of the Central Committee on July 26, 1991 (its last), Gorbachev presented the draft of a revised party program. The paper, stated the *New York Times*, chucked "many of the dogmas of the past . . . [but] offered only broad and general affirmations of perestroika and democracy for the future."

For this fogginess, Gorbachev paid dearly, not least within the governing party. The Communists who were the overpowering majority in the perestroika choir—85 percent of the congressional deputies—rushed headlong into elections and legislative work, real and not ersatz, without preparation or plan. In February 1990 Gorbachev consented to strike out Article 6 of the constitution, which sanctified the CPSU as the only Soviet party. To shore up his authority, the Congress of People's Deputies instituted the office of USSR president and on March 15 selected him to it. Attaining the position as a legislative appointee flew in the face of his pontification about democratization. No one opposed him, but the 495 votes cast against him and the 420 abstentions (out of 2,250 deputies) spoke volumes about his waning authority. President Gorbachev did not abdicate as general secretary of the Communist Party; he remained its leader and clung rhetorically to Lenin and the "socialist choice" of 1917. Morale in the party's professional staff was low. Pessimism percolated into the substrate of the membership, as shown by an exodus from party ranks. Of 19 million members of the CPSU as of January 1990, 4.2 million had by the summer of 1991 turned in their party cards or stopped paying dues.

A sustainable coalition might have taken one of several forms. Gorbachev could have tried logrolling (the trading of favors) or the avenue of compromise (splitting the difference between points of view). In lieu of these, he chose serial cooperation with disparate groups, flitting from one to another. In *Life and Reforms*, he defended this as necessary to outfox entrenched interests: "Without political jockeying, our powerful bureaucracy, formed under totalitarianism, would never have let power be taken away from it." Sad to relate, tactics outdid strategy. The jockeying irked Gorbachev's peers and minions and made every pirouette trickier to execute than the last.

Meantime, he and the CPSU were losing the confidence of common folk. The main irritant was negative economic growth in 1990–91 and the exponential spread of angst about the standard of living. Shortages of goods stoked black markets and hoarding and provoked municipal councils to ration vodka, sugar (scooped up for homebrew), tobacco, and soap. The USSR took on more than $100 billion in external debt. The endemic afflictions of the economy could not be laid on Gorbachev's doorstep, and neither could the depressed petroleum prices that cramped Soviet finances. But he was open to reproach for eschewing hard choices and doling out inflationary wages to mollify workers. In early 1991 his government poured gasoline on the flames through a punitive monetary reform—requiring citizens overnight to document how they had acquired large-denomination ruble notes—and through administered hikes in retail prices that took inflation to 30 percent a month. Gorbachev insinuated that the populace was as much in the wrong as the powers that be. "Profligately generating great expectations," he commented in Oslo, "we did not make allowance for the fact that it takes time for people to realize everybody has to live and work differently and stop counting on a new life being given to them from above."

Wear and tear on the nationality problem synergized with the economic distress. Altered power relations in the Soviet republics allowed grievances to be vented openly. Gorbachev took a cavalier attitude and was sure he could reap dividends from the "popular fronts in support of perestroika" that cropped up in the Baltic in 1988. He could not have been more wrong.

The goals of the Baltic fronts and kindred organizations like Rukh (Movement) in Ukraine and Birlik (Unity) in Uzbekistan escalated from administrative subsidiarity and linguistic concessions to self-determination. Ethnonational identities that predated the Soviets and those energized and spawned by them were of intrinsic value to millions of citizens. More to the point, they gave succor at a time of insecurity and ammunition to vote seekers in the new politics. Public demonstrations took off—a hundredfold over the stagnation-era baseline. Of 6,663 open-air protests in a tidal "glasnost mobilizational cycle" tracked by Beissinger from 1987 through 1992, 42 percent put forth only ethnonationalist demands, 24 percent nationalist demands in conjunction with democratization, and 16 percent only political demands.

In December 1989 the Lithuanian chapter of the CPSU was the first to detach itself from Moscow. A breakpoint for

the fifteen union republics was the procession of parliamentary elections there in 1990. The governments elected were
at first content with a "parade of sovereignties," fencing off
some degree of autonomy. By year's end the Balts, Georgians,
Armenians, and Moldovans were for downright independence
or gearing up for it. In hotspots like Central Asia's Fergana
valley and the South and North Caucasus, the nationalities
were coming to blows over language, land, and past injuries.

With the USSR on the razor's edge, its politics trussed together interest, identity, and ideology. What had started out as
responses to a backlog of economic and social ailments, within
the matrix of Soviet institutions and thought, metastasized
into an existential crisis of the party-state.

Who was Yeltsin and what enabled him to carry the day?

Like Gorbachev, Boris Nikolayevich Yeltsin (b. 1931) came into
the world in a dot of rustic Russia turned upside down by
collectivization, and made his mark vocationally in the local
party apparatus. But there were discrepancies in their résumés
as well.

Yeltsin was a child of the Urals, where rural dwellers
were frontiersmen, never enserfed, and the heritage was self-
reliance. Gorbachev's kin were penurious devotees of the
regime; Yeltsin's four grandparents were enterprising kulaks
evicted to the subarctic taiga by the OGPU, and his father
did time in Gulag for anti-Soviet agitation. Gorbachev went
straight from the farm to the law school of prestigious Moscow
State University, and returned to the capital in 1978. Yeltsin's
profile was at once more urban and more provincial. He left the
village with his parents as a toddler and was a schoolboy in the
smokestack town of Berezniki, in Perm oblast. Studying civil
engineering at a polytechnic in Sverdlovsk (as Yekaterinburg
was then called), he stayed put for thirty-six years. He joined
the Communist Party belatedly at the age of thirty, nine years
later than Gorbachev.

Drawn into the full-time CPSU staff from the building industry in 1968, Yeltsin was promoted in 1976 to party first secretary of Sverdlovsk oblast, a hive for producing nuclear and conventional weaponry. In volume one of his memoirs, *Confession on an Assigned Theme*, he recollected being "god, tsar, and master" of his fiefdom. Yeltsin's repute was as a disciplinarian with a flair for back-and-forth with students and workers, and given to irreverent digs at Soviet problems. He made his way to Moscow at Gorbachev's initiation in April 1985 and in December landed the position of first secretary for the capital city, thrusting him into the national political limelight. In February 1986 he was elevated to candidate member of the Politburo.

Yeltsin was a bundle of energy—administrative ability, unvarnished ambition, and pugnacity in equal portions. Gorbachev knew full well of his excesses but was sure they could be harnessed. To his chagrin, Yeltsin held forth about perestroika's deficiencies and its slowness to bring results. In contrast to the faceless Soviet leadership, he pressed the flesh with Muscovites at factories, in food shops, and on public transit. He made enemies out of underlings and the CPSU's second secretary, Yegor Ligachev, by sacking underachieving officeholders in droves and railing against "undeserved privileges" such as clinics, dispensaries, and delicatessens for the nomenklatura. At weekly Politburo meetings, we know from the archives, Yeltsin lit into the chairman for mistaking verbosity for action.

Yeltsin iterated his complaints in a letter to Gorbachev in September 1987 and demanded to quit his Moscow and Politburo duties. When Gorbachev would not name a date to meet, Yeltsin accosted him on the floor of the Central Committee. At the plenum of October 21, 1987, he rehashed the earlier resignation request, said "the people's faith [in perestroika] has begun to ebb," and scolded Gorbachev for winking at a cult of his personality, to boot. Gorbachev administered a tongue-lashing and turned over the microphone to a phalanx of committee members to elaborate. The plenum indecorously dismissed Yeltsin from the Moscow job and the Politburo. Hospitalized with a nervous breakdown, he apologized to the city committee of the CPSU in November and took a B-list sinecure in Gosstroi (the State Construction Committee).

Yeltsin, given the aura of martyrdom, did not wander in the wilderness for long. Unproven political resources had spun off from glasnost: the ability to voice barbed criticisms that the KGB or the censors in Glavlit would previously have nipped in the bud, and direct election to public office. Once he recovered his equanimity in 1988, Yeltsin brandished free speech, reimagining himself as a prescient reformist ahead of the curve. In 1989 he latched onto elections and people power.

In March of 1989 Boris Yeltsin won the all-Moscow seat in the USSR Congress of People's Deputies, in a landslide. He canvassed against inertia, favoritism, and the creaking bureaucracy, and as a streetwise manager who knew how to get things done. In the Congress, he was coleader with Andrei Sakharov of the proto-oppositional Interregional Deputies Group. In March 1990, during the round of republic-level elections, he took a place in the RSFSR Congress of People's Deputies. Eking out 50.5 percent of the votes, he was chosen as chairman of the Congress and Supreme Soviet on May 29. There was no holding him back: Yeltsin was now the uncontested leader of Russia-in-the-USSR. The RSFSR did not have a Communist Party branch until some weeks later, as Gorbachev, like earlier Soviet chieftains, feared it would pose "a standing threat of a rift" between the Kremlin and Russian leaderships. Once instituted, the Russian Communist Party (RKP) was inimical to reform and a haven for Soviet conservatives. Yeltsin deserted the CPSU in July 1990, in a jeremiad from the podium of its Twenty-Eighth Congress. On June 12, 1991, having steered enabling legislation through parliament, he made short shrift of six rivals for RSFSR president, with 59 percent of the votes cast; Ryzhkov, the stolid ex–prime minister who was the RKP's candidate, was next with 17 percent. A gala swearing in was held in the Kremlin Palace of Congresses on July 10.

Yeltsin's political star shot up on account of his flamboyance, tactical dexterity, and demotic touch. But he also hit on believable answers to two smoldering dilemmas of the day. One pertained to nation and the union. Out of civic Russian nationalism and a hodgepodge of selfish motives, Yeltsin threw in his lot with "sovereignty" for the RSFSR, saying the republic should not be just a handmaiden of the USSR. In doing so, he bared the Achilles' heel of Soviet federalism—the existence of a Russian entity that under the right conditions could be turned against the central Soviet authority. Sovereignty was distilled in a motion of the Russian congress adopted overwhelmingly on June 12, 1990, calling for renegotiation of the federation.

Within the RSFSR, territorialized minorities in single file rehearsed the national awakening that had just roiled the union republics of the USSR, replete with sovereignty resolutions and language laws, and clamored for the same liberties. One of the reasons Russian Communists voted for the resolution of June 12 was fury over Gorbachev trying to draw in the intra-RSFSR autonomous republics (ASSRs) as allies in his contest of will with the union republics. Yeltsin stole the thunder of sovereigntists in a speech in August 1990 at Kazan, Tatarstan. He dared the Tatars and their cominorities to "take as much sovereignty as you can swallow"—implying readiness to decentralize out to some undetermined limit as long as the non-Russians accepted the need to work together with the Russian majority. In April 1991 the RSFSR parliament voted to honor the suffering of the "repressed peoples" of World War II.

On the second focal issue where Yeltsin said his piece, the economy, he shucked glib populism and embraced the marketplace. The summer of 1990, an expert committee advisory to him and Gorbachev hammered out a Five Hundred Days Program. In that timespan, most pricing was to be decontrolled, the industrial ministries scrapped, privatization (euphemistically, "destatization") started, and regulatory control farmed out to an interrepublic committee. Yeltsin accepted the plan. Gorbachev washed his hands of it and lurched off in a dirigiste direction, assigning a more directive role to state planners. In December he purged progressive and centrist ministers and appointed the reactionaries—with Vice President Gennadii Yanayev and Prime Minister Valentin Pavlov leading the pack—who would push the Soviet Union over the precipice.

How was power transferred from the USSR to Russia and the other new states?

For the Soviet Union, a misbegotten coup d'état did in forty-eight hours what World War I took three years to do for the tottering Russian Empire. The coup, in August 1991, was choreographed by a self-appointed State Committee on the State of Emergency (going by the Russian initialism GKChP) fronted by the state leaders Gorbachev had impaneled the previous winter and by *siloviks*, or higher-ups in the security and military services.

The diehards were out of step with Gorbachev. He had zig-zagged again in the spring of 1991, reaching out to Yeltsin and opening "Nine Plus One" negotiations at the Novo-Ogarevo villa in Moscow oblast. There the RSFSR, eight other union republics, and the Soviet government came to agreement in late July on a treaty redoing the USSR into a confederative Union of Sovereign States (USS, or SSG in the Russian initials), leaving only national security, the currency, and the railroads to the central government. In a tête-a-tête with Yeltsin (bugged by the KGB), Gorbachev agreed to run in a public election for USS president in 1992, with Yeltsin in his corner, and to name Nursultan Nazarbayev, the energetic leader of Kazakhstan, prime minister.

The GKChP timed the putsch to derail the scheduled signing of the game-changing Nine Plus One treaty on August 20.

At daybreak on August 19 word was spread through state media that Gorbachev was laid up (he was under house arrest in his mansion at Foros, Crimea), Yanayev was standby president, and the treaty was off. Soldiers and armor flooded into Moscow. The man of the hour was Yeltsin, the RSFSR president with a public mandate. At midday he staged his stand-on-the-tank heroics, reading out an anti-GKChP declaration in front of the Moscow White House, the parliamentary office block. The morning of August 21, Defense Minister Dmitrii Yazov and Nikolai Kryuchkov, head of the KGB, blinked, deciding against an assault on the building. By that evening the troops were returning to quarters and the coup makers were under lock and key.

The dénouement was swift and unforgiving. Gorbachev never bounded back from his betrayal by the GKChP group and from the mortification of being harangued in front of the RSFSR deputies on August 23 and having to watch Yeltsin sign Decree No. 79, suspending the RKP, the Russian wing of the CPSU. The almighty party was taken apart in the weeks to come and its real estate filched by republic governments. The USSR congress voted on September 5 to close shop. A panel chaired by RSFSR Prime Minister Ivan Silayev stood in for the Soviet Council of Ministers. Russia nationalized oil and gas enterprises and impounded ministerial bank funds, so USSR departments depended on its largesse. Bandwagoning away from the enervated center, the union republics declared their independence one by one.

Desultory negotiations over a union treaty, now Seven Plus One, reopened at Novo-Ogarevo in October. Gorbachev was flustered at having to parley with "the new khans from the outer regions of the Soviet Union," as Foreign Minister Boris Pankin said acerbically. The talks were narrowed down to the economy, and even here there was gridlock. After dragging his feet, Yeltsin would have none of the eleventh-hour text Gorbachev tabled on November 25.

A first reason Yeltsin had for saying no was the reception of the center's entreaties in Ukraine (1989 population 51.7 million, second to the RSFSR's 147.4 million). Its parliament had voted for independence on August 24 and the Ukrainians, turning a deaf ear to Gorbachev (whose mother was of Ukrainian Cossack descent), would not budge on separation; it was to be cheered on in a referendum on December 1 by 92 percent of the voters. As Serhii Plokhy shows in *The Last Empire: The Final Days of the Soviet Union,* a divorce with Moscow, which had been thinkable only for Ukrainian "national democrats," took with apparatchiks and captains of industry who felt they had been cast aside after Chernobyl and were petrified that Yeltsin would conduct an anti-Communist witch hunt in Kiev if given half a chance. Yeltsin said then and later that there could be no union state without Ukraine. In a telephone conversation with President George H. W. Bush before the referendum, he griped that most republics in a Ukraine-less confederation would be Turkic and Muslim ("we can't forget the Islamic fundamentalist factor") and in Central Asia ("which we feed all the time").

The second snag concerned the internal affairs of the RSFSR. As the crisis of the union came to a head, Yeltsin firmed up his position on repairing Russia's economy. A coterie around Gennadii Burbulis, a professor and parliamentarian from Sverdlovsk, had his ear. It thought Russia had footed the bill for the non-Russian fourteen, could not do so anymore, and would best make a go of it with a national currency and unimpeded control over its resource bounty and economic rules. What Russia was to do was unparalleled. Instead of putting empire first, as it had done in the past, the country, writes Plokhy, "would start building its own ark to survive the coming flood." Plokhy's nautical analogy is insightful but incomplete. Yeltsin, as I see him, was at this point of time part Noah and part Jason—setting sail not only to stay alive but also to find the Golden Fleece of the good life somewhere across the waters.

The Russian Ark/Argo slipped into uncharted seas on December 8, 1991. Yeltsin met at a hunting chalet in the Belavezha Forest, Belarus, with President Leonid Kravchuk of Ukraine and the Belarusian parliamentary speaker, Stanislav Shushkevich. After some equivocation, the East Slavic troika signed on to an accord that asserted the end of the USSR, quoting rights as parties to the treaty of union of 1922. In its stead they put a minimalist agglomeration. The Commonwealth of Independent States (CIS), based in Minsk, the Belarusian capital, would turn out to be a medium for discussion and little else. The RSFSR Supreme Soviet ratified the agreement on December 12 (188 votes for, 6 against, 7 abstentions) and de-Sovietized the republic's name for the twin monikers of Russia and the Russian Federation. The five Central Asian "stans" and three other non-Slavic republics (Armenia, Azerbaijan, and Moldova) joined Russia, Ukraine, and Belarus at a CIS summit in Alma-Ata, Kazakhstan, on December 21. They agreed that Russia would be the legal continuator to the USSR and would take the Soviet seat in the United Nations, and that the CIS eleven (Georgia became a twelfth member in 1993) would respect each nation's territorial integrity.

Gorbachev made a last-ditch plea to the military brass to back him up and organize a USSR-wide referendum. Only when this fell flat did he see the writing on the wall and submit his resignation. On December 25 he videotaped a farewell and through a go-between handed over to Yeltsin the "nuclear briefcase" carrying electronics and the launch codes for Soviet missile forces. Twenty minutes after the speech was broadcast, the Russian flag, striated in white, blue, and red, was hoisted over the Kremlin. Without much ado, vlast had been transferred. On December 26 an atrophic parliamentary body, the Soviet of the Republics, certified the independence of the twelve union republics (Baltic independence had been granted in August). The day after, Yeltsin moved into Gorbachev's office suite in the former Governing Senate. Given a country house and a personal foundation, Gorbachev sallied forth onto the international lecture and fundraising circuit. His one political project after 1991 was to run for president of Russia in 1996. He finished seventh, with one-half of 1 percent of the popular vote.

Why was the Soviet collapse relatively peaceful?

Gorbachev's most vehement argument against dissolution was that it would be a humanitarian catastrophe—"Yugoslavia squared, raised to the tenth power," as one of his aides paraphrased it. The bloodletting in the Socialist Federal Republic of Yugoslavia started in June 1991, in the midst of the Novo-Ogarevo process in the USSR, and ground on until 1999. By the time the last shoe dropped in 2008, with Kosovo's secession from Serbia, there were seven successor states on the territory of the former Yugoslavia.

The prognosis is borne out if one looks at absolute statistics. On formerly Soviet soil, Russian forces were to wage two wars in the North Caucasus republic of Chechnya, and there were firefights in nearby parts. Tajikistan was torn by civil war from 1992 to 1997, and Georgia from 1992 to 1994 (the contenders were a weak central government, warlords, and militias in the provinces of South Ossetiya and Abkhaziya). There were hostilities in Transdniestria, or eastern Moldova, in 1992 and between Azerbaijanis and Armenians in the Nagorno-Karabakh region of western Azerbaijan from 1992 to 1994, and skirmishes in almost every ex–Soviet republic. In ballpark figures, transition-related violence claimed 250,000 to 300,000 combatants and noncombatants—the 150,000 who perished in Chechnya (toting up the second war of 1999–2002), 50,000 to 100,000 in Tajikistan, 25,000 to 30,000 in Nagorno-Karabakh, 20,000 to 25,000 in Georgia, and 1,000 in Transdniestria. For Yugoslavia, the International Criminal Tribunal for Former Yugoslavia puts deaths at half of the Eurasian total—140,000, the brunt of them in Bosnia-Herzegovina between 1992 and 1994.

In relative quantities, the balance sheet looks different. Yugoslavia's population in 1989, 23.7 million, was only 8 percent of the Soviet Union's. Adjusted for demography, fatalities in the former USSR were five or six times less than in the Balkans—104 per 100,000 (taking the body count as 300,000) as compared to 590 per 100,000 in Yugoslavia. In the Russian Federation, the ratio was right about the pan-Soviet mean.

The Soviet Union had the social tinder to feed a Yugoslav-type ethnonational inferno. It did not have a comparable spark in the leadership stratum.

To the squeamish and waffling Mikhail Gorbachev should go some of the thanks. As the USSR disintegrated between 1988 and 1991, he was implored over and over again to clamp down. A pattern was set at Tbilisi, Georgia, on April 9, 1989. Soldiers clubbed one protester to death outside the parliamentary building, after which nineteen were asphyxiated in a stampede; a Moscow inquiry upbraided the troops; and Gorbachev, saying the killing was without his knowledge, disowned the mess. In China, Deng Xiaoping did not blanch at turning the People's Liberation Army loose on the students in Beijing's Tiananmen Square in June 1989, and took responsibility for it. Gorbachev was reluctant to copy him—dissuaded by pangs of conscience and by a perception that it would boomerang.

Yeltsin had fewer compunctions about ordering out the troops, but was leery about employing them to save the Soviet Union. Yugoslavia's answer to Yeltsin was Slobodan Milošević, the president of the Serbian republic within Yugoslavia and then of the rump Federal Republic of Yugoslavia, consisting of Serbia and Montenegro. Milošević's truculence was the product partly of personality, partly of a Serbian collective memory lush in narratives of victimization (by Austrians, Turks, Croats, Albanians, et cetera), and partly of Serbia's relative weakness in the Yugoslav federation, which had interrepublic parity of voting power. The republic of Serbia counted for 42 percent of the Yugoslav population at the last full census in 1981 (the RSFSR was 51 percent in the USSR), and ethnic Serbs were

37 percent (ethnic Russians were 51 percent in the USSR). Serbia itself was also a more ethnically fractionated place: 34 percent of its people were from minorities (in the RSFSR it was 19 percent). The principal non-Serb community, the Kosovar Albanians, constituted 14 percent of the population; its relationship with the Serb majority was toxic, and Milošević had revoked the Kosovars' autonomy in 1989. Milošević fought for Serbian rights in the dying days of the federation. He then battled, in effect, for a Greater Serbia that would have roped in districts of Croatia and Bosnia and kept sovereignty over Kosovo and the multiethnic province of Vojvodina. Although culpability does not lie solely with him or Belgrade, the most vicious of the intercommunal fighting and ethnic cleansing of the 1990s stemmed from these actions.

Yeltsin had a stronger hand to play and was made of different stuff. Russia proper could not wear the victim's cape and was still a majority in the union. There was no insubordinate minority within it to approximate the Kosovars. The ranking non-Russian nationality, at 5 percent of the population, was the Volga Tatars, the group at which Yeltsin aimed his brash sovereignty offer in 1990. In the terminal years of the USSR, Yeltsin conducted a center–periphery and anti-Communist game and not an ethnonational game. His strategy was much more like that of the Czech leader Václav Klaus in Czechoslovakia, which broke into the Czech Republic and Slovakia peacefully in 1992, than the rancorous divisiveness of Slobodan Milošević. It is difficult to fancy Yeltsin keeping company with Milošević confederates like Radovan Karadžić (head of the Serbian enclave in Bosnia) or Ratko Mladić (commandant at the Srebrenica massacre of Bosnian Muslims in 1995), who were to join Milošević in the dock at the Hague tribunal. Unlike Milošević, Yeltsin took scant interest in past wrongs and none in irredentism, seeing them as diversions from his duty of turning the page of history. His assessment was explicitly postimperial. "A united empire," says *Notes of a President*, the second volume of his memoirs, "is a powerful . . . thing which elicits awe and respect. But how long could it [the USSR] have remained an empire? By now all the other empires of the world—British, French, and Portuguese—had fallen apart.... Russia had to shed its imperial mission." Slimmed down as a normal state, it would earn the high opinion of the international community and "the authority to carry out reforms."

Those reforms would begin with things material. In 1991 the RSFSR was the location for 61 percent of the Soviet economy, 70 percent of manufacturing, 91 percent of oil pumped, and 77 percent of natural gas. Yeltsin wanted Russia to benefit from this cornucopia without appendages which, as he said to Bush, "we feed all the time." If Milošević's object was to keep other Yugoslav units under Serbia's thumb, Yeltsin's was to get other Soviet units off of Russia's back.

Unlike past empires and failed states, the Soviet quasi-empire was armed to the teeth. The possibility of loss of control expressly over its nuclear storehouse gave governments everywhere fits. Providentially, this had a sobering effect on all sides.

Three thousand two hundred of the USSR's strategic warheads in 1991 were in Belarus, Kazakhstan, and Ukraine, in storage bunkers or on ICBMs and bomber aircraft, as were four thousand less destructive tactical weapons. Tactical weapons were shipped to Russia without a hitch by the summer of 1992, as provided for by the Belavezha and Alma-Ata pacts. For the strategic arms, a CIS command was instituted; all codes for unlocking and firing remained with Moscow and Yeltsin. A Russian Ministry of Defense took them over in May 1992, and a couple of weeks later the Lisbon Accord, cosigned by the Western powers, bound Belarus, Kazakhstan, and Ukraine to send their warheads to Russia, where the fissile materials were to be reprocessed for civilian reactors.

With Belarus and Kazakhstan, all went well, but Ukraine had qualms about letting go of its 2,250 strategic nukes. American financial aid for denuclearization was central to incentivizing Ukraine. Pentagon officials put Kiev on notice that if Moscow decided the Ukrainians were unable to maintain missiles or were trying to snatch working control, the Russian military could well bomb silos from the air and spark an inadvertent liftoff—of rockets programmed by the Soviet General Staff to strike American cities. In November 1994 Ukraine gave in and ratified the Nuclear Nonproliferation Treaty. The last warheads were whisked to Russia in May 1996.

What was Russian "shock therapy"?

As regards the economy, Yeltsin was in such a hurry to go where Gorbachev feared to tread that he rolled out a wide-ranging reform plan two months before the Soviet Union cratered. The premises behind his milestone speech to the Russian Congress of People's Deputies on October 28, 1991, went back to the stillborn Five Hundred Days of 1990. A multidimensional "reformist breakthrough" would rewire central planning into "a healthy mixed economy with a strong private sector." Yeltsin said pointblank that it would pay off in a preset time frame, one year in this case. "If we take this path today," was his reassurance, "we'll see real results by the autumn of 1992"—words he had to eat when the year was up. The alternative to "shock therapy" (*shokoterapiya*), as the reform came to be known, would be "to condemn ourselves to poverty and our centuries-old state to annihilation," Yeltsin averred.

Reform particulars were sketched by a brain trust assembled by economist Yegor Gaidar, who was appointed finance minister and deputy premier at the tender age of thirty-five, under the benefaction of Gennadii Burbulis, now first deputy premier. Yeltsin briefly took over chairmanship of the cabinet and gave portfolios to interlopers "without mental and ideological blinkers," as he worded it in *Notes of a President*. Congress on November 1 gave him twelve months to take action by executive fiat.

Shock therapy's heart was the price deregulation begun on January 2, 1992. In one fell swoop, 90 percent of retail and

80 percent of wholesale prices were thrown to the impersonal and decentralized forces of supply and demand. On January 29 a presidential edict unchained trade from governmental dictate, leaving Russians at liberty to buy, sell, and resell almost anything. USSR Inc. was stripped down by the summer of 1992. Gosplan and the bevy of overhead agencies went under the knife; all except for a few of the Soviet industrial ministries were reorganized as holding companies. A State Property Committee under the liberal economist Anatolii Chubais doled out vouchers citizens could use to buy equity in fifteen thousand government-owned companies. Municipalities privatized flats and small houses and freely granted permissions to build family dachas. Collective and state farms were rearranged as joint stock companies and began a slowpoke movement toward the market.

In the months they were given to work, Gaidar and his ministers laid the groundwork for an independent central bank, two stock markets (the misnamed Moscow Interbank Currency Exchange, or MICEX, and the Russian Trading System, or RTS), commodity exchanges, a new civil code, and rules on corporate governance—the organizational and statutory underpinnings of capitalism. A CIS currency union was resisted; by mid-1993 the ruble had been Russified and the other fourteen lapsed republics minted national currencies. Russian trade began to globalize, as commerce with the post-Soviet states tapered off from 59 percent of the total in 1991 to 17 percent in 1995. In November 1996 the telecommunications firm VimpelCom was the first Russian company since 1917 to do an Initial Public Offering (IPO) and the first since 1903 to be listed on the New York Stock Exchange.

There were payoffs to the great reform straightaway: a currency with purchasing power, the end to monetary overhang and to ration coupons and lines for groceries, and attenuation of the shadow economy. Chubais's privatization program would be the largest divestiture of state resources in history. Two-thirds of material and financial assets were taken off the government's books. The incubator of state socialism was now a market economy—distorted yet real—complete with the paraphernalia of modern consumerism.

For the man and woman on the street, the bright news about the economy was eclipsed by the dark. Retail prices spiked by 2,520 percent in 1992. Savings stashed under the proverbial mattress, chiefly in Soviet rubles printed under Gorbachev with nothing to spend them on, were wiped out. Gaidar's remedy was tight money, as per the gospel of liberal economics. Yeltsin vacillated. Goaded by supplicants from industry and the old-school nomenklatura, he was fearful that a shortfall in operating funds would bankrupt producers and cause layoffs and mass protest. In July 1992 he installed Viktor Gerashchenko, the last head of the USSR State Bank, as governor of the Russian Central Bank. With gusto, Gerashchenko for two and one-half years expanded the money supply, making it hard to put a damper on prices and weed out unproductive firms. The consumer price index increased by a still astronomical 840 percent in 1993 and stayed in triple digits through 1995. A multitude of transactions in the wholesale economy were done, and about half of government taxes were paid, through barter or monetary surrogates.

Macroeconomic volatility coalesced with fiscal indiscipline and the shattering of the Soviet economic space to bring about a relentless downswing, in output and welfare, which rated with the Great Depression of 1929–33 in the United States. The slump was exacerbated by a deus ex machina—softening of the Brent monthly price for crude oil from $23.54 per barrel in January 1991 to $13.56 in December 1993, dragging down the value of Russia's primary generator of hard currency. Real GDP was dialed back by 15 percent in 1992, 9 percent in 1993, and 13 percent in 1994, and wages and government pensions were routinely in arrears. The freefall put a dent in the allure of a leader, Yeltsin, who told the people about pulling in their belts for one year and not more. The downturn abated to 4 percent in 1995 and 1996, as inflation fell and the Brent index recouped pre-1991 values. Only in 1997 was there finally an uptick, of 0.8 percent. The field was plowed for future prosperity, but in the here and now most Russians lived hand-to-mouth.

Why was there a constitutional crisis after 1991, and how was it resolved?

Contestation over an institutional blueprint for the state is a marker of regime change anywhere. Old instruments have malfunctioned; new ones have yet to be devised and debugged; uncertainty abounds. Jon Elster has likened governmental reform after Communism to rebuilding a ship on the open sea, with no chance of putting it into dry dock.

In the Russia born-again in 1991, the shards of Soviet institutions were suspect. Novel ones not infrequently came to fruition through "institutional isomorphism," a fancy formula organizational primers use for the imitation of forms verified to have succeeded somewhere else. As Yeltsin was to observe in *Notes of a President*, the products were as often as not castles in the ether, "beautiful structures and beautiful titles with nothing behind them." Foreign counsel on political reform was decontextualized and accepted sight unseen. The CPSU was not there to patch together impromptu solutions. Input from the citizenry was sporadic.

Russia's legacy constitution was antiquated and riddled with inconsistencies. It dated from 1978 and had been amended 230 times. A constitutional commission, originally chaired by Yeltsin, never found common ground. When the presidency was established in 1991, the constitution now referred to it and the Congress of People's Deputies both as the final authority in the state, without demarcating roles or providing for conflict resolution.

Parliament had peccadillos on its side of the aisle. Only the RSFSR and Kazakhstan replicated the ungainly upstairs-downstairs format of the USSR legislature, with overlapping roles for a large Congress and a smaller Supreme Soviet. The

Russian Congress convened three or four times a year amid fanfare and posturing. Its 1,051 deputies, elected in 1990 as individuals and not as party nominees (there were no opposition parties at the time), had few preset preferences and often cycled in rollcalls between opposing positions. The Supreme Soviet, its 251 members in continuous session, was a more businesslike body. The parliamentary speaker chosen after Yeltsin went off to be president, economist Ruslan Khasbulatov, made the best of a murky division of labor to wring personal control over budgeting, staff, and the legislative calendar.

Institutions interlocked with money matters. Since radical economic reform emanated from an activist executive branch, the separately elected legislature was the predictable place for counteractivism. Khasbulatov and a goodly share of Yeltsin's parliamentary bedfellows from 1990 to 1991 denounced shock therapy and its socioeconomic effects. A month after the year for making reforms by decree ran out, the deputies vetoed Yeltsin's nomination of Yegor Gaidar, now the lightning rod for dissatisfaction, as prime minister. A deal was cut to select Viktor Chernomyrdin, the middle-aged founder of the state gas corporation, Gazprom, and a political centrist; Gaidar and Burbulis left the government.

Come the spring of 1993, the two camps were at daggers drawn. Yeltsin's 1991 running mate and vice president, Alexander Rutskoi, a former air force pilot who had two jets shot out from under him in Afghanistan, aligned himself with Khasbulatov. On March 26 a motion to impeach Yeltsin missed the required two-thirds majority in the Congress by seventy-two votes. In April a referendum gave a yes to Yeltsin (57 percent) and his program (53 percent), but failed to clear the air. A Kremlin-selected "constitutional conference" produced a presidentialist rough copy by July. Yeltsin took a breather, as he was wont to do when stressed. More than was wise, he found a security blanket around this time in alcohol—"The load eased after several glasses," he was to concede as ex-president.

The end came through bullets and ballots. On September 21, 1993, Yeltsin stole a march on the lawmakers by issuing Decree

No. 1400, which dissolved parliament and called an election for December 12 to a new, bicameral Federal Assembly; the assembly's first act would be to approve a constitution. He had no illusions about the legality of his decree: "Here I was, the first popularly elected president, infringing the law—bad law . . . but in any case the law." He was, he said, cutting a Gordian knot, as he had in 1987 when he spoke out against Gorbachev and in 1991 at Belavezha. The opposition in the legislature went through a form of impeachment on September 23, pronouncing Rutskoi to be president. Deputies holed up inside the White House on the Moskva River, the very building where Yeltsin barricaded himself during the 1991 putsch.

The night of October 3–4 was one of mayhem on the streets of the capital. Yeltsin ordered Defense Minister Pavel Grachev to send tanks into central Moscow. Ten of them shelled the parliamentarians' lair, and soldiers rushed it. Khasbulatov and Rutskoi were bused to jail in handcuffs. The death count was 187, none of them elected deputies.

Yeltsin on October 7 "suspended" the Constitutional Court inaugurated with his approbation in 1991. The next week, he reconsidered the plan to have a post-Soviet constitution adopted by the Federal Assembly after its election on December 12, ruling that a plebiscite, on the draft of a presidential advisory group, would be held as an add-on to the parliamentary balloting. Turnout in the plebiscite on election day was 54 percent, and 58 percent of them voted yes on the Yeltsin draft—32 percent of the electorate. His pride and joy, the constitution for a Russian Federation/Russia (the name order was inverted from 1991), took effect on December 25, 1993, two years to the day after Gorbachev's resignation. Yeltsin bowed to advice to write the Constitutional Court into the new charter.

Was Yeltsin's Russia really a democracy?

For Yeltsin, the termination of the crisis was bittersweet. His constitution had been riveted in, and the election tournament was between political parties and movements as well as individual candidates. But the Federal Assembly was anything but a presidential poodle. Half of the 450 members of the lower house, the State Duma (the name of Nicholas II's lower chamber from 1906 to 1917), were elected on national party lists and half in single-member districts. The propresident Russia's Choice bloc chaired by Gaidar, which started the campaign with high hopes, netted only 16 percent of the party-list vote and 96 seats. Vladimir Zhirinovsky's demagogic Liberal Democratic Party of Russia (LDPR) received 23 percent of the vote. The Duma retained Chernomyrdin as prime minister but kept his government at arm's length. One of its first legislative acts was to amnesty Khasbulatov, Rutskoi, fourteen accomplices from 1993, and the kingpins of the 1991 GKChP.

The Yeltsinesque regime is not easily stereotyped. Most political scientists would call it a crossbreed of democracy and authoritarianism. A whole glossary of terms has been applied to systems of this ilk—illiberal democracy, competitive authoritarianism, patronalism, and the like—without any unanimity reached on definitions or the forces at work.

A statistical metric can be found in the yearly reports of the monitoring organization Freedom House. They emphasize individual freedom and equality and are frequently cited as a decent approximation of the truth. Two ratings are assigned, for political rights and civil liberties, on a scale from 1 to 7 where 1 is the freest and 7 is the least free. These are averaged into a composite freedom score.

In 1986, as perestroika was getting airborne, the Soviet Union rated a summary 7 from Freedom House. For 1992, Russia's first year of independence, the count was 3.5 (3 for political rights and 4 for civil liberties): on a continuum between democratic and authoritarian rule, nearer the democratic pole. The index held steady through 1997. It was at the midway point on the scale, 4, in 1998 (when bickering between president and parliament changed the political rights score to 4), and 4.5 in 1999 (when renewed combat in Chechnya changed civil liberties to 5), slightly nearer the authoritarian end. One may quibble with the arithmetic. Freedom House is too generous to Russia's early 1990s, when Yeltsin used the army to knock out an elected parliament, and too ungenerous to Russia's late 1990s. Just the same, this method of judgment and others like it concur that the Russian regime throughout the 1990s merged some properties of democratic and authoritarian orders.

At a minimum, it accommodated a cluster of democratic practices that stand against the monism and absolutism of yesteryear. Article 1 of Yeltsin's constitution proclaimed Russia "a democratic, federal, law-bound state with a republican form of government." Forty-eight articles in the constitution, often lifting lines from the Universal Declaration of Human Rights of 1948, enshrined personal freedoms. In the new system, political parties appeared, disappeared, and altered hue like beads in a kaleidoscope and compulsory membership in official mass organizations fell by the wayside. A skeleton law on "nonprofit organizations" (the Russian acronym is NKO, the closest thing to an NGO or nongovernmental organization in Western parlance) was passed in January 1996. But well before then a civil society genie was out of the bottle. Unconventional voluntary groupings, headless movements, and formal associations sprang up by the thousands, and international NGOs and donors also set up shop. Some of the more intrepid players were organizations for human rights—for example, the Union of Soldiers' Mothers Committees, Rights of the Child, and Prison and Liberty. Russia subscribed to the Council of Europe, an intergovernmental group for law and rights, in 1996. In 1998 it ratified the European Convention on Human Rights and committed to execute judgments of the European Court of Human Rights (ECHR) in Strasbourg, France.

The dreaded KGB was scissored into a half-dozen agencies (domestic counterintelligence was accommodated in a Federal Security Service, or FSB), and phone tapping was curtailed.

Yeltsin encouraged the security services to jostle with one another for access to information and to him. The process was less like intelligence oversight in a consolidated democracy and "more like the competition of viziers in the medieval Middle East or Napoleon's France, where several secret police agencies spied on each other," yet was an improvement on Soviet practice.

In a startling deviation from the empire and the USSR, Yeltsin's Russia had no political prisoners outside of Chechnya-related arrests, and no political exiles. The most renowned Brezhnev-era expatriate, Alexander Solzhenitsyn, showed up in Moscow from Cavendish, Vermont, in 1994 and built a dacha next to those that had belonged to Mikhail Tukhachevskii, Mikhail Suslov, and Konstantin Chernenko. He had a biweekly talk show on Russian television for a year, turning it into a monologue after seven months. Solzhenitsyn died in 2008 and was interned in the yard of Donskoi Monastery, an NKVD killing field in the 1930s and where the cremated ashes of Nikolai Yezhov of the Great Purge and the Great Terror were dumped in 1940.

Russians in the 1990s were free to work overseas or emigrate, and to assemble and petition. Except for national television, the mass media were mainly capitalist businesses, and even in that market a for-profit network, NTV, took to the airwaves in 1993. One of its most watched programs was *Kukly* (Puppets), a Sunday-night spoof written by Viktor Shenderovich and produced by Vasilii Grigoriev in which costumed dolls poked fun at the political class. Young computer buffs laid the basis for the Runet, the Russian segment of the newfangled Internet. The country code top-level domain (.ru) was introduced in 1993 (.рф, Romanized as. rf, for Russian Federation, came in 2010). MSK-IX, Russia's first Internet exchange point, working out of the Kurchatov Institute for Atomic Energy, was up and running in 1995, a Russian search engine (rambler.ru) in 1996, and Yevgenii Kaspersky's international software security group (Kaspersky Lab) in 1997.

The democratic or democratizing factor in the Yeltsin equation was most upfront in the electoral realm. "Russians," as Freedom House's *Freedom in the World* said in its country essay for 1999, "can change their government democratically." "Though marred by irregularities, the 1995 and 1999 parliamentary and 1996 presidential elections were deemed generally free and fair by international observers." The 1996 election was a point of no return. Yeltsin, egged on by his boon companions, the silovik (security official) Alexander Korzhakov (chief of the presidential guard) and Oleg Soskovets (first deputy premier), had considered abrogating the vote and ruling by diktat for several years. At the end of the day, Yeltsin faced the electorate and fired Korzhakov and Soskovets.

The costs of entry into the electoral ring were low to nonexistent—239 parties and political movements were registered in 1999, and State Duma candidates in local districts could sign up as nonpartisans. Yeltsin took a dim view of ventures to form a "party of power," and they fizzled. Prime Minister Chernomyrdin's Our Home Is Russia in 1995 underperformed Gaidar's Russia's Choice party from 1993, raking in but 10 percent of the Duma party-list vote; a Communist Party of the Russian Federation (KPRF) took 22 percent of the vote and 35 percent of the seats. In 1996 Yeltsin, running as an independent and fearing he would go down to defeat by the KPRF's Gennadii Zyuganov, trudged through a four-month campaign and involved "political technologists" from the budding public relations and advertising industries to carry the qualifying round by 3 percentage points and the runoff by 14 points. The 1999 version of the party of power, the Unity bloc, was formed three months before the election; it received 23 percent of the party-list votes but was again bested by the Communists with 24 percent.

Warts and all,' the system was competitive. Yeltsin envisioned his administration as a big tent, with space for intelligentsia democrats of every stripe, ex-apparatchiks, tech-nocrats and "red directors" from Soviet industry, practitioners of the new mass politics, and intransigents from the security services. He was tolerant of interpersonal and interfactional competition, setting up crisscrossing jurisdictions that referred conflicts to him for final resolution.

This is not to say that the pluralistic and democratic ele-ments in the Russian polity were a coherent whole or were embodied in full-bodied institutions or wholehearted popu-lar acquiescence. Rule of law, upheld by an impartial judi-ciary, might have glued together the regime. It was poorly developed in transitional Russia, as Yeltsin had the acumen to admit. "Having jettisoned the command principle of rule," he said in February 1994, "the state has not fully assimilated the law-based principle." "This has brought forth such men-acing phenomena as . . . the imbuing of the state and munici-pal apparatus with corruption . . . a low level of discipline in implementation . . . lack of harmonization in the work of the ministries and departments." Other symptoms of a dysfunc-tional state did not need listing—thievery and violent crime, protection rackets and mafias displacing law-enforcement agencies, porous borders, tax evasion and a budget drafted in red ink, bills of exchange as stand-ins for the ruble, and the ragged retreat of the army from a caved-in empire. "We must confess openly," Yeltsin said, "that democratic principles and the organization of our government are being discredited."

To call the Yeltsin constitution presidentialist is an under-statement. The Federal Assembly was weak if not toothless. Its powers were thinnest regarding oversight of the executive branch; its role on legislation, government spending, and con-firming a prime minister was greater. The president was head of state, director of the executive branch (with the right under Article 90 to issue binding decrees), and commander-in-chief. What's more, Article 80 stipulated that he was "guarantor" of the political order and "shall determine the main directions of domestic and foreign policy" in keeping with the law. Yeltsin exercised these powers with restraint.

Was Yeltsin's Russia really a federation?

The division of powers in the vertical dimension, between levels of government, was as much contested as the horizontal division of powers between executive and legislature in Moscow. The USSR, after all, had been done in by disharmony with its republics. The two post-Communist federations in Eastern Europe, Yugoslavia and Czechoslovakia, had gone bust in 1991 and 1992.

The RSFSR of 1918 was the primal Soviet ethnofederation, and retained this feature when it was encased in the USSR in 1924. With the Soviet carapace and the other union republics gone, the Russian remnant post-1991 sheltered twenty-one homeland republics (*respublikas*), as the old ASSRs were now called, with an almost thousandfold range in area from 1,400 square miles (Ingushetiya) to 1.2 million (Sakha). Eleven ethnically tagged districts (ten "autonomous *okrugs*" and one "autonomous oblast") sat lower on the totem pole. The republics covered 29 percent of Russia's surface area and the lesser minority units 25 percent, though the latter were subject to knotty legal arrangements.

The minority homelands were far less impressive demographically than geographically: 17 percent of the Russia-wide population mass for the republics in the 1990s and a trifling 2 percent for the minor units. Among the people of post-Soviet Russia at large, the 81 percent who were ethnic Russians were 30 points above their share in the Soviet Union and more than the titular ethnicity's share in all of the new states except Azerbaijan and Armenia. In only five Russian republics—late-acquired Tuva in Siberia, Chuvashiya on the Volga, and Chechnya, Ingushetiya, and North Ossetiya in the North Caucasus—were members of the titular group over 50 percent of the population. This was so in just two of ten autonomous okrugs; in the Jewish autonomous oblast on the Amur River, once envisaged as a colony for Soviet Jews, 1 percent of the populace was Jewish, 3 percent Ukrainian, and 93 percent Russian. What is more, the lesser ethnic entities, rich in natural resources but poor in human and political resources, were with the passage of time to be whittled down in number and territorial extent. Between 2005 and 2008, after Yeltsin's retirement, six of the autonomous okrugs would without furor be merged into adjoining regions—halving their share of Russia's surface area to 13 percent while leaving their share of the population statistically untouched, since they had a piffling four hundred thousand people between them.

In raw numbers of square miles and especially population, then, the Russian majority was in an impregnable position. Yet the demise of the Soviet Union had not been about numbers. The impertinent Baltic republics had 7.9 million people in toto on sixty-seven thousand square miles of land, and they led the charge away from the USSR. The Soviet governmental federation was overlaid by the Communist Party, which was unitary and not federative. For political process if not sociology and culture, the CPSU failsafe made federalism a polite fiction. Its extinction made for governance woes all over post-Soviet Eurasia. In far-flung Russia, where the Politburo and Secretariat had dealt directly with regional actors, without union republic–level mediation, it made for a governance crisis.

Intergovernmental relations were muddied by the inter-branch rivalry capped by Yeltsin's shelling of the parliament in 1993. The regions shamelessly played one central faction off against the other, and the claimants in Moscow bid for support by appeasing subnational governments. Yeltsin was no stranger to this dalliance, having told the republics to take as much sovereignty as could go down their throats.

Still another wrinkle was an asymmetry in the vertical distribution of powers. Most territories were populated principally by ethnic Russians and had nothing in common with ascriptive identities or ethnofederalism. Of the catalog of eighty-nine regional "subjects of the federation" (eighty-three by 2008), fifty-seven were ethnically neutral. Forty-nine of the fifty-seven were oblasts, and six larger units, usually with subunits within their boundaries, were called *krais* (there were nine krais by 2008, and forty-six oblasts). These regions were simply provinces, named after their administrative seats (Novgorod oblast after Novgorod, Krasnoyarsk krai after Krasnoyarsk, and so on); they had "governors" (*gubernators*) and not the pretentiously titled "presidents" (*prezidents*) most republics had until the 2010s. Russian law also recognized two "federal cities," Moscow and St. Petersburg (back to its pre-1914 name), which had the same rights as regions. The leaders of the oblasts, krais, and federal cities saw some pickings for themselves in the interplay between the ethnic republics and the center but were unsympathetic to the demands of the republics for special status, to say nothing of the underpopulated lower-tier units.

In one of the brighter chapters of his presidency, Yeltsin improvised a fuzzy federalism that served 1990s Russia passably well. He seized the high ground by bullying and cajoling the regions into signing a "federative treaty" in the Grand Kremlin Palace on March 30, 1992. During the 1993 political stalemate, he removed governors who bet on the opposition and ordered elections for new regional councils. His constitution, unlike past Soviet constitutions (but like the US constitution), did not assign rights of secession, and it flunked a legal test of federalist probity for not reserving any policy areas wholly for the regions. But it did inscribe rudiments of a federal state. Article 72 enumerated fourteen fields that the regional and federal governments would share; Article 73 granted residual rights to the regions; and Article 125 had the Constitutional Court arbitrate jurisdictional disputes. The constitution also gave Russia a standard accoutrement of federalism, an upper chamber of parliament to represent the federal units, like the US Senate or the German Bundesrat. Members of the Federation Council, two per region, were directly elected in 1993; after 1995 one was the governor or president and the other the chair of the legislative assembly.

The fuzzily federalist stopgap was intertwined with hard-headed adaptations to circumstances—"political first aid" for the system, as Yeltsin expressed it. Tatarstan on the Volga and Chechnya in the North Caucasus, both with Muslim titular groups, drew back from signing the 1992 treaty, and a Tatarstan referendum voted to treat Russia as a foreign country. But the Tatar president, Mintimer Shaimiyev—a former CPSU apparatchik and a supporter of the GKChP in 1991—was agreeable to negotiations. In February 1994 he and Yeltsin came up with a "Treaty on Delimiting the Jurisdictions and Mutual Transmission of Authority between the Organs of State Power of the Russian Federation and the Republic of Tatarstan." It highlighted the Tatars' free association with Russia and rights on raw materials and taxation. Other republics and soon enough nonethnic provinces demanded bilateral agreements for them. By 1998 treaties, some with unpublished codicils, had been concluded with forty-seven regions.

The treaties were complemented by fiscal and political de-centralization. In 1991 about 60 percent of budgetary revenues were remitted to the federal government and about 40 percent to the regions; by 1999 the balance was vice versa. In politics, the sea change was firsthand election of provincial governors and presidents, which went into effect countrywide in 1995. In a sign of Yeltsin's disposition to live and let live, one of the governors elected in 1996, in Kursk oblast on the Ukrainian border, was Alexander Rutskoi, his deposed vice president.

Why and with what results did war break out in Chechnya?

If Tatarstan was the showcase for fuzzy federalism, Chechnya was the horror story. The Chechens, a mountain people just under 1 million in 1989, had come into the empire late, toward the end of the Caucasian War of 1817–64, and resisted Sovietization. During World War II, German troops, looking to take oilfields and refineries, occupied part of the area; in February 1944 the Chechens were piled by the NKVD into unheated freight cars and transported to Central Asia. The CPSU Presidium allowed them back in 1956–57 and reinstated the Chechen-Ingush republic, shared with the closely related Ingush nationality, who had also been exiled in 1944. Ethnic riots between Russians and Chechen returnees, fueled by competition over housing and jobs, tore Grozny, Chechen-Ingushetiya's capital, in August 1958.

The rearview mirror gets us only so far toward elucidating Chechnya's tribulations in the 1990s. Other minorities in and near the Caucasus fought the empire, and six were expelled en masse in the 1940s, but only the Chechens took up arms against post-Soviet Russia. Latter-day happenstance, misconstructions, and personae offer superior leads.

Chechen-Ingushetiya was an inveterately conservative region and one of the last in the RSFSR to be ruffled by perestroika. Turmoil at the turn of the 1990s led to a bisection of the hyphenated unit and an exit of Russians. Jokhar Dudayev, a headstrong general in the Soviet air force and a political neophyte, who had lived in Chechnya only as an infant (like his fellow Chechen Ruslan Khasbulatov), returned there in 1990 and took over a counterparliament, the All-National Congress of the Chechen People. In September and October 1991, Dudayev's congress dislodged the official administration and he was elected president. On November 1 he claimed independence from the Soviet Union. Unable to agree with Yeltsin on a riposte, Gorbachev pulled Soviet troops out, leaving behind a mound of military hardware and ammunition.

Opting out of the federative treaty of 1992 (Chechnya and Tatarstan were the only regions to do so), Dudayev declined to follow the example of Tatarstan's Shaimiyev and bargain with the center. Yeltsin did not bestir himself to meet Dudayev halfway and assigned Russian special-operations units to stir up trouble in Grozny. Promised an easy victory by the military high command, he ordered in the armed forces in December

1994. There was no easy victory to be had. The Russian aerial and artillery bombardment of Grozny was the heaviest of any European city since World War II. The army took Dudayev's life with a radio-guided rocket and chased the Chechen insurrectionaries into the hill country, but it and the MVD had no stomach for the errand and were unable to finish it. Yeltsin walked away from the unpopular war during his 1996 reelection campaign and sued for peace. A preliminary agreement was reached in August. On May 2, 1997, a peace treaty with a new Chechen headman, Aslan Maskhadov, postponed setting of a final status for the republic until 2002.

The shambolic First Chechen War, with its tens of thousands dead and maimed and hundreds of thousands displaced, had secondhand ramifications in many directions. Performance in the field and the war's abject wrap-up telegraphed a decay of Russian military power. And the war induced something else—a brush with large-scale terrorism. On June 14, 1995, a ragtag band of Chechen fighters under field commander Shamil Basayev took fifteen hundred hostages at a hospital in Budyonnovsk, a sleepy town in Stavropol krai seventy miles north of Chechnya. Premier Chernomyrdin, on live television, negotiated safe passage for Basayev's men. One hundred and sixty-six died before the Chechens left on June 19.

Respite for Chechnya was fleeting. Left to its own devices, it careened into lawlessness. Maskhadov had no sway over highland clans, militias, and mobsters who ran amok and kidnapped for fun and profit. Islamists supplanted secular nationalists. Basayev and guerrilla leader Movladi Udugov organized to "liberate" other North Caucasus republics. Moscow hardliners itched to put them in their place. All the fixings were there for a second war.

How did post-Soviet Russia come to terms with its past?

Yeltsin did not pigeonhole his changes as a revolution, preferring the tab "reforms." He had a visceral reaction against the "disorder, looting ... and anarchy" of 1917, says *Notes of a President*. "I saw continuity between the society of the Khrushchev-Brezhnev period and the new Russia. It was not in my plans to smash and bust up everything as the Bolsheviks did." By Bolshevik standards, the human resources he took over from the Soviet state were handled with kid gloves. Russian sociologists found that "more than 80 percent of the former Soviet nomenklatura ... moved [after 1991] into positions that were either in the first or second rank of the post-Communist elite, and conversely that almost 80 percent of the post-Communist elite had enjoyed elite or 'pre-elite' positions in the late Soviet period."

Yeltsin did establish a blue-ribbon presidential commission for "rehabilitation of victims of political repression" under the CPSU, which exonerated 4.5 million individuals over the next ten years, 90 percent of them posthumously. History textbooks and school curricula were rejiggered. But Yeltsin had no appetite for the lustration, or unmasking and purging, of officials affiliated with the party and security organs of the old system, as in the former East Germany and the Czech Republic—a policy plank that might have been trouble for him personally. He continued to pay respects to Great Patriotic War veterans and to hold an annual Victory Day parade on Red Square. US President Bill Clinton stood beside him on the dais in May 1995.

One thing Yeltsin was impatient for was a reckoning with the patrimony of the founding father of the Soviet Union. He had a two-ton bronze statue of Lenin taken out of the Kremlin garden, his lovingly conserved Kremlin study carted away to a museum, and the goose-stepping ceremonial guard at the Lenin mausoleum in Red Square removed. He had hoped to have Lenin's body extricated from the shrine and entombed in a Moscow graveyard. But he prevaricated on implementation, aware that public opinion was riven, and nothing came of it.

Stymied on the Lenin tomb, Yeltsin pushed through semiotic links with pre-Soviet Russia. The tricolor flag, adopted by the still-RSFSR on August 22, 1991, had been the flag of the empire from 1896 to 1917 and of the Provisional Government of 1917. In March 1992 Yeltsin substituted a Hero of the Russian Federation award for Hero of the Soviet Union. Later edicts Russified Soviet medals, restored several from the empire, notably the Order of St. Andrei, and registered traditional Cossack guard formations. A presidential proclamation in November 1993 made an image of the two-headed eagle of Byzantium and Muscovy the Russian Federation's coat of arms. In December the "Patriotic Song," composed by Mikhail Glinka in 1833, was instituted as an unloved national anthem (without lyrics, which were never written). Nineteen ninety-three also saw commencement of renovations to the Kremlin buildings of state, which had fallen into desuetude.

A sidebar to the romance with tradition was a revival of religious practices and belief, anathema to the CPSU. An unstitching of controls by Gorbachev in 1988, the thousand-year jubilee of the Christianization of Kievan Rus, was continued under Yeltsin. Antireligious propaganda was halted, scores of churches reopened, and the injunction against building new ones was lifted. The prime beneficiary was the Russian Orthodox Church, which had three or four times the congregants of all others combined. Yeltsin, who was from a religious family, took a liking to attending services and lighting a votive candle on holy days. From 1995 to 2000, workers knocked together a carbon copy of the largest church in Imperial Russia, the Cathedral of Christ the Savior. The cathedral, several blocks from the Kremlin, was dynamited by Stalin in 1931 to clear the way for a USSR Palace of Soviets that was to dwarf the Empire State Building; work on the palace was stopped in 1941, and after 1945 the foundation was converted into an outdoor swimming pool. The Soviet-appointed patriarch, Aleksii II, was an indefatigable spokesman for his flock. His crowning achievement was a Law on Freedom of Conscience and Religious Associations passed in 1997. It codified the "special role" of Orthodoxy and fast-tracked the "traditional confessions of Russia"—Orthodoxy, Islam, Buddhism, and Judaism—in registering congregations. Protestants, Catholics, and others faced stricter rules. Yeltsin would have liked a more ecumenical statute but put his presidential signature to the bill to placate the patriarch.

The most poignant act of reconciliation was the reburial with pomp and ceremony of Russia's last royal household. The bones and skulls of Nicholas II, Alexandra, three of their daughters, and four loyal retainers had been exhumed from an unmarked woodland grave near Yekaterinburg in 1991. DNA testing confirmed their authenticity. On July 17, 1998, the eightieth anniversary of the regicide, coffins holding them were buried in a chapel in St. Petersburg's Peter and Paul Fortress, where emperors had been laid to rest from 1725 to 1894. The bell rung that day had been cast from melted-down Russian cannon by order of Nicholas. The final rites, said Yeltsin, were an act of atonement for all: "The gunning down of the Romanov family was the result of the implacable schism within Russia into one's own and the others.... The burial ... is a symbol of the unity of the people and expiation of our common guilt." The skeletal remains of a fourth girl and of the tsarevich, Alexei, were found in 2007 but have not yet been interred.

How did post-Soviet Russia come to terms with its place in the world?

Russia's first order of business was to call a halt to economic autarky and buy into globalization. It signed up for the International Monetary Fund and the World Bank on June 1, 1992, and got seats on their boards of trustees. In August the Yeltsin government was granted an IMF stand-by arrangement for $1 billion, the first of $22 billion in credits. Russia took in circumscribed foreign assistance from Western nations—much of which went to pay consultants from the donors. Accession talks with the World Trade Organization (WTO) were opened in June 1993. Russia courted foreign direct investment, which came to $6 billion by 1995, and sent record volumes of gas to Europe through twelve pipelines. In 1997, after rescheduling its debts, it took out membership in the international clubs of creditor countries: the Paris Club for public lenders and the London Club for private.

If Yeltsin was grateful for entry into the exchange-based world market, national security was all about strength, a different game. Here the Russian Federation, downscaled, problem-ridden, and relieved of the grandiose conceptual goal of safeguarding socialism, had fewer cards to play. Russia as a middle-rank power or "a world without Russia," as the maxim went, were hot subjects on the conference circuit. One diplomat carped to Strobe Talbott, President Clinton's director of post-Soviet affairs, that Russia had "been downgraded from a great power to a status lower than Chad's."

An opportunity was wasted to give shape and definition to a forward-looking role for Russia in the post–Cold War international system, and one that had political legs domestically. This was up to a point Yeltsin's doing. A novice in foreign affairs, he was as excited about hyping his authority as about policy. At a first summit meeting with Clinton, in Vancouver in April 1993, he "galloped through the agenda in a way that suggested he was interested more in creating the overall effect of being in charge than he was in achieving concrete results," Talbott was to recall. Consumed by domestic headaches, and with a dearth of grand strategy, he mounted a charm offensive and personalized relations with partner countries, striking up a rapport with Clinton, Helmut Kohl of Germany, and Jacques Chirac of France.

But much of the fault for Russia's not getting its bearings falls with the extant superpower, the United States, and the Western nations. The wedge issue was a security architecture for Europe. When the Warsaw Pact voted itself out of business in February 1991, NATO was the only security collectivity left on the continent. Not only did it survive victory, as few alliances do, NATO was to grow from sixteen members to twenty-eight; all twelve recruits had been, or been in, Communist countries. In talks with Bonn and Washington in 1990, Gorbachev was furnished unwritten assurances by Secretary of State James Baker that, when Germany was reunited, NATO would not expand "one inch" to the east. They were never formalized in a protocol or treaty—Gorbachev insisted on neither, a baffling dereliction of duty—and Baker was to claim he had been misquoted. A unilateral pullout of Russian forces from the bloc began in 1989 and was completed under Yeltsin in 1994.

The position of Russia was that the promises to Gorbachev still held and a revised European order should be worked out by negotiation among all parties. But, disordered and unfocused, it did not come up with a solid alternative. Foreign Minister Andrei Kozyrev, a liberal and internationalist, favored a security covenant with NATO, which he judged more workable than inclusion within it; the conceit withered on the vine. The fifty-three-nation Organization for Security and Cooperation in Europe (OSCE), the Conference on Security and Cooperation in Europe (CSCE) until 1996, might have been an acceptable locus for pan-European collaboration spanning the old bloc lines. Russia wanted a strong OSCE board, and veto rights on it, but the rest found this unpersuasive.

The Euroatlantic community let a sterling chance slip. The Russians were not wrong to think that trundling NATO eastward was a breach of trust and the application of a formula dreamt up in and for another age.

In what it considered its "Near Abroad," the former Soviet republics, Russia maintained a high profile with little protestation from the West throughout the 1990s. The vehicle was not the CIS but a cat's cradle of bilateral accords. After pulling 150,000 troops out of the Baltics, the Russian military kept bases in all the CIS states except Turkmenistan and Uzbekistan and was embroiled, as peacekeeper and conciliator, in the Tajik civil war and the "frozen conflicts" in Azerbaijan (over Nagorno-Karabakh), Georgia (over South Ossetiya and Abkhaziya), and Moldova (over Transdniestria). The touchiest relationship was with Ukraine, with whom Russia wrangled over oil and gas sales, pipelines, and the Soviet Black Sea Fleet based in Sevastopol, Crimea (part of Ukraine), which had one hundred thousand personnel and 835 ships in 1991. A Treaty of Friendship, Cooperation, and Partnership sealed with President Leonid Kuchma in May 1997 partitioned the fleet, with Moscow buying out the much of the Ukrainians' share in exchange for debt relief. Russia was given a twenty-year lease on the navy yard at Sevastopol and the right to billet twenty-five thousand sailors, aviators, and marines in Crimea.

With regard to NATO membership, Yeltsin briefly signaled some give for the Poles, but recanted. The USSR's former dependencies, led by Václav Havel of the Czech Republic and Lech Wałęsa of Poland, pressed for inclusion as a hedge against Russian revanchism. In Washington, Strobe Talbott, Secretary of State Warren Christopher, and military planners were at first resistant to the idea, but it found fervent backers in the White House, on Capitol Hill, among conservative Republicans, and with voters of east European origin. Clinton at a January 1994 conference in Prague, having notified but not consulted with Yeltsin, announced that NATO expansion was a fait accompli, the issue being "not whether but when." Yeltsin imparted to Clinton, and repeated it to the press, that the post-Communist states should enter NATO or a post-NATO consortium, at an opportune time, as a bloc. Viktor Chernomyrdin suggested to Vice President Al Gore a go-slow timetable of ten to twenty years. This was not in the offing from the United States. A ticking time bomb had been set.

The most Russia could muster was a stalling action. In Paris in May 1997, Yeltsin grudgingly acceded to a NATO–Russia Founding Act on Mutual Relations, Cooperation, and Security, establishing a Permanent Joint Council for discussing issues of concern. NATO, without reference to Russia, invited the Czech Republic, Hungary, and Poland to become members; they did in March 1999.

More NATO may have been good for Eastern Europe. Few if any members of the Russian elite felt or feel it did anything for their country. The joint council was inconsequential. Some on both the Russian and the Western side saw entrance into the G7 club of industrial democracies as a consolation prize, after Russia's loss of the argument over NATO. The G7 (the United States, Japan, Germany, France, the United Kingdom, Italy, and Canada) voted to admit Russia and become the G8 at Denver, Colorado, in June 1997. Yeltsin, who had craved admission, made cameo appearances at G8 conferences in Birmingham in 1998 and Cologne in 1999.

The honeymoon with the West over, Yeltsin in January 1996 canned Kozyrev for the chief of foreign intelligence, Yevgenii Primakov, an Arabist and a trouper from the Soviet nomenklatura. Primakov took inspiration from Alexander Gorchakov, the foreign secretary to Alexander II who maneuvered deftly between the great powers after the debacle of the Crimean War in the 1850s; he kept a bust of Prince Gorchakov on his desk. Primakov accepted the Founding Act with NATO as damage limitation only. Ill feeling seethed over the Kosovo crisis of 1998, where Russia sided with Milošević and the Serb-controlled Federal Republic of Yugoslavia, while NATO supported the Kosovo Liberation Army, and in 1999 over the three-month, US-led air bombardment of the federal republic that forced the Serbs to quit Kosovo. In June 1999 there was a tense standoff between Russian and NATO peacekeepers at the Pristina airport in Kosovo.

Yeltsin, at a gathering of the CSCE in Budapest in December 1994, had found the most eloquent term for the reconfigured relationship. The Cold War, he said, had yielded to a Cold Peace. He accused the United States of wanting a Pax Americana: "History demonstrates it is a dangerous delusion to suppose that the destinies of continents and of the world community in general can someway be managed from one single capital." Yeltsin batted down as a slur President Clinton's justification for a bigger NATO as an insurance policy and made an avowal of the interdependence of foreign and domestic policies: "We hear explanations to the effect that this is the expansion of stability, just in case there are undesirable developments in Russia. If the objective is to bring NATO up to Russia's borders, let me say that it is too early to bury democratic Russia."

Who were the oligarchs?

Laissez-faire economics and changing mores turned Russian society topsy-turvy. In the popular culture, the effects of stratification of rewards were netted in the trope of the "New Russians" (*novyye russkiye*). The New Russians were arrivistes who gained from capitalistic pursuits that were legal but still disreputable, such as running a streetside kiosk or doing "shuttle trade" (importing cheap foreign goods, often in suitcases, for resale). As the cliché had it, they also strutted their tawdry belongings, wore crimson jackets and gold chains, and patronized the nightclubs, casinos, and boutiques popping up in the cities.

Another term came on-stream mid-decade. The tycoons or "oligarchs" (*oligarkhs*) were construed as the most affluent subclass of the maligned New Russians. The oligarchs ran the gamut from shrewd entrepreneurs and managers to conmen. More than a few were red directors who by hook or crook won proprietary rights to the firms they once ran as agents for Gosplan. Another pathway started in finance and trade; gains from speculation on currency and commodities, commissions, and kickbacks were parlayed into command over physical assets.

The act of privatization that cemented the oligarchs' reputation was the "loans-for-shares" plan of 1995. The hobbyhorse of banker Vladimir Potanin, it delivered twelve large properties to private banks to run (a thirteenth was added later), in return for loans to the government. Six were in the oil industry, three apiece in metals and shipping, and one in telephone communications. Two years later, the same banks were cleared to stage auctions in which they bid for and acquired, at knock-down prices, the shares deposited with them as collateral for the loans—the acme of self-dealing. True, the companies, once privatized, were well run and therefore profit mills for their owners. To evade Russian regulators and taxmen, their accountants made a habit of shunting winnings to shell companies, offshore accounts, and "inland offshores" (provincial tax havens).

In 1997 *Forbes* for the very first time put Russian citizens, six of them, on its world roster of dollar billionaires. The most well-heeled, arrogant, and cynical was Boris Berezovsky, a former mathematician and software engineer. Berezovsky earned his first millions through a dealership for Lada automobiles, and scraped through a gangland car bombing in 1994 that decapitated his driver. As main shareholder in the Sibneft oil company, he was worth $3 billion. Others atop *Forbes* listings were Potanin (Norilsk Nickel, the world's leading smelter of nickel and palladium), the former Komsomol activist Mikhail Khodorkovsky (Bank Menatep and Yukos Oil), and Vagit Alekperov (LUKoil). The amenities purchased were eye-popping for Russians indoctrinated on CPSU puritanism. Downtown Moscow gentrified as developers and their governmental allies emptied communal flats and put in luxury housing. Deluxe dachas went up in exurban hideaways for the Politburo and the Soviet upper crust, their occupants commuting to work in chauffeured sedans. The Russian language now rang out on the Côte d'Azur, in Miami Beach, and in "Londongrad," to the wags.

Apart from making money hand over fist, the oligarchs, if Russian tabloids are to be taken seriously, wielded almost otherworldly influence in politics. The standard Western telling sounds a like note of the "capture" of the state by plutocrats. The *Financial Times* of November 1, 1996, regaled readers about briefings from "a tightknit group" of businessmen who had paid for Yeltsin's second election and "portray themselves ... openly as the main force shaping Kremlin policy." The in-group was "debating how to exercise its power" and had "decided [that] the new moguls had to assume authority in their own right. The banks had to have their men in government."

That the magnates had political clout is undisputable. Yeltsin met with six of them in February of 1996, as his re-election fight went into motion; they coaxed him to step up the campaign and promised to donate to it, and did. At the time of the *Financial Times* article in November, Berezovsky was deputy secretary of the president's Security Council and Potanin was first deputy premier. Oligarchs used media holdings to propagandize their corporate interests and, in 1996, to back candidate Yeltsin. Vladimir Gusinsky, a former cab driver and theater producer, and comanager of one of the USSR's first business cooperatives, owned the NTV television network; Berezovsky had operational control over ORT, the channel with the most viewers (the majority shareholder was the state).

The more breathless exposés are to be taken with a grain of salt. The robber barons were never the cardinal force in Russian politics. Most of the time, they were at each other's throats and not a united front. Yeltsin was not in regular communication with them; besides the election-related huddle in 1996, he met with business representatives only two other times, in 1995 and 1997. Potanin's and Berezovsky's postelection appointments were by the president, not by vote of a cabal. Potanin left the government in March 1997 and Berezovsky in March 1999; nonbusinessmen took their places. There was no love lost between the hyperactive Berezovsky and Yeltsin. "I never liked and I do not like Boris Abramovich," Yeltsin groused in the third volume of his memoirs, *Presidential Marathon*. "He always got lots of airtime. And the people would think, this is who is truly governing the country." "There were no mechanisms," Yeltsin said, "through which Berezovsky could exercise influence over the president." This sentence may shave the truth, but no more so than the hearsay about oligarchic invincibility.

What were the causes and effects of the financial crash of August 1998?

On August 14, 1998, Yeltsin was at his histrionic best on an outing in Novgorod. Rumors were flying that the ruble was going to be devalued. Not so, Yeltsin trumpeted, "firmly and concisely." It was all a bluff. Three days later Moscow floated the exchange rate, defaulted on its sovereign debt, and inflicted a ninety-day moratorium on payments by Russian banks to foreign creditors. After the squirt in growth of 1997, the ruble had been redenominated on January 1, 1998, lopping three zeros off, as a demonstration of reinvigoration. Seven months later, the government's economic program was in tatters. Russians lined up at bank wickets to cash out their savings. The currency lost half of its value by September and two-thirds by October. Other meters kept it company. The RTS's index, a capitalization-weighted price average for fifty stocks listed on its Moscow exchange, set at 100 at inception on September 1, 1995, plummeted to 38 on October 6, 1998; at its apogee on October 2, 1997, it had been 572.

The financial crash did not come out of the blue. Unsound public policy and presidential politicking were largely to blame. To fund income transfers and easy credits that would keep loss-making firms alive, and fulfill the promises Yeltsin made in his 1996 campaign, the Russian government stiffened tax collection and expenditure discipline. When this was insufficient, it issued ruble-denominated treasury bills, or GKOs. Introduced in 1993, the GKOs were distinguished by their quick maturation times and high payouts. They were peddled to Russian banks and also to nonresident portfolio investors, who had the right to convert to hard currency, at will, any earnings made. Yields on the bills were 18 percent in July 1997; as the budget deficit and perceived risk to lenders rose, they spurted to 65 percent in June 1998 and an untenable 170 percent in mid-August. Eurobonds and cash loans repayable in dollars further jacked up the cost of servicing the debt. Debt charges were 34 percent of the federal budget by July 1998.

The crunch was not all the Yeltsin administration's doing. The new, open Russian market lay exposed to adverse external trends. These started in 1997 in the overheated economies of East and Southeast Asia, battered by low commodity prices and runs on their currencies. The "Asian flu" rubbed off on Russia when Wall Street shied away from all developing markets. The fever was heightened by the tumbling price of Russia's most precious resource and export—petroleum. Brent crude traded at $23.47 per barrel in January 1997, $15.09 in January 1998, and $11.88 in August 1998. Export levies and tax revenues shrank and the budget deficit ballooned.

Yeltsin's political footwork as the economic storm clouds loomed was too clever by half. He decided to keep Viktor Chernomyrdin in the prime minister's chair but to "get him going" by stocking him with "young and in a good way pushy" deputy premiers who would keep him under "high tension" (quotations from *Presidential Marathon*). The two tension providers were archprivatizer Anatolii Chubais and Boris Nemtsov, recruited from the governor's mansion in Nizhnii Novgorod. The multiheaded cabinet could not agree on a reform package, and the State Duma, where pro-Yeltsin deputies were in the minority, was unreceptive. Yeltsin at long last decided in March 1998 to ease Chernomyrdin out and put in his place Sergei Kiriyenko, a thirty-five-year-old protégé of Nemtsov. Majority confirmation in parliament, on April 24, came only after a war of words and three cliffhanger rollcalls, with Yeltsin promising to send the Duma to the hustings if it turned him down.

A $5 billion rescue from the IMF in July 1998 was too little, too late. When default hit, the political lightweight Kiriyenko was a casualty; Yeltsin relieved him of the premiership on August 22. But the Duma would not countenance his chosen substitute—the heavyweight Chernomyrdin, ousted in March. In a Hobson's choice, Yeltsin made do with Foreign Minister Yevgenii Primakov, whose politics were leftish and who had once sat on Gorbachev's Politburo. The Duma ratified Primakov's appointment on September 11. Demands blared in the press for Yeltsin's resignation and a government of national salvation.

While Yeltsin was hamstrung and on the defensive politically, the economic tidings after the cold shower of default took a turn for the better. Primakov, holdovers from the Chernomyrdin and Kiriyenko cabinets, and Viktor Gerashchenko, put back in the Russian Central Bank, managed to calm the financial panic. With a presidential carte blanche, they printed money, trimmed the deficit in the budget, canceled the GKOs, and negotiated new terms for the national debt. Currency devaluation, an embarrassment in August, was a fillip to recovery by the end of the year, as it helped Russian industry compete with pricy imports and aided exports. Output, down again in 1998, by 4.9 percent, was up by 5.4 percent in 1999, only the second growth year since 1991, and the ruble stabilized at twenty-seven or twenty-eight to the US dollar. For once, the gods of the oil market smiled on Russia. The Brent index for crude, from a nadir of $9.80 per barrel, bounced to $25.48 in December 1999.

Post-Soviet Russia was poised for better days. A counterfactual is fascinating to consider. Had the economic about-turn been a year or two quicker in arriving, with Chernomyrdin or Kiriyenko as prime minister and president-in-waiting, it would have fed into a much more democratic politics.

Why did Yeltsin relinquish power?

The term for which Boris Yeltsin took the oath of office on August 9, 1996, had been reduced from five years to four by Article 81 of the 1993 constitution. There remained a ghost's chance that he would stand in 2000 for a third term. Article 81 specified that a president could serve only two terms consecutively. The Constitutional Court entertained arguments from Kremlin lawyers that, seeing as how Yeltsin was first elected, in 1991, under the Soviet-adopted constitution, he could run a second time under the Russian constitution if he so chose. In November 1998 the justices found against them. The qualifying round of a presidential election was to be held without Yeltsin's name on the ballot by June of 2000 and a new president to be sworn in by August.

Yeltsin, having said he had no intention of going for a final term, was known to change his mind, and there were clients who preferred him to stay on. He seems not to have considered the option of trying to rule by decree, which he had debated in the spring of 1996. Nor did he give thought to the roundabout but constitutionally permissible way of staying in command that Russia's second president was to take when faced with the same choice—sit out several years in a lesser position and then reclaim the presidency.

Yeltsin by now was fixated on the notion that his mission was finished and he would be poorly served by overstaying his time. He knew his Russian history books: no ruler in all these centuries of statehood had ever of his own volition handed vlast to another. He would go a different route. "I have often heard it said," as he was to articulate it in his retirement speech, "that Yeltsin will cling to power by any means possible and will never give it up. That is a lie." He meant to honor the letter of the law for posterity's sake and "set the invaluable precedent of a civilized, voluntary transfer from one president of Russia to another, newly elected."

Had Yeltsin been primed morally to trample on the constitution, or interested in charging back into office after a timeout, he would not have been equal to it physically. On November 5, 1996, after a run of heart attacks, he had undergone a cardiac bypass operation (the nuclear briefcase was in Chernomyrdin's custody overnight). He gave up tennis and overindulgence in alcohol, obeyed doctor's orders, and took frequent vacations, but never returned to full strength. Susceptible to spinal and chest pain and bouts of respiratory disease, he was in and out of hospital and many days stayed away from the Kremlin, receiving ministers and signing documents at his residence. To help tide him over, he relied on his younger daughter, Tatyana Dyachenko, who was made a Kremlin adviser in 1997 and in some wonks' rankings was one of the five most influential people in Russia.

Yeltsin was even weaker in the political arena than he was medically. KPRF deputies in the State Duma took steps to impeach him under the constitution's Article 93. By February 1999 a committee had lodged five counts: unlawfully signing the Belavezha accord that disbanded the USSR in 1991; abetting murder during the 1993 showdown with parliament; abusing his power in Chechnya; subverting the army; and "genocide of the Russian people." A two-thirds majority of 300 on any one charge would have taken an indictment forward, and the resolution on Chechnya got 283 votes on May 15 (the genocide resolution got the least votes, 238).

At this near-miss moment, Yeltsin orchestrated a last hurrah. He was unwavering about setting up someone like-minded, and from the younger generation, to succeed him in 2000. His ace in the hole was the prime minister's office. On May 12, 1999, three days before the Duma was to vote on impeachment, he drummed out Premier Primakov, who was two years older than he. The youthful liberal Kiriyenko, his name blighted by default, was not salvageable. Neither was the quirky Boris Nemtsov, whom Yeltsin once spoke of publicly as a possible successor. As prime minister, Yeltsin nominated Interior Minister Sergei Stepashin. True or not, Yeltsin was to write in his memoirs that the mild-mannered Stepashin was a placeholder only and his heart was set on another silovik he had on the sidelines. He intimidated the Duma into ratifying Stepashin, with an ultimatum that, if not, he would force an election.

On August 9, 1999, Yeltsin reshuffled the deck one final time, sacking Stepashin after only fourteen weeks. As head of government he submitted the name of Vladimir Putin, director of the FSB, Russia's neo-KGB, with the addendum that he wanted the hitherto unknown Putin to run for president with his support in 2000. The Duma accepted Putin on the first ballot on August 16. A corner had been turned.

A positive showing by the pro-Kremlin Unity bloc in the Duma election of December 19 persuaded the lame-duck Yeltsin to bow out early. On December 31, 1999, on the cusp of a new century and a new millennium, he resigned. A retirement packet, covering perks and immunity from prosecution for acts as head of state, was worked out by aides. Pursuant to Article 92 of the constitution, Prime Minister Putin was interpolated as acting president and an election was scheduled for March 26, 2000. "I have attained my life's goal," Yeltsin said with some satisfaction in his onscreen valedictory. "Russia will never return to the past, Russia from now on will proceed only forward." In midstream, he shifted gears to a mea culpa: "I beg your forgiveness for not making many of your and my dreams come true. What seemed simple to do proved to be excruciatingly difficult. I beg your forgiveness for letting down the hopes of those who believed that in one leap, with one stroke, we could hurtle from the gray, stagnant, totalitarian past into a cloudless, prosperous, and enlightened future.... One leap was not enough to do it. I was in some respects naïve. Some problems revealed themselves to be incredibly thorny. We slogged ahead through trial and error. Many people were shaken by these trying times." "I am departing," he said. "I did all I could."

5

TRANSITION WITHIN
THE TRANSITION

Who is Putin and what were his credentials to be leader?

A new president took it upon himself to craft a transition within Russia's transition. The jury is out on whether it will make it to the level of the critical junctures of 1917 and 1991, using those years as shorthand for the arc of events that constructed and deconstructed Communism.

Vladimir Vladimirovich Putin (b. 1952 in Leningrad), was the first ruler of Russia to be a child of the latter half of the twentieth century; the first since Lenin to be city-born, to be fluent in a foreign language, and to have lived abroad; the first to have cut his teeth in the special services; and the first to enter politics after Soviet rule capsized.

Putin's working-class father was gravely wounded during World War II, behind enemy lines; his mother almost starved during the Nazi siege, and an older brother died of diphtheria. Putin had a hardscrabble childhood. The family shared a thin-walled, cold-water flat, heated by a wood-burning stove, with two other households. In journalistic interviews in 2000 (*From the First Person*, in English), he recounted walloping rats with a stick and "petty kitchen squabbles." Putin was a "hoodlum" as a boy, he said; only in his teens did he buckle down to his books and to workouts in martial arts clubs. "You can consider me," he went on about his political attitudes, "the product of a patriotic Soviet upbringing." Animated by "romantic tales about the work of secret service agents," the ninth-grader asked a desk officer at the city KGB office if he could train as a spy. He would need a college education, he was told. In 1975, when Putin got his law diploma from Leningrad State University, already a member of the CPSU, the KGB recruited him.

Little has come to light about the decade and a half in the KGB. After six months monitoring foreign tourists and Soviet dissidents, Putin was appointed to the intelligence directorate, boned up on his grade-school German, and attended the agency's Red Banner Institute; he was de-enrolled from the institute after one year as punishment for getting into a fistfight with hoodlums on the Leningrad subway. In August 1985 Putin was sent to Dresden, East Germany's third city, where he liaised with the Ministry of State Security (Stasi) of the German Democratic Republic. Posting to a backwater was not the badge of a wunderkind. Putin missed out on perestroika back home—he and his wife, Lyudmila, "watched it only on television," she says in *From the First Person*—but he did express support for Gorbachev's political reforms. Dresden was a hothouse for the local opposition. When the Stasi compound was stormed by protesters in December 1989, Putin requested instructions from Moscow; he was aghast that no one picked up the phone. "I realized that the Soviet Union was ill. It had a terminal, incurable disease called paralysis, a paralysis of power."

Putin was stoical about the downfall of Soviet Communism, doomed by the system's congenital imperfections, as he saw it. But when it came to results, he felt the losses more than the gains, above all in geopolitics. "To be honest, I had nothing but regret for the loss of the Soviet Union's position in Europe, although I understood intellectually that any position based on walls and barriers cannot last forever. But I had hoped that something different would rise in its place, and nothing different was proposed. That's what hurt. All we did was toss everything away and leave."

Back in the Soviet Union in 1990, Putin was reassigned to his alma mater, Leningrad State, as a low-status watchdog in the department handling contacts with foreigners—another sign of mediocre grades from the KGB. A turning point was the confidential relationship he struck up with Anatolii Sobchak, a department head in the law school where Putin had studied in the 1970s. Sobchak was a member of the USSR Congress and, with Yeltsin, of the Interregional Deputies Group; chair of city council in May 1990; and in June 1991 mayor of what was again St. Petersburg. Putin trailed him to city hall and "made himself indispensable" in a quiet way. By 1994 he was first deputy mayor. Putin's remit, for international trade and investment, put him in touch with Russia's newfound capitalists— breeding possibilities for corruption about which biographers have endlessly conjectured. Putin also got his feet wet in electoral politics in Sobchak's repeat campaign in May 1996.

Putin made it through a second career hiccup when Sobchak lost the election (he was to die in obscurity in 2000). Out of a job for three months, Putin made the trek to Moscow. Coworkers from St. Petersburg found a spot for him in the Kremlin business office. Over the next half-year he somehow ingratiated himself with Yeltsin, who in March 1997 made him deputy head of the presidential administration. In July 1998 Putin vaulted to directorship of the FSB.

What possessed Yeltsin to make the momentous decision to select Putin as his seventh prime minister and heir-apparent? Did an interested party put him up to it? The oligarchs, Tatyana Dyachenko and Yeltsin's next-of-kin, a shadowy politico-economic "Family" around Dyachenko and Boris Berezovsky, Kremlin courtiers—there are whodunits involving all of them and more, and no substantiation for any. Berezovsky identified himself publicly as the kingmaker, but exaggeration of his role was Berezovsky's stock-in-trade; declassified US government files indicate he had but a nodding acquaintance with Putin and told diplomats he liked Foreign Minister Igor Ivanov as prime minister. Was it all because Putin promised Yeltsin and his biological family to exempt them from prosecution? This makes no sense. Any pretender to the brass ring would have agreed to the limited decree of December 31, 1999, which made no mention of family members. No one was so foolish as to think this scrap of paper would protect Yeltsin in a pinch.

Putin had checked out of the KGB's active reserve in 1991 at the middling rank of lieutenant-colonel. Some thought him unequipped to govern the Lubyanka, let alone Russia. But he was nothing if not quick on his feet. To politics he applied the mindset of a lifelong practitioner of judo, where the fighter turns his opponent's physique and energy into a force to disarm him. Fiona Hill and Clifford G. Gaddy's *Mr. Putin: Operative in the Kremlin* brings out his knack for "working with people," much cherished in Yurii Andropov's KGB. Working with people was about reconnaissance, evaluation, and a quarry's vulnerabilities. As Hill and Gaddy write, the retro toolkit of the secret police required no special talent, "just brutality"; the newer, more sophisticated technique "was a difficult task requiring skill, delicacy, patience, and, importantly, leverage."

Putin completed his meteoric ascent by working with a selectorate of one—Boris Yeltsin. His leverage inhered in being acceptant of Yeltsin's endorsement but not presumptuous, and in satisfying the president's desiderata for a successor. Yeltsin was adamant that the next leader be from the coming generation of "new faces," as he said in his goodbye speech, and have the qualities to keep Russia in one piece after its whirlwind of change. In 1998 he had appointed Nikolai Bordyuzha, a career KGB officer, as chief of Kremlin staff. Bordyuzha ran afoul of Yeltsin months later for being too cozy with Primakov, and was removed. As Yeltsin wrote in *Presidential Marathon*, he hoped for someone who combined an understanding of the un-Soviet Russia with a "steely backbone that would strengthen the political structure of authority." "We needed a thinking person who was democratic and innovative, yet steadfast in the military manner. The next year such a person did appear . . .

Putin." In retrospect, "steely," "thinking," and "innovative" sit well with Putin; "democratic" does not.

How did Putin consolidate his power?

To solidify his lease on power into lasting ownership, Putin was compelled to take action. The financial, impeachment, and prime ministerial crises were only months in the past. The summer of 1999 begot another threat—to national unity, again radiating out from the inflammable republic of Chechnya.

In August, days before Putin was made prime minister, an "Islamic International Brigade" rampaged into Dagestan, the polyglot republic between Chechnya and the Caspian. It was commanded by Shamil Basayev, of Budyonnovsk fame, and Ibn al-Khattab, a Saudi national who had warred in Afghanistan and Tajikistan. Apartment-house explosions in Moscow and the provinces, charged by the government to Caucasus terrorists, killed three hundred in September.

Putin rendered the situation in apocalyptic language in *From the First Person:* "My take on ... the bandits' attack on Dagestan was that if we did not stop it right away Russia as a state in its current sense was finished." But Chechnya offered opportunity and menace in equal measure. Yeltsin entrusted Putin with a military counterpunch stronger than the 1994 operation and more in tune with a public burned by the fiasco of the 1996–97 accords. The army repulsed the Islamist Brigade's sortie in Dagestan and progressed to bombing strikes on, and in October an infantry invasion of, Chechnya. In February 2000 it raised the tricolor over Grozny, a moonscape ravaged by war for the second time in five years. Khattab was hunted down that March, Maskhadov in 2005, and Basayev in 2006. The battlefield if not the social results of the war of 1994–96 had been upturned.

Chechnya was the backdrop for a brawny decision-making style that set Putin apart from the burned-out Yeltsin. On September 23, 1999, he uttered one of his trademark vulgarisms, exclaiming about the insurgents that he would "rub them out in the outhouse" if need be. His approval ratings raced to 80 percent. In November, during the mudslinging campaign for the Duma election, Putin gave the Unity bloc's list of candidates a photo-op and some kind words. The endorsement accounted for half of Unity's vote on December 19 and boxed out the left-leaning Fatherland–All Russia (OVR) slate headed by Mayor Yurii Luzhkov of Moscow and Yevgenii Primakov.

For the presidential election, 2 percent of the electorate intended to vote for Putin as of August 1999 but 51 percent by New Year's. With the other candidates on the stump, Putin, who had never run for office, made a show of sticking to his desk. "I have no special campaign measures on my calendar," he said smugly in an open letter on February 25. When the electorate spoke on March 26, the acting president sewed up 53 percent of the officially recorded vote, to Gennadii Zyuganov's 29 percent, and managed without a runoff round. He was inaugurated under the chandeliers of the Grand Kremlin Palace on May 7.

Foretaste of a transition within the transition, and not merely snaring the presidency, was given by Putin's treatment of the Russian press. The one private television network, NTV, supported OVR for the Duma and the liberal Grigorii Yavlinskii for president, showed unflinching reportage on Chechnya, and did hilarious sendups of Putin, as a jug-eared gnome, on its satirical program *Kukly*. On May 11, 2000, a truckload of policemen, flak-jacketed and masked, raided the offices of Media-Most, the holding company for NTV. In June the Media-Most president, Vladimir Gusinsky, was detained on suspicion of a scam during negotiation of a large loan guaranteed by Gazprom. Cooling his heels in prison for three days, he agreed to emigrate and unload his equity in Media-Most as quid pro quo for prosecutors ditching the charges; he has since then lived in Israel and the United States. The Strasbourg-based ECHR found in 2004 that the arrest contravened Gusinsky's "right to liberty and security," Russian law, and the European

Convention on Human Rights. *Kukly* continued without a Putin doll until taken off the air in 2002.

Consolidation of power was facilitated by the constitutional setup bequeathed by Yeltsin. The superpresidency gave Putin a bully pulpit for setting the national agenda and let him take initiatives proactively. The decree power, and flimsy rule of law and legislative oversight, made for few institutional hurdles.

To firm up his grip, Putin reached out to people with whom he felt camaraderie and whose viewpoints on policy were compatible with his. A good many hailed from the security services or from his hometown. In an inauguration-eve interview with American ABC News, he was matter-of-fact about manning his administration with "people whom I've known for many years" and, he tacked on, "people whom I trust." It was not about nepotism or ideology but about "professional qualities and personal relationships." The magic word was "trust," a rarity in what was still a protean polity. Silovik promotees from the security and defense fields included Sergei Ivanov (defense minister), Viktor Ivanov (Kremlin personnel department), and Igor Sechin (coordinator for the energy sector); all three were from Leningrad/St. Petersburg. St. Petersburgers not from the KGB fraternity included Dmitrii Medvedev (Putin's fill-in for president from 2008 to 2012), Viktor Zubkov (a transient prime minister in 2007–8), and Alexei Kudrin (finance minister from 2000 until 2011); all were workmates of Putin and Sobchak in the St. Petersburg municipality.

How did Putin compare to Yeltsin in leadership goals?

Be it out of filial piety, magnanimity, or some ulterior motive, Putin never once reprimanded Yeltsin ad hominem. Yeltsin lived out his days at a state chateau west of Moscow. He mouthed well-mannered support for Putin's program and harbored private misgivings. The one criticism he expressed openly was about the decision in December 2000 to bring back the familiar descant of the Soviet national anthem, with

Russified lyrics—by the same Sergei Mikhalkov, a writer of schoolchildren's books, who composed them for the USSR hymn in 1944. Yeltsin traveled widely but gave no speeches and few interviews, and the good works of his Yeltsin Foundation were nonpolitical. When Putin threw a ritzy seventy-fifth birthday party for him in 2006, he said to the press that once in a thousand years a past Russian leader "did not have his head chopped off" and got to enjoy an evening of accolades in the Kremlin.

Yeltsin died of pneumonia on April 23, 2007, and was buried out of the re-created Cathedral of Christ the Savior. Putin eulogized him as "the rare person who is given the destiny to become free himself and at the same time to carry millions along behind him, and to make historic changes in his homeland and change the world." How heartfelt these words were can only be guessed. Putin was to cut the ribbon for a budget-funded memorial center for Yeltsin in Yekaterinburg, in November 2015. It overlooks the church on the spot where Nicholas and Alexandra were murdered in 1918.

Gleb Pavlovsky was a tactician and spin doctor for the Kremlin from 1996 to 2011, with political antennae second to none. He has typecast Putin as "one of those who were passively waiting for the moment for . . . resurrection of the great state in which we had lived, and to which we had become accustomed." "We didn't want another totalitarian state . . . but we did want one that could be respected." This was in an interview in 2012, and there may be some backward induction to the statement, but the track record bears Pavlovsky out.

A glimmering of Putin's statism can be found in the four-thousand-word essay "Russia at the Turn of the Millennium," posted over his name on the government website on December 30, 1999. Known as the Millennium Manifesto, it is the fullest compendium of his opinions as he donned the presidential robes.

The manifesto emphasized incremental change and steadiness of purpose. Russia was rounding out "the first, provisional stage of its economic and political reforms." Despite "problems and mistakes" on the go, "we have entered onto the highway down which humanity is traveling.... There is no alternative to it."

For Putin, the outgoing century had been unkinder to Russia than to any country. A main reason was that change so often took the form of "political and socioeconomic shakeups, cataclysms, and total makeovers." "Only fanatics or political forces absolutely aloof from Russia and its people can make calls for a new revolution. Whether the next splintering of everything and everyone be carried out under communistic, national-patriotic, or radical liberal slogans, our country and our people would not be able to withstand it." The diatribe against revolution bled into an ode to evolution. "Responsible civic and political forces," wrote Putin, "ought to offer a strategy for Russia's revival and prosperity. It should be based on all the positives created in the process of market and democratic reforms, and be implemented by evolutionary, gradual, and balanced methods. It should be carried out under conditions of political stability and not worsen the living conditions of the Russian people."

The reference to living conditions can be read as a jab at Yeltsin, but other paragraphs in the Millennium Manifesto are dismissive of socialist economics. Russians, Putin intoned, still "reap the bitter fruits of those [Soviet] decades, both material and mental." About politics, he had less to say. He was for "democracy," pluralism, and fidelity to the constitution but against "metaphysical models and schemes lifted from the pages of foreign textbooks."

The manifesto's most-quoted passages—and the most evocative of Pavlovsky's backdated comments—are about the state and its centrality to Russia's flowering and brute survival. "Russia will not soon if ever become a second edition of, say, the United States or Britain, where liberal values have deep historical roots. For us, the state, its institutions, and its structures have always played an exceptionally important role." For

Russians, "a strong and effective state" is not an anomaly or a nuisance. On the contrary, said Putin, it is "the font ... of order and the initiator and main driving force of change." "Society wants to see the guiding and regulating role of the state replenished to the appropriate degree, in accordance with the traditions and present condition of the country." "Our hopes for a worthy future will work out only if we prove capable of combining the universal principles of a market economy and democracy with Russian realities."

There was little here Yeltsin would have opposed in theory. But the devil would be in the details and in the meaning of "to the appropriate degree" and "Russian realities." Putin's second-generation model of governance would diverge unmistakably from Yeltsin's first-generation model.

How did Putin compare to Yeltsin in leadership style?

As persons and political animals, there was a world of difference between the second and first post-Communist occupants of the Kremlin. Whereas Yeltsin was ursine in bearing and had a sonorous, staccato way of speaking, Putin was a half-foot shorter and expressed himself quietly and fluidly. Yeltsin made his way in the old system as an engineer and learned government and politics as a spinoff; Putin studied law yet steeped himself in the KGB. Yeltsin left the CPSU; the CPSU left Putin. If Yeltsin was punctual, Putin was maddeningly tardy. Yeltsin did the team sports of volleyball and pairs tennis, Putin the solo sports of judo and swimming. Yeltsin relied in his verdicts on instinct and Putin on the intelligence officer's meticulous store of information. Yeltsin acted in fits and starts and was a maestro of surprise; Putin acted with a steady hand and was a maestro of dosage.

Putin, like Yeltsin, often found himself calming the waters in response to exogenous stimuli and shocks. Chechnya was behind a slew of them. The Russian seizure of Grozny was followed by intermittent fighting and by two hideous assaults outside the republic: on the Dubrovka Theater in Moscow on October 23–26, 2002, when 133 hostages and about 40 militants were killed; and at Beslan, North Ossetiya, on September 1–4, 2004, where Chechen and Ingush gunmen took some 1,100 pupils, teachers, and parents captive in a public school gymnasium and the death toll was 385. Both incidents were mishandled by law enforcement. In Moscow, most hostages died from a toxic gas the FSB pumped into the theater to tranquilize the terrorists; in Beslan, tanks and thermobaric flame throwers were fired into the space where hostages were confined and efforts to set them free were uncoordinated.

If Yeltsin, facing his crises, scrambled for a compromise or face-saving device, Putin was more inclined to deepen resolve and rely on the panacea of strengthening the state and its leadership. In a Putin telecast to the nation after Beslan in 2004, the lesson was that Russian government needed to be more rugged and more unyielding. "We have shown ourselves to be weak," he said, coming close to parroting Stalin from 1931, "and weaklings get beaten." There were forces out there salivating "to tear a strip of 'fat' from us" and anonymous malefactors that assisted them, "in the belief that Russia as a major nuclear power still poses a threat to them."

The response to Beslan was to eliminate the direct election of regional governors, professedly so the Kremlin could aim higher on law-and-order questions. The restrictive trend was boosted by Putin's reaction to the Orange Revolution in Ukraine in December 2004. Mass protest on Maidan Nezalezhnosti (Independence Square) in Kiev overturned a presidential election a pro-Russian candidate, Viktor Yanukovych, was initially said to have won; Viktor Yushchenko, promising to bring Ukraine into the European camp, finished first in a rerun. Impugning the revolution as the work of locals on the payroll of Western governments, Russian legislation toughened bureaucratic controls over NGOs.

And yet, it would be a misconception to say Putin only reacted to crises of others' making. On his own steam, he made decisions that shook the ground of Russian politics and government. They could be theatrical—an early case in point being the arrest and prosecution of Russia's wealthiest citizen, Mikhail Khodorkovsky, in 2003—but most were more subtle and graduated.

One dissimilarity with Yeltsin was regarding political and administrative personnel. Yeltsin, as a wisecrack of the day went, changed ministers and assistants like someone else might change neckties or hats. From 1991 to 1999 he went through seven different prime ministers, four defense ministers, seven Kremlin chiefs of staff, and nine finance ministers. Putin was predisposed to work with an orb of political stalwarts, apolitical technocrats, and role players recruited ad hoc, and to get what he could from them over a period of years—a stance not unlike Brezhnev's in a generation past. Putin from 2000 to 2008 had three different prime ministers, three defense ministers (one of them a carryover from Yeltsin), three chiefs of staff (one also a carryover), and one finance minister.

Did Putin kill Russian democracy?

At the dawn of the Putin era, Russia's political regime had, by a democracy barometer, been regressing little by little. In 1992 the Freedom House end-of-year report rated it at 3.5 on its scale from 1 to 7 where 1 is the most democratic (using averages for subratings for political rights and civil liberties) and 7 the least. In 1999 Russia was placed at 4.5, or a touch worse than the halfway point on the scale, 4. It continued to be reckoned in gross terms as "partly free," an equitable judgment.

The 2001 *Freedom Report*, stating results for 2000, revised Russia's rating for political rights from 4 to 5 and its composite rating from 4.5 to 5, "due to ... serious irregularities in the March presidential elections and President Putin's increasing consolidation of central government authority." The document for 2003 reproved Russia for "increased state pressures on the media, opposition political parties, and independent business leaders"; the government received a "downward trend arrow" but the scores were unchanged. The bulletin for 2004 recoded Russia from 5 to 6 on political rights, "due to the virtual elimination of influential political opposition parties within the country and the further concentration of executive power." The new summary index of 5.5 placed Russia under the "not free," or undemocratic, heading. There it persisted until the end of Putin's second term in 2008.

The same story is spun by the Worldwide Governance Indicators, prepared by World Bank staff from surveys of households and firms, business information providers, and NGOs. One of the six main measures is for "voice and accountability," understood as "the extent to which a country's citizens are able to participate in selecting their government, as well as freedom of expression, freedom of association, and a free media." By this statistic, the Russian Federation placed in the fifty-sixth percentile globally in 1996 and in the sixty-third percentile in 2000. Its slot was then in the seventieth percentile in 2004, the seventy-fifth in 2008, and in 2013 the eighty-first—one-fifth of the way from the bottom of the barrel.

Until Putin publishes memoirs and the archives are unsealed, we will not know how much of this backsliding was by premeditated design and how much the result of a learning process, political undercurrents, or contingency. The results do not amass into a cogent theory or image. While Vladislav Surkov, the ideological arbiter of the Kremlin executive office from 1999 to 2011, spoke of "sovereign" (*suverennaya*) and "managed" (*upravlyayemaya*) democracy, his idol used neither term. Putinism was at heart about praxis and not about ideology, and about depoliticization and not politicization. He looked for positives in the Russian past without wedding himself to any single approach—both praising accomplishments of the Soviet decades, for example, and organizing the reburial in Russia of anti-Soviet White leaders who fled after the Civil War.

Surkov, who had worked in PR in Khodorkovsky's bank in the 1990s, vacuumed up ideas, claiming proprietorship for Putin but tying him down to none. The journalist Peter Pomerantsev writes of this surreal eclecticism: "One moment Surkov would fund civic forums and human rights NGOs, the next he would quietly support nationalist movements that accuse the NGOs of being tools of the West. With a flourish he sponsored lavish arts festivals for the most provocative modern artists in Moscow, then supported Orthodox fundamentalists, dressed all in black and carrying crosses, who ... attacked the modern art exhibitions." Surkov's and Putin's Kremlin, in Pomerantsev's take, sought "to own all forms of political discourse, to not let any independent movements develop outside of its walls. Its Moscow can feel like an oligarchy in the morning and a democracy in the afternoon, a monarchy for dinner and a totalitarian state by bedtime."

It started with the mass media and elections. The encroachments on media freedoms stage-managed by Mikhail Lesin, minister of communications until 2004, were worst for national television, where 90 percent of Russians get their political information. The taming of Gusinsky's private NTV and of ORT or Channel One, editorially in Berezovsky's pocket, was completed in Putin's first year. The printed press and the Internet had more leeway.

When it came to the electoral process, the transgressions Freedom House detected in the 2000 presidential election were not dispositive. One of the most censorious studies of Putin as a politician, *Putin's Kleptocracy*, by Karen Dawisha, outlines sundry misuses—sweetheart treatment of Putin in the state media, *adminresurs* ("the administrative resource" of the bureaucracy and state budget), and fudging of the vote count—but finds Putin to have been "a viable and charismatic candidate who all conceded would have won against Zyuganov, whether in the first or the second round." This also applies to Putin's reelection, hands down, in 2004. He drubbed the KPRF nominee, Nikolai Kharitonov, by 72 percent to 14 percent.

Even though fabrication of turnout and of the pro-Kremlin vote did take place, the essence of Putin's method was not the numbers on the scoreboard but about preparing the electoral playing field, and determining who was to play.

The creation in 2001 of an effectual and overweening party of power, United Russia, bolted in position a crucial political lever. Yeltsin had frowned on the 1993 and 1995 renditions, Russia's Choice and Our Home Is Russia; in 1999 he approved of the Unity slate but took no part in the campaign. Putin went all in for the new organization. United Russia fused the Unity bloc and Fatherland–All Russia, which had brawled with Yeltsin, Putin, and Unity in 1999–2000 but came to the conclusion that teamwork with the victor was better than ostracism. In parliament, United Russia worked through pacts with minor parties and with deputies elected as independents in local Duma districts. In the 2003 election, riding Putin's coattails, it took 38 percent of the party-list vote, winning 223 of 450 seats. In 2007 it had a bumper crop of 64 percent of the popular vote and 315 of the 450 seats, 15 more than a two-thirds constitutional supermajority.

United Russia provided the regime with a well-oiled electoral appliance, a domesticated legislature, and lopsided majorities in regional dumas. The party was a site for sharing out the loaves and fishes of office, political access for business, and naked corruption. Its platform—"Freedom, Legality, Justice, and Harmony"—was a mishmash of euphonious goals ranging from firming up the state to entrepreneurialism, rule of law, interethnic accord, and the new century as one of "greatness and well-being for Russia."

A hammerlock on parliament gave Putin the ability to rewrite and so to manipulate the rules for national elections and for apportionment of the spoils. It was a circular flow of power custom-built for the post-Communist age.

A supine Federal Assembly fine-tuned the regulations: banning last-minute electoral blocs and limiting campaigns to registered parties; devising a bureaucratic sieve that made it unrealistic to form any new party; hemming in existing parties through finicky rules and regulations; raising the threshold for seating in the Duma from 5 percent of the party-list vote to 7 percent in 2003; and abolition of the Duma's 225 geographic districts in 2007, leaving all 450 deputies to be elected from national party lists. The gaggle of political parties and near-parties on the books in 1999 had been winnowed a decade later to United Russia and six tame groups known collectively as the "in-system [*sistemnaya*] opposition." United Russia, the neo-Communist KPRF, the poseur Zhirinovsky's LDPR, and the left-of-center A Just Russia sat as a four-party cartel in the Duma. The KPRF and the LDPR were fossilized organizations incapable of bidding for real power. A Just Russia, led by Sergei Mironov from St. Petersburg, speaker of the Federation Council from 2001 to 2011, was antigovernment but pro-Putin, and had been set up with active participation of the Kremlin.

To posit Putin as the gravedigger of Russia democracy performs an intellectual service if it silhouettes his responsibility for tilting a hybrid political system, by degrees, away from inclusiveness and competition and toward exclusiveness and collusion. It is a disservice if it exculpates Yeltsin for bringing him to the fore, or implies that Putin de-democratized Russia single-handedly after 1999.

Russia's autocratic turn fell back on Muscovite, imperial, and Soviet patterns of thought and behavior. It did not reestablish the monarchy or totalitarianism or, for that matter, set up a vintage personal dictatorship. Putinism was more an intermingling of ingredients—the attachment to order and past achievements, reflexive nationalism, casting aspersions on alien influences, and neopatrimonial reverence for the state as a provider and regulator—than a recombinatory, organic whole. Fragments of a more open politics endured. They were vestiges of an adjourned democratization process under Yeltsin and Gorbachev and reflective of Putin's belief that he was best served by access to a mixed bag of opinions.

Majorities marked off their ballots for United Russia and Putin; tens of millions (34.1 million in the 2003 State Duma election, 13 million in the 2004 presidential election) voted for others. Day to day, uncounted millions more bobbed on the authoritarian tide. The tacit bargain was that the resurgent state, unhampered in the public domain, would stay out of people's private lives. Putin on the whole held up his end. Russians were at liberty to think, pray, spend, read, and pass their spare time as they pleased. Relative prosperity left them freer than before to soak up property and goods, and to see the world. In 1999 12.6 million Russians went abroad as tourists. This figure nearly doubled to 24.5 million in 2004, trebled to 36.5 million in 2008, and quadrupled to 47.8 million in 2012. A fair share of them flew in charter flights to previously unattainable destinations such as Turkey, Egypt, Spain, and Thailand.

Channels for interpersonal communication also teemed. In 1999 there was 1 cell phone in use per 100 Russian citizens; in 2004 there were 51 per 100, in 2008 there were 139, and in 2012 there were 145. Only one Russian in a hundred had regular access to the Runet in 1999. Thirteen did in 2004, twenty-seven in 2008, and sixty-four in 2012. Fast-moving, nonhierarchical, and transnational, the Internet is an unrivaled agent of sociocultural globalization, a pervasive process about which Putin is fretful but which accelerated on his watch. The FSB eavesdropped on electronic networks through black boxes plugged into a blandly titled System of Operative Search Measures (SORM), which had been around since the 1990s, but did not impede their growth. A whopping 80 percent of Russians with Internet access use social networks, which is 30 points more than the European Union (EU) average. Social media market leaders as of the fourth quarter of 2014, by count of statista. com, were VKontakte (In Contact), which had a 28 percent penetration rate, Odnoklassniki (Classmates) with 24 percent, Facebook with 18 percent, Google+ with 15 percent, Skype with 12 percent, and Twitter with 10 percent.

Gleb Pavlovsky in 2008 borrowed the emblem "creative class," coined by American economist Richard Florida, to stand for Russians who work in science and technology, the arts, business and management, or the professions and have diverse and individualistic lifestyles of a piece with the Internet. Like it or not, the modern creative class made its entrance in Russia during the Putin years.

Did Putin kill Russian federalism?

Putin's apprehension about state weakness was at its most tangible with respect to metropole and periphery, which was his beat in the Kremlin front office for several months in 1998. As he gathered the reins of power, he was vexed by two developments he took as proof that Yeltsin's "political first aid" and its liberality with subnational governments were ripe for revision. The intercession of provincial figures in the leadership politics of 1999–2000, acting through the Fatherland–All Russia electoral bloc (OVR), might be thought more an annoyance than a hazard. But, excepting Primakov, the leading lights of OVR were all decentralizing regionalists—Mayor Luzhkov of Moscow; Presidents Shaimiyev of Tatarstan, Murtaza Rakhimov of Bashkortostan, and Ruslan Aushev of Ingushetiya; and Vladimir Yakovlev, the St. Petersburg governor (mayor) whose upset of Anatolii Sobchak in the 1996 city election had forced Putin to relocate to Moscow. The more unnerving challenge was a second war over Chechnya.

Looking back in an interview in 2011, Putin spoke of the do-or-die reasoning behind his turning of the screws, a pungent simile he had not permitted himself a decade earlier: "We had lived through the collapse of the state. The Soviet Union fell apart. And what was the Soviet Union? It was Russia, only by another name. There was a period in our state's development when ... we came under enormous threats, and these threats were so bad that the very existence of the Russian state was in question. For that reason, we had to 'tighten the screws,' to be blunt, and introduce strict regulatory mechanisms, most of all in the political sphere. How else could it be if the [regions] referred in their constitutions and charters to everything you could imagine except for the fact that they were . . . constituent parts of the Russian Federation?"

Putin drew first blood on May 13, 2000, with a decree superimposing seven "federal districts" on the then eighty-nine units of the federation; an eighth district for the North Caucasus was separated out in 2010. All were under a "plenipotentiary representative" of the president. Five of the seven envoys were uniformed siloviks from the army or the security agencies; the only prominent civilian was the former prime minister, Sergei Kiriyenko. The plenipotentiary representatives were the centerpiece of what Putin dubbed his "power vertical" (*vertikal vlasti*), a term hewed for federal officialdom but generalized to riding herd on the regional governments.

Next, Putin clipped the wings of the Federation Council, the upper house of the national parliament. Since 1995 it had been an assemblage of the regional governors/presidents and legislative chairs, ex officio, who had a say in federal lawmaking and, as positive externalities, residences in Moscow and immunity from criminal prosecution. A bill introduced in May 2000 called for them to be replaced with two delegates per unit to be selected by the region's leaders. The Federation Council blessed it once Putin let sitting members fill out their terms and created a well-victualed, advisory State Council of regional dignitaries. The appointed members of the Federation Council were mostly decorative, and two-thirds were chosen through political horse-trading with the Kremlin and had no ties to their territories.

The sharpest rupture with Yeltsinesque federalism was the nullification of elections for regional heads in the wake of Beslan. Putin signed the new procedure into law in December 2004. The president of Russia was to nominate a candidate for provincial governor or president, and the local duma could take or leave his nominee. The nominations were tantamount to appointment: no region was ever to reject one. This act of centralization problematized the very idea of Russia as a federal state, although city mayors continued to be elected.

Centripetal modifications to the federal compact dribbled out year by year. Regional laws were "harmonized" with national legislation and the Russian constitution. No new bilateral treaties were forged and agreements from the 1990s, for five- or ten-year spans, were not renewed; by 2010 only Tatarstan still had a working pact. Fiscal decentralization was reversed, so that by 2008 60 percent of state revenues were collected by the center and 40 percent by the regions. As mentioned above, six sparsely populated ethnic units (autonomous okrugs) were amalgamated with ethnicity-blind units.

But it would be an overreach to say that power sharing with the regions was deleted down to the last whit. Putin's frenemies Luzhkov, Shaimiyev, and Rakhimov from OVR all kept their places until 2010; even Yakovlev of St. Petersburg had a major position until 2007. The presidential stranglehold over central decision-making deformed the power vertical in action. When a directive is issued, lower-down careerists often "are afraid to ask for clarifications or detailed instructions, fearing such inquiries might make them appear incompetent. Hence, they resort to . . . independent interpretations that often distort the original concepts devised in the highest offices." Variation in regional resource endowments and traditions enables political trades at the subnational level. Russian specialists on federalism write of a modicum of between-the-lines decentralization; of "a new political triangle" that enmeshes the Kremlin, governors, and large corporations; and of the continuance into the 2010s of "clientelistic exchange" between the executive in Moscow and the leaders of regional political machines and of social groups, like pensioners and public sector workers, reliant on them for favors.

Practical autonomy was above average for Moscow (2010 census population 11.5 million) and St. Petersburg (4.8 million), the ethnic republics, and the ten or twelve resource-rich regions not dependent on federal subventions. One of the ironies was that the most flexible arrangement was in postwar Chechnya, which remained under military occupation as the central government reconstructed Grozny. To defuse conflict, Putin wagered on a strongman to whom a maximum of decision powers would be devolved in return for rock-solid fealty. His choice was Akhmad Kadyrov, the former head mufti of the republic who had fought for the rebels in the 1990s. He was assassinated in 2004 in the Grozny soccer stadium and succeeded after a waiting period by his son Ramzan. Ramzan Kadyrov had commanded the Kadyrovtsy (Kadyrovites) militia and ran an amnesty program for guerrillas who laid down arms. Chechnya is to this day a financial ward of Moscow, with transfers from federal coffers constituting 81 percent of its budget in 2013. It was at Kadyrov's suggestion that, starting in 2010, the republics suffered a semantic demotion. One after another, all but in Tatarstan, their legislative organs renamed the chief executive "head" (glava) of the territorial unit, reserving "president" for the leader of the Russian Federation.

What was behind the economic boom of the 2000s, and what difference did it make?

Every statistical trendline about the Russian economy after 1991 was negative in slope. Every trendline after 1999 had a positive slope. The GDP soared by 10 percent in 2000 and by a mean of 7 percent per annum from 2000 through 2008, or a cumulative 90 percent. Inflation fell from 72 percent in 1999 to 38 percent in 2000 and 15 percent after that. Food production more than doubled. The RTS equities index (MOEX or Moscow Exchange in 2011, after a corporate merger) finally chugged back to its 1997 peak (572) in the summer of 2004, and to almost 2,500 in May of 2008. IPOs of Russian companies went from one or two a year in the late 1990s to twenty-seven in 2007, with the London Stock Exchange being the preferred foreign location. The country reeled from the world's Great Recession of 2008–9, with an 8 percent dip in 2009, but growth restarted at a faltering pace and the RTS/MOEX average steadied at approximately 1,500. The World Bank has a fourfold ranking of countries by level of development: low, lower-middle, upper-middle, and high income. In 2013, applying a floor of $12,616 in nominal GDP per capita, it slotted Russia into the high-income category. Compared to three-quarters of the world, the perennial Eurasian laggard was now well-off.

What explains the toggle from bust in the nineties to boom in the noughties? The 1998 ruble devaluation that made Russian goods more competitive could have had only a near-term effect, as would the availability of slack production capacity. The fact is that Yeltsin and the shock therapists of the 1990s had laid the institutional foundation for an economic miracle. The reforms, for all their faults, had the effect of co-ordination through market fingers rather than administrative thumbs, a business infrastructure, and openness to global processes.

Few would disagree that the new administration, taking direction from Finance Minister Kudrin, Economic Development Minister German Gref, and Andrei Illarionov, Putin's small-government libertarian adviser for economics, did its part. In selective strategic sectors, Putin pushed the aggregation of firms into state-dominated "national champions" like Gazprom (gas), Rosneft (oil), Rosatom (atomic power, run by Sergei Kiriyenko), the United Aircraft Corporation, and the United Shipbuilding Corporation. In the main, though, he accepted private ownership and the market—never reneging on the profit motive, market pricing of goods and services, and a fully convertible currency. His first year in the Kremlin, Russia lowered customs tariffs, replaced the graduated income tax with a flat tax of 13 percent (the lowest in Europe), and deflated the corporate tax rate to 24 percent from 35 percent. Lower rates were instrumental in reducing tax evasion. In 2002 a rephrased land code legalized the sale of urban and rural land to individuals and companies, which had been forbidden since 1917. A 2003 statute entitled every citizen to a personal plot, free of charge, measuring two to seven acres depending on region.

The macroeconomics of the Putin government were judicious and progrowth. Its budget was in surplus every year. In 2004 it established a rainy-day Stabilization Fund to squirrel away savings against future recessions. All oil and gas export income above a cutoff point of $20 per barrel (the amount was later adjusted) was decanted into the fund. The Stabilization Fund was divvied in 2008 into a Reserve Fund strictly for stabilization purposes, with about $140 billion in capital, and a Norwegian-type sovereign wealth account, the National Wellbeing Fund, with about $90 billion. The Russian Central Bank held on deposit $475 billion in hard currency and gold at the end of 2008 and $540 billion at the end of 2012—a far cry from the $7.8 billion in its vaults in 1998. Russia also discharged its sovereign debt. To the public lenders in the Paris Club, an informal collection of government officials from creditor countries who seek out affordable solutions to payment difficulties, the $22 billion still owed was paid down in 2005–6. Russian debt to the private creditors in the London Club was restructured and the last $1 million reimbursed in 2010.

Deferred returns to the reforms of the 1990s and policy stewardship in the 2000s do not fully explain the U-turn. Weight also goes to a windfall not under Russia's control. The bane of Yeltsin's existence was a monthly Brent price for crude oil below $20 per barrel, and below $10 in 1998. By August 1999, when he named Putin prime minister, Brent had returned to $20 per barrel. It wheeled above $30 in September 2000, $40 in August 2004, and $50 in March 2005. The $60 barrier was broken in March 2006, $70 in April 2006, $80 in October 2007, $90 in November 2007, and $100 in March 2008. In July 2008 the price of oil reached a pinnacle of $133.90. The Great Recession was a rollercoaster, but Brent was back up over $100 a barrel by 2011.

The bull market stimulated production and had a multiplier effect on the flow of petrodollars. Russian oil, having fallen off from 9.0 million barrels per day in 1991 to 5.9 million in 1996 through 1999, caught up with the 1991 level in 2006 and reached 10 million barrels per day in 2009, 10.5 million in 2013, and 10.8 million in 2015. Gas production, which was off by only 10 percent in the 1990s, mended to 607 billion cubic meters in 2011, two-thirds of it by Gazprom. As of 2012, oil and gas, constituting 16 percent of GDP and 70 percent of Russian exports, contributed 52 percent of federal budgetary revenues. Oil rents and exuberant growth were a bonanza for Putin's sacrosanct state apparatus. With its books in the black and taxes and royalties pouring in, the government could afford to engorge the federal civil service (from 1.2 million civilian positions in 2000 to 1.8 million in 2007 and more than 2 million in 2012), fatten paychecks, put departments online, and fix up office buildings and courthouses. Arrears in social assistance payments were a thing of the past. Old-age pensions, after a reorganization in 2002 and an infusion of funds, came to 9 percent of GDP in 2010, not much short of the advanced economies. In September 2005 Putin initiated four "national priority projects" to expand outlays for public health, education, housing, and agriculture.

Enough was left over in the till for big-ticket spending to brighten Russia's international image. In 2004 the Kremlin launched the Valdai Discussion Club, an experts' forum at which Putin puts in an annual appearance. In 2005 Mikhail Lesin, now his media adviser, supervised the birth of Russia Today, a television channel tasked, as Putin said later, with "breaking the Anglo-Saxon monopoly on the global information streams." Putin played host to Russia's first (and, as chance would have it, last) G8 summit in July 2006. It was held out of the eighteenth-century Konstantin Palace on the outskirts of St. Petersburg, ostentatiously reconstructed with ministerial funds. An American PR firm, Ketchum, was hired to publicize the event; Russia was a client until 2015. In 2007 Putin talked the International Olympic Committee into awarding the 2014 Winter Olympics to Sochi, a resort city in Krasnodar krai near where the Greater Caucasus Range meets the Black Sea. Yeltsin's government had tried such a bid in

1995 but failed. The decision, Putin told reporters, was "not just a recognition of Russia's sporting achievements, but . . . of our country." He would be "intimately, obsessively, involved in the Olympic project, awarding contracts . . . approving designs, and policing construction schedules." The games cost taxpayers a world-record $51 billion. Lesser jewels would be the Association for Pacific Economic Cooperation (APEC) summit held at an island off Vladivostok in September 2012, for which two cable-stayed bridges and a university campus were constructed, and the World Cup scheduled for 2018, for which twelve soccer stadiums are to be built or rebuilt.

The long-suffering populace, too, was treated to a decade of plenty. Disposable incomes in 2008 were twice what they had been in 1999 and more if dollar-denominated, since the ruble appreciated in value by one-third after 2003. The population living below the official poverty line dropped from 29 percent in 2000 to 16 percent in 2008. Sales of new motor vehicles went through the roof, from 903,000 in 1999 to 1,807,000 in 2005 and 3,142,000 in 2012, bringing with them atrocious traffic congestion. An expansion of credit extended purchasing power; it was made possible by rising incomes, lower inflation, and the banking system running serviceably well out of the glass-clad office towers studding Moscow's skyline. Russians held 10 million plastic cards, first issued in the Soviet Union in 1989, at the end of 2001 but 54 million at the end of 2004, 119 million by 2008, and 150 million by 2010. The lion's share of these were payroll, debit, and automated teller machine (ATM) cards until Sberbank, the state-held savings bank, introduced revolving credit cards. Russians' pocketbooks contained 30 million credit cards by 2014, and they could take out cash or pay bills at more ATMs per capita than any country other than Canada or San Marino. A related innovation was the home mortgage. By 2014 one-quarter of Russian residential properties were being bought with the aid of a mortgage.

The retail economy supplied shoppers through mom-and-pop stores, supermarkets, department and big-box stores, auto showrooms, and roofed malls, of which there were eighty in Moscow by 2012. While local firms were prevalent, foreign companies took positions: the French Auchan, the German Metro AG, the Swedish IKEA, the British Debenhams, and, for fast food and drinks, the American McDonalds (which has five hundred Russian restaurants), KFC, Subway, Starbucks, and Pinkberry. For those who could pay for the dolce vita, there were gourmet restaurants, pet salons, artisan bakeries, and boutiques purveying haute couture apparel and accessories, fine wines, and cosmetics, with 60 to 70 percent of the market in Moscow and 10 to 15 percent in St. Petersburg. The first international fashion house to do direct sales in Russia was Louis Vuitton, a division of Moët and Hennessy, in 2002. An Ogilvy & Mather ad for LV luggage in 2007 showed a photo by Annie Leibovitz of a balding gentleman in the rear seat of a limousine, an unzipped bag at his feet, smiling as the car drives by a leftover of the Berlin Wall. The passenger was, of all people, Mikhail Gorbachev; the footer was, "A Journey Brings Us Face to Face with Ourselves." Ten years before, Gorbachev and his granddaughter had filmed a TV commercial for Pizza Hut.

What happened to the oligarchs after 1999?

In a word, Putin happened to the oligarchs. The takedown of NTV's Vladimir Gusinsky was but an opening salvo. On July 28, 2000, Putin met with twenty members of the Russian Union of Industrialists and Entrepreneurs (RSPP), the mouthpiece for big business. Only snippets of the discussion were leaked, but they all have Putin's bottom line as "mutual noninterference." He would leave the moguls' money and firms alone on the proviso that they left his government alone and paid their taxes. True to form, Putin embroidered the status quo ante. "You yourselves," he rebukes the businessmen, "have to quite an extent formed this state, through political and quasi-political structures under your control. Perhaps what one should do least is blame the mirror." Now, "We will prevent anyone from glomming onto political authority and using it for their own goals. No clan, no oligarchs should come close to the regional or federal authorities—they should be kept equidistant from politics."

Boris Berezovsky, on the outs with the president, had re-signed his Duma seat, decrying "the imposition of authoritarian rule" and retroactive justice: "Only people who have been asleep for the past ten years have willingly or unwillingly avoided breaking the law. And those sitting in the Kremlin are in the same spot." In August those sitting in the Kremlin told Berezovsky to divest himself of his shares in ORT television. By November 2000 he had done so and decamped for the United Kingdom, which gave him political asylum in 2003. Beaten down by the failure of haphazard dabbling in Russian politics, in absentia, and by lawsuits over contracts and property, Berezovsky would hang himself at his home in Ascot, Berkshire, in March 2013.

If any doubts lingered about Putin's willpower, they were dispelled by the prosecutorial blitz against Mikhail Khodorkovsky. Such had Khodorkovsky's Midas touch been that upon his arrest in October 2003 *Forbes* magazine valuated his net worth at $15 billion—first in Russia and sixteenth in the entire world (seventh among non-Americans). He had acquired Yukos Oil for a pittance ($350 million) under loans-for-shares and modernized it with the help of McKinsey & Company and PricewaterhouseCoopers. Taken to court on charges of tax fraud and theft with his business partner Platon Lebedev—the two sat through the thirteen-month trial in a metal cage, as Russian defendants often do—he was found guilty in May 2005 and sentenced to nine years. Yukos went into receivership for tax delinquency in 2007, upon which Khodorkovsky faced new accusations of embezzlement and money-laundering; in 2010 a judge gave him seven years more in a penal colony. In 2013, right before the end of his sentence, Putin pardoned him on compassionate grounds (his mother was dying of cancer).

Anti-Putinites were to lionize Khodorkovsky as a crusader for freedom. Amnesty International put him on its ledger of prisoners of conscience in 2011. Khodorkovsky had given munificently to charity and higher education before his arrest, but was hardly a poster child for business responsibility or a candidate for sainthood. As Thane Gustafson remarks in his definitive book on Russian oil, Khodorkovsky for the most part lived out "a personal creed that gave the entrepreneur absolute license and made greed not only good but the supreme good." On the subject of business–government relations, Khodorkovsky was oblivious. Without Kremlin clearance, he attempted to merge Yukos with the Russian company Sibneft, US-based Chevron, or ExxonMobil. He pulled strings for tax breaks through a business partner, Vladimir Dubov, who chaired the Duma's taxation subcommittee; laced into the Ministry of Finance for closing tax loopholes; and demanded a license to build an oil pipeline to China, saying he would not export to East Asia in a state-owned pipe. The last straw may have been Khodorkovsky's hubris at a televised Putin audience with the RSPP in February 2003. He lectured Putin on the China pipeline and sparred openly with him over malfeasance by Rosneft, the state-controlled oil company—which was to acquire most of Yukos's property in 2007. "In one flash, Khodorkovsky's incaution, his underestimation of the forces against him, and his contempt for the president himself were on display for all to see."

The message Khodorkovsky's comeuppance sent to the business class was that, as Mikhail Kasyanov, the then prime minister who was present at the ill-fated February meeting, said in 2013, they were "dependent people." Putin "had begun in the strongest possible terms to threaten them all, inferring that, 'Look here, to keep bad things from going on I will personally take care of the whole bunch of you.' " Putin was to fire the liberal Kasyanov in early 2004; his economics aide, Andrei Illarionov, left in 2005. But the progressive bloc in the government apparatus sat tight, and the Kremlin regularly solicited business input on policy matters, behind closed doors, from the Union of Industrialists and Entrepreneurs, the Chamber of Commerce and Industry, the Union of Business Associations, and Business Russia.

As positions opened up in state-owned corporations and lucrative orders flowed to firms and individuals connected one way or another to the chief, the composition of the Russian economic elite changed. Daniel Treisman has thought up "silovarch" as a portmanteau of silovik and oligarch. A series of entrants to the charmed circle, their pasts in state security and intelligence, fit it to a T, men like Igor Sechin (Rosneft) and Sergei Chemezov (Rostec, aerospace and armaments). Others qualified as childhood friends of Putin, as cottage owners in the Ozero Dacha Cooperative (lakeside cabins on the Karelian Isthmus), or as officemates under Sobchak in the 1990s. Samples would include financier Yurii Kovalchuk of Bank Rossiya (personal banker to Putin, so they say), Arkadii Rotenberg (Putin's judo sparring partner when they were youngsters, who made his money in oil and pipelines), Gennadii Timchenko (of the Dutch-registered oil trader Gunvor), and Vladimir Yakunin (president of Russian Railways until 2015, who also had worked in foreign intelligence).

One should not weep for the Russian oligarchs, old and new. The regime never tried to liquidate them "as a class," as Stalin did to the kulaks and the NEPmen. Putin, reports Gleb Pavlovsky, based on his interaction with the leadership, felt that a reason the Soviet Union lost the Cold War was not having "our own class of capitalists," "the kind of predators described to us [in Soviet propaganda] ... who would ... devour their [the West's] predators." Russia now had omnivorous predators of its very own. The bashing of Khodorkovsky notwithstanding, Putin's was a gilded age for all of the nouveaux riches except any who chose to cross swords with him. There may have been dissension over slices of the pie, but the pie grew year after year and there were seats for many at the repast. The Russian Federation boasted 2 *Forbes* billionaires in

1998 but 36 in 2004 and 87 in 2008. There were 110 of them in 2013, third only to the United States' 422 and China's 122, and they had amassed $427 billion in capital, second behind the United States' $1.87 trillion. Capping the Russian list were Alisher Usmanov ($17.6 billion, mining and miscellaneous activities), Mikhail Fridman ($16.5 billion, banking and oil), and Leonid Mikhelson ($15.4 billion, Novatek natural gas). Of Putin's chums, Timchenko had salted away the most ($14.1 billion, fifth), with Rotenberg ($3.3 billion) and Kovalchuk ($1.1 billion) in more modest niches.

Nor need tears be shed over less-than-oligarchs in the Russian Federation who are rich but not filthy rich. Credit Suisse Research in its *Global Wealth Report 2014*, with data for 2013, stamped Russia as a "very high-inequality country." One hundred and fifty thousand persons had a net worth of over $1 million and 2,800 qualified for "ultrahigh net worth" of over $50 million. Not a single Russian would have been worth 1 million dollars in 1991. A Gini index, or economists' measure of inequality, estimated by the World Bank in 2012, placed Russia as the fifty-first most unequal place out of seventy-four countries studied.

What made Putin and his policies so popular?

On one level, Russians related to their second president through his personality, or what they took it to be. Putin has persistently disseminated a persona tailored to his power and policy needs.

As the research of Helena Goscilo, Valerie Sperling, and Elizabeth Wood has set out, a defining element was machismo, as come to life in athleticism, male bonding, and thuggish and mildly profane one-liners. An Internet search will turn up visuals by the bushel of Putin performing the part—pumping iron and slamming judo partners to the mat; riding a horse bare-chested in Siberia; in the cockpit of a Su-27 jet; driving a Formula One race car or a motorcycle with the Night Wolves bikers club; telling OSCE election monitors they would be better off teaching their wives how to cook *shchi* (cabbage soup) than teaching Russia democracy. Some of the opposite sex were smitten. The chart-topping "Someone Like Putin" (2002), recorded by the girl band Singing Together—with how much musicological help from Putin's handlers we do not know—tells of deciding to throw over a worthless boyfriend for a virile and faithful teetotaler: "I want someone like Putin, full of strength / Someone like Putin, who doesn't drink / Someone like Putin, who won't treat me badly / Someone like Putin, who won't up and leave me." A 2012 poll by the reputable Levada Analytical Center found that 20 percent of Russian women told interviewers they would like to marry Putin.

The image makers were at pains to show up a kindhearted side as well. Funnily enough, they did it through programs to protect rare and endangered fauna, systematized in Putin's term two. Excursions to remote locations were half scientific probe and half publicity stunt. In September 2009, in a visit to Chkalov Island in the Sea of Okhotsk, Putin pinned a radio transmitter to a calf beluga whale and carried her into the surf in a net. In September 2012 he piloted a motorized hang glider over the northern tundra, pointing six red cranes raised by the Russian branch of the World Wildlife Fund in the direction of their winter habitat in Uzbekistan; the birds later got lost and had to be flown south in the hold of a government airplane. The Kremlin website posts links to programs to nurture populations of Amur tigers, belugas, Far Eastern and snow leopards, and polar bears.

Putin made sure to ascertain what Russians think by way of opinion polls, focus groups, and scrutiny of the press and Runet. To communicate his strengths, he hit upon a two-way formula that took advantage of his stamina and command of detail. On December 24, 2001, national television broadcast a "Direct Line with Vladimir Putin" in which he responded, live, to questions from Russian citizens, filtered by staffers. He has continued year in year out, except for 2004 and 2012, when he held press conferences instead. At the marathon session in 2011 he fielded ninety queries over four hours and thirty-three minutes.

There was more to Putin's popularity than PR, polls, and Q&A screenings. Bill Clinton's jingle from 1992—"It's the Economy, Stupid!"—could not have been more germane to Russia in the 2000s. Defensibly or not, most Russians associated the economic upsurge with the chief executive. Putin also won kudos for delivering a more stable state and a more shred-proof social safety net. And he delivered geopolitical deference and awareness that Russia stood tall in world affairs. Only 31 percent of Russians in a Levada poll in 1999 felt Russia had the status of a great power (*velikaya derzhava*); by November 2007, 53 percent did; by November 2015, 65 percent.

If Putinism put the state and Putin in the driver's seat, it had much less to say about the passenger's seat. An untold number took comfort from the fact that someone was at the steering wheel and, concomitantly, that the passenger could do what she or he wanted, provided no spitballs were thrown at the driver. From this angle, Putin brought some semblance of normalcy, one in which private affairs again take precedence over public affairs and, by temporal comparison, go relatively well.

A glimpse at what Russians make of their life situation comes from the World Values Survey (WVS), which social scientists have executed in almost one hundred countries. The WVS studies carried out in the Russian Federation in 1995–96, by the ROMIR firm, and in 2011, by the Levada Center, offer grist for the mill. Asked in the Yeltsin decade how "happy" they were, Russians were evenly divided: 6 percent said they were very happy and 44 percent were moderately happy; 40 percent were not very happy and 8 percent unhappy. The mood on Putin's watch was unquestionably more cheerful, with 73 percent very or moderately happy and only 23 percent not very happy or unhappy. Russians were less upbeat than Americans, but the gap was less in 2011 than in the 1990s.

Only a minority of Russians take much of an interest in the political process. The World Values data for 2011 show 5 percent telling interviewers they were very interested in politics and 28 percent that they were rather interested, almost unmoved since 1995. Few people found fulfillment in things political: 7 percent said in 2011 that politics was very important to them and 20 percent that it was rather important (compare with 11 percent and 42 percent in the United States). Away from politics, Russians had a much higher satisfaction quotient than Americans for family (very or rather important to 98 percent), friends (80 percent), leisure time (75 percent), and work (74 percent).

How did Russian foreign policy change under Putin?

It should not come as a revelation that the underlying storylines for foreign and domestic policy were so alike. The state collapse Putin lamented at home had in the international realm taken the contours of the literal dismantlement of the Soviet Union and the abandonment of its forward positions—"the greatest geopolitical catastrophe of the century," as Putin called it in an address to the Federal Assembly in 2005.

A presidential Foreign Policy Concept dated June 2000 set the stage for revisions. It recited a litany of "challenges and threats to Russia's national interests" that transcended Yeltsin's Cold Peace oration of 1994. "The trend grows," said the concept, "toward creation of a unipolar structure for the world . . . dominated by the United States." Western institutions such as NATO were usurping the UN Security Council and global forums. Russia would work for "formation of a multipolar system of international relations reflective of the diversity of the contemporary world and the variety of interests in it." The document committed to seven "basic goals." Beefing up Russian "sovereignty and territorial integrity" was put first. Making "favorable external conditions for Russia's continuing development," which would have been first-ranked for Yeltsin or Gorbachev, was third. Russia was also to weigh in on decisions of world import (second), build "a good-neighborly belt" on its perimeter (fourth) and partnerships with amenable states (fifth), defend "the rights and interests of Russian citizens and compatriots" (sixth), and burnish its national reputation and promulgate its language and culture (seventh).

Putin was slower to put his imprint on international statecraft than on national politics. Like Yeltsin, he worked at building personal relationships with foreign leaders: George W. Bush of the United States (who in Slovenia in June 2001 legendarily stared him in the eye and read his soul), Tony Blair of the United Kingdom, Jacques Chirac of France, and Gerhard Schröder of Germany. After 9/11, Putin was the first to get through to Bush with condolences; when the American military went after al-Qaeda in Afghanistan, Putin offered to assist access to bases in Central Asia. In November 2001 the Russian president paid a visit to Bush at his ranch in Crawford, Texas.

Combustible episodes one after the other frittered away the good feeling, all in synthesis with Putin's priors and with magnified Russian capabilities. The Bush administration notified Russia in December 2001 that the United States was pulling out of the 1972 ABM Treaty, so it could test and install missile-defense technology. An agreement on offensive nuclear weapons was reached in 2002, but the bloom was off the rose. The Russian Federation ferociously resisted a US antimissile shield in Europe. In 2003 it opposed as unwise and illegal the American-British invasion of Iraq.

What really curdled relations, however, were differences over Russia's Near Abroad in Eurasia. In November 2003 the United States, the EU, and the chairman of the OSCE convinced President Vladimir Voronin of Moldova to torpedo a Moscow-drafted plan to federalize that country and formalize considerable autonomy for the pro-Russia Transdniestria section, where Russian peacekeepers were to remain until 2020. The rejection came as a Kremlin airplane was preparing to fly Putin to Moldova to witness the signing. "What was for most Western capitals a relatively minor incident for the Russians was a personal affront to their president and a denial of Russia's right to play an independent political and diplomatic role in a part of the world that had once been theirs exclusively." Normative disagreement and recriminations over Moldova dirtied Russia's view of the "color revolutions"—the Rose Revolution in Georgia in 2003 (already in train when Putin nixed his trip), the Ukrainians' Orange Revolution in 2004, and the Tulip Revolution in Kyrgyzstan in 2005. Accompanied by civil disobedience and reorientations in foreign policy, all of them were savaged by Putin and the siloviks as pro-Western infringement on Russia's interests and pernicious for its internal stability. More unwelcome yet were the 2004 and 2009 rounds of NATO expansion, bringing into the alliance not only six East European countries but the three ex-Soviet Baltic countries, and NATO agreements on "intensified dialogue" with Ukraine in 2005 and Georgia in 2006.

In an acid-tongued speech at the Munich Security Conference of February 2007, Putin lashed out at the United States and its allies for unilateralism in Europe and beyond and for disregarding organizations like the UN and the OSCE that were not at their beck and call. Western adventurism was bringing the world "to the abyss of one conflict after another." "Countries that forbid the death penalty even for murderers and dangerous criminals are lightheartedly participating in military operations that are difficult to consider legitimate." That month Putin appointed a civilian defense minister, Anatolii Serdyukov, and ordered him to reform the military. Later in 2007 he put on ice Russian obligations to the Conventional Forces in Europe (CFE) treaty of 1990, citing American plans for missile defense and for bases in Bulgaria and Romania. A last effort at getting agreement on cooperative missile defense ran aground several months after that. Russia was to withdraw completely from CFE in 2015.

Putin's Russia has employed external military force three times. It is no fluke that two times out of three it has been in

Eurasia, where, as Dmitrii Medvedev said in 2008, the Russian Federation claims "privileged interests." Medvedev, deputizing by then for Putin as president, spoke weeks after the war with Georgia (population 3.6 million), which began on August 8 and was over in five days.

Russian–Georgian relations had soured after the 2003 revolution against Eduard Shevardnadze swept Mikhail Saakashvili to power. A Columbia University L.L.M. who had been Shevardnadze's justice minister, the impetuous Saakashvili dissociated himself from Russian policy and hired a Washington consulting firm to lobby for NATO membership. In 2006 Russia interdicted imports of Georgian wine and mineral water and closed its embassy. A bone of contention was the status of the two minority districts within Georgia long trapped in interethnic frozen conflicts. The Lilliputian republics of South Ossetiya (population fifty thousand) and Abkhaziya (two hundred thousand) both lay on the international border with Russia and had been self-governing under Kremlin auspices since the early 1990s. Many residents had been issued Russian passports.

Saakashvili touched off the 2008 war by endeavoring, not so different from Putin in Chechnya, to reassert central preeminence over South Ossetiya. Russia's retort to Georgian shelling of the South Ossetiyan capital, Tskhinvali, and an attack on a Russian peacekeepers' base was to send in ground forces through the Roki Tunnel beneath the mountain range. They routed the Georgians even with substandard intelligence, coordination, and weaponry and slowness in transporting forces to the theater. Russian tanks revved their engines from August 13 to 22 in Gori, Stalin's birthplace, an hour's drive from Tbilisi. President Bush turned down advice to use American airpower against a Russian armored column. On August 10 the Russian military barged into the seaside and more important Abkhaziya and sealed it off from Georgia. Moscow recognized both entities as sovereign states on August 26. Georgia had lost one-fifth of its territory and two-thirds of its frontage on the Black Sea, and its suit for NATO admission had been short-circuited.

The uneven performance of Russian forces underscored the necessity of defense reform, which Defense Minister Serdyukov began in earnest in October 2008, fresh from the messy victory in Georgia. By six or seven years later he and Sergei Shoigu, who succeeded him in 2012, had effected what a European Council on Foreign Relations report terms a "quiet military revolution," reformatting Russia as "a military power that could overwhelm any of its neighbors, if they were isolated from Western support." Troop strength was lowered from 1.2 million to nine hundred thousand, ground and airborne forces were repackaged into forty maneuverable and fully manned brigades, and key combat roles were reserved for professional soldiers (*kontraktniks*) and a new body of noncommissioned officers. The officer corps was also cut, by one-half, while officer training was upgraded and pay was quintupled. In 2009 the Russian General Staff began a cavalcade of war games simulating offensive operations against the Baltic countries, Georgia, and Poland. In 2010 the government matched military reorganization and rethinking with a no-expense-spared rearmament program. Twenty-three trillion rubles ($725 billion at the 2010 exchange rate) were earmarked to replace 70 percent of the Defense Ministry's armaments with next-generation systems by 2020—procuring 2,300 T-14 Armata main battle tanks, 1,200 airplanes and helicopters, 50 surface ships and 28 submarines, and 100 spy and communication satellites. The latest Russian ICBMs and SLBMs (submarine-launched ballistic missiles) have individually guided, maneuverable warheads to skirt American missile defenses.

After the Georgia war Russia also throttled up economic integration in the post-Soviet expanse. Until then it had been the subject of interminable verbalizing but little action. Russia, Belarus, and Kazakhstan first agreed in principle to a pact to legislate away tariff and nontariff barriers to trade in 1993. Discussions were renewed in 2006 and quickened in 2008, with the Russian president committed and an implementing staff formed. Protocols for a Customs Union of Russia, Belarus, and Kazakhstan came into effect with uniform tariffs in 2010, the scrubbing of internal border controls in 2011, and in 2012 a tripartite Eurasian Economic Commission. The union, given the new name Eurasian Economic Union (EEU), enrolled Armenia and Kyrgyzstan as members in 2015.

Who is Medvedev and what was "the tandem" of 2008 to 2012?

Dmitrii Anatolevich Medvedev (b. 1965 in Leningrad) was president of Russia from 2008 until Putin regained the office in 2012. For the four years, Putin was prime minister, in principle serving at Medvedev's pleasure but in actual fact having the last say. *Tandem*, a loanword the same in Russian and English, stuck as a label. As things stand, the Putin–Medvedev duumvirate—sometimes lampooned as *tandemokratiya* (tandem democracy)—will be consigned to the historical footnotes.

Medvedev was an alumnus of the same Leningrad State University law faculty as Putin and met him in 1990 in the employ of Anatolii Sobchak. He taught civil and Roman law there until 1999 and was legal counsel for a forestry firm, Ilim Pulp; he made a tidy profit when he sold his shares. Appointed deputy head of the Kremlin staff on December 31, 1999, Medvedev managed Putin's (non-)campaign that winter. Stints followed in Gazprom, as presidential chief of staff, and from 2005 to 2007 as first deputy premier responsible for national priority spending.

Medvedev had intelligentsia parents, was younger than Putin by a half-generation and came of age during perestroika, has no known silovik affiliations, and had tried his hand in private business. He was a self-confessed fan of the English rock band Deep Purple. He was and is one of the more broadminded members of the Putin inner circle.

Putin was in an unaccustomed bind as his second term closed out. Article 81 of the constitution stated that a president could serve two four-year spells in a row; a return was not disallowed, but there would have to be a hiatus. Sixty percent of Russians in 2007 favored revising the constitution. Putin shirked this, out of worry, he said, it might unbalance the system: "When each new head of state customizes the constitution to suit him, before you know it there will be nothing left of the state."

Putin had three questions to answer. Would his exit be irreversible, like Yeltsin's, or just a furlough? What would he do with himself once he was out of the Kremlin? And who would replace him as president or, more truthfully, who would be on the 2008 presidential ballot with his endorsement?

Putin kept his options open on the first question, not wanting to be put out to pasture in his mid-fifties. To the second, there were not so many potential answers. For a president of Russia, given the majesty of the office, any other domestic job would be a comedown. The delicate question was the third: on whom could he lean to be true to his legacy, were he to go for good, or to make way for him to come back if that was his wish?

When news of the solution broke in December 2007, Putin held his tongue on any life plans. He knew the nuts and bolts of the premier's job, having had it for four months in 1999. It would keep him in the public eye and let him keep tabs on the president. We do not know what secret handshake if any the two had about life after the tandem. Medvedev let slip in 2011, when Putin's impending return was divulged, that they had "discussed this possible turn of events when we formed our comradely union." "Possible" implies that the matter was left open and is consonant with his hints about wanting to stay put for another term.

Why precisely did the needle spin to Medvedev? Putin volunteered no explanation in 2007, other than that United Russia was in favor and "I have known him closely for more than seventeen years." Medvedev was an establishmentarian and a Putin man through and through, but so, too, were a throng of other functionaries. Putin may have felt the need to slacken the screws on society, for which Medvedev, a circumspect liberal, was more fitting than the other first deputy premier, Sergei Ivanov, an ex-spy and Putin clone. This is the omniscient and levelheaded take of the insider Pavlovsky: Putin intuited that "the country needs change, it can't be ruled by generals." With hindsight, we can say one other wheel was grinding in Putin's head. For a proven leader who was genuinely getting out, the desirable qualities in a successor would be strength and resolve. Medvedev's malleability suited a Putin loath to part with power and for whom it was an article of faith that, as he said in 2005, "weaklings get beaten."

The presidential election of March 2, 2008, was as anti-climactic as they come. Medvedev chalked up 71 percent of the national vote, within 1 percentage point of Putin's score in 2004. Inspectors from the Parliamentary Assembly of the Council of Europe noted aberrations yet said the election was best seen as a plebiscite on the past eight years: "The people of Russia voted for the stability and continuity associated with the incumbent president and the candidate promoted by him." Medvedev was inaugurated on May 7 and Putin confirmed as prime minister on May 8.

The tandem years were an opportunity squandered, a Machiavellian ploy by Putin, or a farce, depending on your point of view. Medvedev took with him into the Kremlin a more brainy, garrulous, and faddish approach, attuned to the creative class and its lingo and gadgets. As the prolific Russian-American correspondent Masha Gessen writes, he "talked of what his speechwriters thought to call 'The Four I's': institutions, infrastructure, investment, and innovation. Flashing an iPhone and, once it had been introduced, an iPad, Medvedev seemed to be trying to imbue his dense vocabulary with a modern, Western spirit." In point of fact, the third president talked up a storm about almost everything. He condensed his thoughts in "Go, Russia!," an essay in the online newspaper gazeta.ru in September 2009. It voiced displeasure at Russia's "primitive raw-materials economy, corruption, and incorrigible habit of looking for solutions to our problems to the government, to foreigners, to an invincible doctrine, to anything or anybody but ourselves." The Putin administration itself was not given an A grade: "We did not do all we ought to have in recent years, and ... not all we did was done correctly."

Under the rubric of *modernizatsiya* (modernization), Medvedev launched a flurry of reform initiatives. He declared "war on corruption" and forced federal officials to file income declarations. He took civil servants off the boards of state corporations. He enlivened the Presidential Council for Civil Society and Human Rights formed by Putin in 2002 and had parliament curb pretrial detention for suspects in economic crimes. Billions went to bank bailouts, relief for company towns, and other countercyclical measures to mitigate the 2008–9 recession. The government funded the Skolkovo Innovation Center in the Moscow suburbs, billed as Russia's rejoinder to Silicon Valley (which Medvedev visited in October 2010). In foreign policy, Medvedev responded to the Obama administration's "reset" of relations. There were palpable if unexciting benefits: a US–Russia Bilateral Presidential Commission; a New START treaty, reducing deployed strategic warheads by about one-third; and collaboration on multilateral issues such as nonproliferation, climate change, Iran, and Afghanistan. Washington worked to get Russia into the WTO in 2012, after nineteen years of negotiations.

How, then, did Medvedev's fifteen minutes of fame go awry? He did not make good on his most ballyhooed promises. For Russians who expected little, the reaction was unconcern. Where he raised hopes of positive change, the reaction was frustration, as Gessen's book conveys, with a vignette: "When Medvedev [in 2011] told a group of activist historians he would finally approve a long-stalled plan for a national museum in memory of victims of Stalinist terror, the historians dropped everything to draw up plans, draft documents, and do the work federal bureaucrats should have been doing, all to enable Medvedev to sign the decree—which he never did. What he did was keep giving speeches, promising to fight corruption and modernize the country, while nothing changed." In forthright interviews before stepping down, Medvedev admitted that nothing much had changed. About his anticorruption policy, for example, he said, "if we are talking of results, then they are . . . modest."

They were modest in part due to personal foibles. Medvedev, he confessed in interviews with the journalist Nikolai Svanidze in 2008, often formulated his ideas "as if I were giving a lecture." "One gets the impression," Svanidze wrote with some empathy, "that Medvedev the scholar takes precedence over Medvedev the politician." Bookishness found outlet in frivolous hobby projects. Examples would be the renaming of cops on the beat from the *militsiya* or militia, the Soviet term, to the European-sounding *politsiya*; subtraction of two of Russia's eleven time zones; year-round daylight saving time; and an even more ludicrous bill to lower the required membership for registration of a political party from fifty thousand to forty-five thousand. All were all the butt of jokes and cartoons; the second, third, and fourth were called off after him.

Medvedev the politician could not act freelance. Having no opportunity to build his own power and patronage base, even had he wished it, he was as dutiful a cog in the Putin machine as ever. His office was staffed by old hands who played musical chairs between the Kremlin–Old Square area and the white-marbled governmental tower a ten-minute ride away. Putin's dramaturge, Surkov, stayed in his Kremlin position until December 2011. Putin himself put in as much travel as Medvedev, gave innumerable speeches, and still did his televised hotline (Medvedev had none). The tandem's big policy success—the antidote to the economic crisis of 2008–9—was primarily worked out, publicized, and defended at trouble spots by Putin.

Nor did Medvedev strive for a separate political program. There was one contretemps in March 2011, during the Arab

Spring. Russia abstained in the UN Security Council on two motions okaying aerial attacks on the forces of the Libyan dictator, Moammar Gadhafi, to prevent him from massacring civilians. Putin publicly called the resolution a benighted "call for a crusade"; Medvedev bit back that such language was "absolutely insupportable." Gadhafi in October was mutilated and killed by paramilitaries with NATO air support. The flap over Libya blew over. Medvedev the next year castigated the UN decision and said he had been hoodwinked by Western governments.

On the majority of issues, the most we can find between Medvedev and Putin are differences of nuance and pacing. Asked about the relationship in late 2011, Medvedev put it this way, in mangled syntax: "We belong to the same political force and have very similar convictions, although we are different people with our own habits. ... Our positions are very close on most strategic questions, on all strategic questions related to the country's development, and on tactical questions, too." One gauge of his attachment to the Putin line was meek acquiescence in Putin's presidential comeback and in a more illiberal palette of policies afterward. The continued ability to work with Putin is why it is not yet time to pen his political obituary.

Why and how did Putin's line harden after he recaptured the presidency in 2012?

Medvedev's statement to a United Russia congress on September 24, 2011, that he would back Putin for a third presidential term was met by a standing ovation. "This applause," he proclaimed, "spares me the need to explain Vladimir Vladimirovich Putin's experience and authority." He was also spared the need to explain his political calculations and why he would occupy the office of prime minister about to be emptied by Putin. It took eight months for the trade to be consummated. The Duma election returned a truncated United Russia majority. Putin won the presidential election of March 4, 2012, against perfunctory opposition. He and Medvedev took their chains of office in early May.

Most items of policy under Putin redux were familiar. The proportions were unfamiliar, as a suppressive and vindictive strand gained strength. He changed the mix because his thinking had evolved and because he believed it necessary to thwart a multipronged affront to his power.

Surveys of public opinion had charted a sagging of Putin's popularity in 2011. His confidence ratings, say pollsters in the politically neutral Levada Center, flagged from 79 percent in December 2010 to 63 percent in December 2011; 51 percent thought Russia was headed in the right direction in 2010 and 38 percent in 2011. Losses were most noticeable in the big cities, among women and high earners, and in the creative class (better-educated, mobile, and digitally savvy). Research by Daniel Treisman shows the decline does not correlate with economics or any narrow grievances. The moving force was "a general loss of faith among the discontented that the Kremlin team would address the sources of their discontent. Those with grievances became less willing to give the country's leaders the benefit of the doubt."

One might surmise a 63 percent favorability rating to be envied, but Putin fastened on the trend. He also had to intercede in a parliamentary election campaign where United Russia was suddenly scavenging for votes. When the ballots for the Duma were counted on December 4, the party's stated vote share came in at 49 percent, 15 points less than in 2007, and it elected 238 out of 450 deputies, 77 fewer than in 2007. Allegations of vote rigging had been made in earlier elections, but in 2011 they were more intense and were instantly diffused on the Internet. Independent researchers were later to confirm tampering that affected maybe 7 or 8 percent of the tally. Had the official result been 40 to 45 percent, United Russia would have forfeited its legislative majority.

The grassroots response to the claims of misconduct was a political bombshell. A carnivalesque rally of sixty thousand people on Moscow's Bolotnaya (Swamp) Square was held on December 10, 2011; one hundred thousand attended another, on Sakharov Prospect on December 24. This was the loudest public uproar in the capital since 1991. Unhappy citizens and a Who's Who of oppositionists waved banners and took in speeches and performance art. Many had been alerted by social media. The celebrity TV talk-show host Kseniya Sobchak, daughter of Putin's patron in the 1990s, was a vocal picketer and spokesperson. Organizers demanded that a new election be held and impediments to opposition parties be lifted.

The post-tandem Putin made countermoves on four fronts. For one thing, he rallied all available resources to ensure his election as president in March 2012. He settled for 64 percent of the vote (versus 72 percent in 2004). Skullduggery, by all accounts, was less rampant than in December.

Second, while sticking to its guns on the validity of the Duma election, the government did enact changes to electoral law. Retracing its steps, it eased registration of political parties; accredited parties rose in number from seven in the spring of 2012 to seventy-six by late 2013 and seventy-eight by 2015. The 225 territorial districts were reintroduced for succeeding Duma elections and the threshold for representation on the party lists lowered from 7 percent to 5 percent. And, by popular demand, Russia reverted to direct popular election of provincial governors and heads of republics.

Thirdly, and contrarily, Putin yet again tightened the screws politically. A boisterous inauguration-eve demonstration on Bolotnaya Square led to pushing and shoving with the police. Four hundred protesters were detained and interrogated; twenty-eight were charged and twelve given prison sentences. New codes broadened the legal definition of high treason, levied stiff fines for unsanctioned gatherings and disturbing the peace, forced all Runet blogs and social media sites with three thousand visitors to register as media outlets, required online companies to store users' data on Russian servers, and gave government bureaus the right to block politically objectionable online content (for example, calls for public actions). In most cases of blocking and filtering websites, Freedom House reports in *Freedom on the Net 2015*, "the legal framework offers no clear criteria for evaluating the legality of content, and public authorities do not always offer a detailed explanation for blocking decisions. The lack of precise guidelines sometimes leads telecom operators, which are responsible for complying with blocking orders, to carry out the widest blocking possible so as to avoid fines and threats to their licenses." On a scale of 0 to 100, where 0 is the best score and 100 the worst, Internet freedom in Russia has deteriorated from an index of 49 in 2009 to 52 in 2012 and 62 in 2015 (in the 75th percentile for the sixty-five countries surveyed).

Leaving nothing to chance, Putin, fourthly, grounded his regime in conservative social values that go over and above his long-standing infatuation with the sturdy state. He sidled in this direction when he sent out feelers to provincial, blue-collar Russia before the 2012 election. The arrest in February and the trial that summer of five members of the feminist rock band Pussy Riot, for an impious performance in the Cathedral of Christ the Savior (a video clip, "Punk Prayer—Mother of God, Chase Putin Away!," went viral), were well received by the hierarchy of the Russian Orthodox Church. Nadezhda Tolokonnikova and Maria Alyokhina, convicted of "hooliganism motivated by religious hatred," were sent to prison for two years.

Anti-Western and anti-American content deluged the official media as the Obama–Medvedev reset with the United States went into disuse. In September 2012 the US Agency for International Development was ordered out of Russia, on a few weeks' notice. A Dima Yakovlev Law, in response to the Americans' Magnitsky Act punishing Russian factotums held to be responsible for the ordeal of accountant and lawyer Sergei Magnitsky, was approved in December 2012. Magnitsky, who had acted for a Guernsey-based investment fund, Hermitage Capital Management, died in a Moscow prison in 2009.

Dissonantly, the chairman of Hermitage, William Browder, was the grandson of a Stalin-era general secretary of the Communist Party U.S.A. The Yakovlev law, named after a Russian-born baby who died in Virginia in 2008, forbade all adoptions of Russian orphans by Americans. A bill in 2013 proscribed the "propagandizing of nontraditional sexual relationships" to minors. Another set down fines for people who "offend the religious feelings of believers," and added up to three years in prison if the offensive act takes place in a place of worship. In 2014, 5 million employees in security and law enforcement were barred from visiting the United States, and 107 countries that have extradition treaties with it, without permission from superiors.

In his speechifying, Putin has stirred tried-and-true themes of patriotism and remembrance together with heretofore embryonic civilizational themes about God, traditional families (never mind that he and the Russian first lady divorced in 2014), and primordial ethnicity. In a televised speech to the Valdai Discussion Club in September 2013, he took a swipe at moral "degradation and primitivism" in the EU and the United States. "As we can see, many Euroatlantic countries are rejecting their roots, including the Christian values on which Western civilization rests. They are refuting moral principles and all traditional identities: national, cultural, religious, and even sexual. They are implementing policies that equate multichild families with same-sex partnerships, faith in God with Satan worship." His Russia, like Byzantium or Muscovy—and with a resemblance to the conservative thought of Viktor Orbán of Hungary and Jarosław Kaczyński of Poland in the 2010s— would be a bastion of the old and true ways against a debauched West. "Without the values implanted in Christianity and other world religions, without the standards of morality that have taken shape over millennia, human dignity will be lost. We consider it natural and correct to defend these values. One must respect every minority's right to be different, but the rights of the majority must not be placed in question."

To demonize the post–2012 Putin would be too easy. Russia's silent majority does have values and interests that deserve respect. There have been no roundups of dissidents and no extrajudicial killings. Tolokonnikova and Alyokhina were set free under a presidential amnesty in 2013, on the twentieth anniversary of the constitution, which also pardoned Mikhail Khodorkovsky and dropped charges against eleven of the Bolotnaya defendants. Contra some hyperbolic reporting in the West, Putin is not waging a holy war on gays. There has been almost no enforcement of the 2013 statute, which makes the propagation of alternative sexuality a misdemeanor and not a crime. The Yeltsin-period decriminalization of homosexual acts has not been reversed. For what it is worth, 85 percent of Russian adults in a 2013 Levada Center poll were antipathetic to same-sex marriage and 87 percent to gay pride parades in their cities.

By the same token, it would be shortsighted to sugarcoat Putin's behavior. Conservatism should not be equated with repression, and particular Russian measures may have unique rationales, but in their totality they aim to hem in personal freedoms and muzzle dissent. "There is discussion at present of a new social contract," gazeta.ru wrote despondently on September 14, 2015. If the contract once was "about a majority of Russians trading improvements in the quality of life and higher incomes for apoliticism"—sausage for freedom—then what is in store for Russians tomorrow is "stability at a lower level, more like Soviet stagnation."

In its report on Russia in 2014, Freedom House marked its score for civil liberties down to 6. "Russia's civil liberties rating," says Freedom House, "declined from 5 to 6 due to expanded media controls, a dramatically increased level of propaganda on state-controlled television, and new restrictions on the ability of some citizens to travel abroad." Russia's composite rating was now 6, its worst score yet and putting it on the same shelf as Afghanistan, Burma, the Democratic Republic of Congo, and Iran.

6

A BETTER EDITION OF ITSELF?

Why did Russia annex Crimea?

The short- and long-term challenges facing Russia are legion. In the short haul, one of the most daunting is to sort through repercussions of events to its immediate southwest. The decision to commandeer Crimea from independent Ukraine in 2014, belying legal obligations and international norms, was the most breathtaking and incendiary yet taken by Putin and his power elite.

Crimea has been described as a bauble dangling from the northern shores of the Black Sea, connected to the mainland by the slender Isthmus of Perekop. Its 10,400 square miles is just about the area of Belgium or the state of Maryland. The bulk of it is arid steppeland; the southern coast offers picturesque outcrops and cliffs, beaches, palm trees, and a balmy climate. A cultural crossroads since antiquity, Crimea passed in the 1400s into the hands of the Muslim and slave-trading Crimean Tatar Khanate, under the sultan in Istanbul. Catherine the Great subjugated it in 1783 and had a naval station and fort built at Sevastopol, at the peninsula's tip. Crimean Tatars were driven out in large numbers at the time, by force or fear, to the Ottoman Empire. It was on an inspection trip to Crimea that Catherine's governor-general and paramour, Grigorii Potyomkin, tried to impress her with his portable "Potyomkin village." The two-year siege of the Sevastopol garrison was the fiercest battle of the Crimean War and the topic of Tolstoy's

Sevastopol Sketches and of Russia's first full-length movie, directed by Vasilii Goncharov, in 1911. Crimea was a summer playground for the nobility and royal family, and its seascapes inspired Russian writers and painters. During the Civil War, it was a last-chance sanctuary for the White armies. Nicholas II's Renaissance-style Livadia Palace was the venue Stalin chose for the Yalta Conference of 1945.

Under the Soviets, Crimea was an autonomous republic or ASSR (in recognition of the Crimean Tatars) in the RSFSR, its economy centered on agriculture, vacationing and health spas, and servicing the navy. From 1923 to 1938, Moscow, cooperating with the Joint Distribution Committee and American Jewish donors, encouraged the formation of Jewish agricultural settlements, and suggestions were put before the Politburo to lay out a "Soviet Zion." After two years of German and Romanian occupation, Stalin and Lavrentii Beria sent away the Tatar indigenes to Uzbekistan in 1944 as collective punishment, and the republic was demoted to an oblast. The Tatars were kept from returning until 1989, by when non-Tatars had tilled their former fields and lived in their former homes for forty-five years; the procrastination bred an unshakable distrust of all things Soviet and Russian. For many human rights campaigners, the problem of the Tatars of Crimea was "the issue that first sensitized them to the national question."

In February 1954 Nikita Khrushchev and the CPSU Presidium took the step of deeding Crimea to Soviet Ukraine. Uncontentious at the time, the decision was partly homage to the tercentenary of the Treaty of Pereyaslav (between Alexei I and the Ukrainian Cossacks) and partly about economic planning. There was talk in the perestroika period about a reversal of the 1954 ruling. Mikhail Gorbachev was opposed, telling the Politburo in July 1987 it "would create a fissure in a place where it would not at all suit our purposes now, that is, within the Slavic nucleus of the 'socialist empire.'"

Crimea's land link was with Ukraine. Across it a North Crimean Canal, to siphon off Dnieper water for rice growing and vineyards, was dug between 1957 and 1971. Crimea was separated from the RSFSR's Krasnodar krai by the Kerch Strait; a rickety bridge jerrybuilt during the war was washed out by ice floes in 1945. But culturally and linguistically Crimea remained a distinctively Russian abode. Ethnic Russians were 67 percent of the population in the 1989 USSR census and 60 percent in the 2001 Ukrainian census; ethnic Ukrainians were 26 percent and 24 percent, and the returned Tatars 2 percent and 10 percent. Seventy-seven percent of Crimeans in 2011, and 60 percent of Crimea's Ukrainians, considered Russian their native language.

A separatist movement in the early 1990s drew interest from nationalists and parliamentarians in Russia. The pre World War II republic was relegalized by Ukraine in 1992; in 1994 Yurii Meshkov, an ethnic Russian proponent of peaceable reunification with Moscow, was elected its president. When Kiev called off an independence referendum in March 1995 and removed him from office, the Yeltsin administration gave Meshkov asylum but did not demur. The Yeltsin–Kuchma treaty of 1997 left the Crimean issue dormant but for frictions over Black Sea Fleet armaments (Kiev had veto rights over all upgrades), lighthouses, and customs inspections. Russia's anxiety about Chechnya made it think twice about throwing any post-Soviet borders into question.

The presidential tenure of Viktor Yushchenko was a trough for the broader relationship between the two countries. Elected in the course of the Orange Revolution of 2004, he pushed for NATO membership—unthinkable in the 1990s—and an economic turn toward Europe. Tiffs over pricing of natural gas led to Russian deliveries being cut short in 2006 and 2009. Viktor Yanukovych, the 2004 runner-up who was elected president in 2010, propitiated the Kremlin by foreswearing NATO and spinning out the Sevastopol lease to 2042, but sat on the fence in economics, playing along with the European Union's Eastern Partnership program. In 2013 he was set to sign a free trade and association agreement with the Europeans, having rebuffed repeated demands from Putin, backed by threats of economic reprisals, to join the Russian-led Customs Union.

The EU agreement would have been unpalatable to the Russian Federation but not a casus belli. In the event, Yanukovych's government in November 2013 put it in limbo in order to haggle further with Moscow. Pro-European demonstrations blew up on the Maidan, the location of the Orange Revolution protests. When riot squads turned clubs, flash grenades, and tear gas on a meeting the night of November 30, the movement radicalized, called for Yanukovych's resignation, and organized sit-ins at official buildings. About one hundred lives were lost in January and February, mostly to police snipers but some to marchers with Molotov cocktails and firearms. Attempts to broker a coalition government and early elections came to naught when the Maidan crowd booed down a power-sharing agreement and public order in Kiev collapsed. On February 22, 2014, Yanukovych made a getaway from his rococo presidential estate. Within days he was at a Kremlin safe house near Moscow. One of the Ukrainian parliament's first decisions after his departure was to annul a 2012 law making Russian a second official language.

The Americans and Europeans were euphoric about the turnabout and recognized the "Euromaidan" government pro tem. For the Russians it was an "unconstitutional coup" by extreme nationalists (who were undeniably movers and shakers on the Maidan) and fascists (who were much less in evidence). Whatever the view from Washington and Brussels, Yanukovych was the legitimately elected president, well within his rights to change government policy, and his overthrow was closer to mobocracy than to Jeffersonian democracy. But public disgust with Yanukovych was real, whatever the view from Moscow, and his decision to mow down demonstrators and passersby was a callous and maladroit abuse of police power.

Putin disclosed in an on-camera interview in March 2015 that the choice to act in Crimea was made at an all-night brainstorming, with four unnamed colleagues, over how to get

Yanukovych to refuge. It broke up the morning of February 23, the day of the closing ceremony of the Sochi Olympics, whereupon he told his aides, "The way it has gone in Ukraine, we have to start on returning Crimea to Russia. We cannot leave this territory and the people who live there to fend for themselves under the roller of the [Ukrainian] nationalists." If it were so, he made the move on the supposition that ethnic Russians and Russophones were on the verge of grievous harm, which they were not. As best we can tell, Putin's keynote speech on Crimea on March 18, 2014, is more reliable. It situates the gambit in geopolitics and waxes indignant over years of ill-treatment of Russia by the West: "They're incessantly painting us into a corner because we have an independent position, because we stick to it and call things like they are without hypocrisy. But everything has its limit. In Ukraine, our Western partners crossed a line.... Russia found itself in a position from which it could not retreat. If you compress a spring as far as it will go, it will snap back hard."

From this standpoint, Crimea, a glittering prize in its own right, was the tool closest at hand for snapping back against a perfidious Ukraine and a West heedless of Russian interests. Pushback was an easy sell internally because Crimea housed so many Russians and Russophones and because of its beauty and cultural connotations, the whimsicality of the 1954 transfer, and memories of imperial grandeur and wars won and lost. Among the Crimeans, not a few were bound to come out for union with Russia once they saw it as a credible possibility. Russia had forces on site, about half of the twenty-five thousand permissible under the 1997 treaty, and planeloads and boatloads more a few minutes away. And the Russian sword had been sharpened by post-2008 reequipping and reform.

The geostrategic variable was by and large about securing the naval base in perpetuity and getting the chance to modernize the fleet, which Ukraine had blocked under articles in the 1990s leasing agreement. But the General Staff in Moscow could not have been uninterested in Crimea's 470 miles of seaboard.

The Black Sea coastline under the effective control of the federation was to grow from the 260 miles inherited from the
RSFSR in 1991 to 860 miles, counting Crimea and Abkhaziya,
Georgia, a Russian protectorate since the five-day war of 2008;
Ukraine's shrunk from 1,090 miles to 620, and Georgia's from
200 miles to 70. The Kerch Strait, over which Russia now has
undivided control, is egress for the Sea of Azov, a saline lake
fed by the Don River; the Don waterway has a large catch-
ment basin in European Russia and a canal connection to the
Volga and Caspian. And Moscow claims under the Law of the
Sea Treaty of 1982 a thirty-six-thousand-square-mile economic
zone in a semicircle around Crimea. The oil and gas reserves
beneath the seabed may be worth a fortune.

Tactically, it went like clockwork. Anti-Euromaidan protests
broke out in Sevastopol on February 23. On February 27–28
well-coached marksmen in green uniforms without national
insignia—commandos from Russian special forces—took hold
of public buildings and the airport in the Crimean capital,
Simferopol. The Federation Council in Moscow authorized
Putin to use force in Ukraine until "normalization" there, and
on March 2 the Russian fleet and airlifted troops began to force
the surrender of Ukrainian ships and military units. The republican legislature set an independence referendum, first for
May 25, then pushed forward in unbecoming haste to March
30 and finally March 16; a dubious 96 percent were said to vote
on the 16th for separation. The morning after, the Crimean
authorities, claiming self-determination, requested voluntary
"accession" (*prisoyedineniye*) to the Russian Federation—the
wording "annexation" was studiously avoided. This was duly
accomplished by statute on March 21, with Crimea admitted
as Russia's twenty-second republic and Sevastopol separately
as its third federal city. On March 24 the new Ukrainian government ordered its remaining forces to withdraw.

The solitary person killed was a Ukrainian ensign; three civilians died in a street mêlée. The commander of the Ukrainian
navy, Rear Admiral Denis Berezovsky (no relation to the

oligarch), defected to the Russians after twenty-four hours on duty, as did three-quarters of all Ukrainian servicemen and officers in Crimea. Russia hunkered down to internalizing Crimea administratively: a ninth federal district, Russian passports, a Russian area code for telephones, Moscow time. Crimeans first voted in a Russian regional election in September (70 percent for United Russia). A minicensus in October 2014 registered 65 percent of them as ethnic Russian, 15 percent as Ukrainian, and 10 percent as Crimean Tatar.

If the results were clear tactically, strategically they were not. A low-hanging fruit had been plucked, but with tremendous reverberations and at a tremendous cost.

What are the repercussions of the Ukraine crisis?

Ukraine is a lower-middle-income country with a 2013 GDP 8 percent the size of Russia's in US dollars, GDP per capita at 27 percent of the Russian level, and high foreign indebtedness—all this before its economy wasted away by up to one-quarter in 2014–15. The countries share a 1,230-mile land border. Russia is nuclear-armed and outspends Ukraine on defense by thirty to one. The mismatch in hard-power terms is why governments in Kiev never ratified the CIS charter of 1991 and have maintained their distance from Moscow and counterbalanced third parties against it. The Ukrainian domestic political scene is convoluted and changeable. Interregional fissures have been the most profound. They grow out of a past divided between empires, with the east and south sharing more history with Russia and the west and center more with East-Central Europe.

The Euromaidan revolution ignited months of unrest and abraded the self-control that had damped down previous Ukrainian set-tos. Even before the swallowing of Crimea was complete, antigovernment demonstrators took over town halls and police stations in the east, where there is a strong regional subculture among local Ukrainians, the Russian ethnic minority is about 40 percent, and the language of business and daily life is Russian. They were urged on by the Moscow media and their ranks augmented by volunteers and government agents who crossed the open border from the Russian Federation by road or rail.

The east's two frontier oblasts, Donetsk and Luhansk, are known jointly as the Donbass. With a pre-2014 population of 6.5 million, the Donbass is home turf to the Ukrainian coal, steel, and chemical industries. It was the electoral and patronage base of Yanukovych, who was Donetsk governor from 1997 to 2002, and his Party of Regions. On the Crimea example, militants proclaimed people's republics in Donetsk and Luhansk in April and organized referendums on May 11; 90 percent ostensibly endorsed independence from Ukraine, much more than forecast by public opinion surveys. The self-declared republics had self-appointed governments (elections were held months later) riven by factions. Russia provided diplomatic and logistical aid but did not take them over directly, preferring to leave them within a decentralized Ukraine as hotbeds of pro-Russianism.

In late March 2014 the interim Ukrainian government began an "antiterrorist operation" in the Donbass with regular army forces and militia battalions. The oligarch elected president on May 25, Petro Poroshenko, tried a ceasefire but soon called it off and went for the military solution. Pitched battles raged back and forth all summer and Ukrainian units advanced. The separatists, who may have numbered thirty thousand in the field, pretended to have taken all their heavy weapons in battle, but there was no hiding that Russia was also supplying matériel and intelligence and that Russian officers and soldiers were with them in force (some covering their tracks by taking leave from active duty), as were mercenaries, Cossack squadrons, and Chechen Kadyrovites. Moscow has hotly and futilely disclaimed official involvement.

The insurrectionaries regrouped in the last ten days of August 2014. With their help, Russian firepower and paratroopers broke the back of the Ukrainian offensive. A ceasefire hashed out at Minsk on September 5 broke down and was succeeded by another on February 12, 2015. Nine thousand four hundred were known dead in the Donbass by May 2016 and twenty-two thousand injured. Gunfire and raids continued along the ceasefire line. The region's physical plant was in ruins. About half of the population was under rebel control, about a quarter had relocated, and a quarter was in Kiev-overseen areas. Opposition investigators reported in May 2015 that some 220 Russian military personnel had been killed (some Ukrainian estimates are much greater). Grieving families were getting hush money from the army—about fifty thousand dollars in exchange for signing a nondisclosure agreement.

As a result of the war, Russia found itself at loggerheads with Ukraine more than ever. Ukraine signed the EU association pact in 2014 (it went into effect in 2016) and bailed on all CIS arrangements in 2015. Parliament revoked Ukraine's neutrality law, and Poroshenko declared it should join NATO by 2022, with which a popular plurality now agrees. Ukraine and Russia have waged a beggar-thy-neighbor trade war and closed their skies to each other's flights and overflights.

The Ukrainian imbroglio also snowballed into a confrontation between Russia and the Euroatlantic nations. The West and Ukraine have the law on their side. In 1994, when Ukraine agreed to go nonnuclear, Russia (with the United States and the United Kingdom) gave its assent to a Budapest Memorandum solemnly obligating it "to refrain from the threat or use of force against the territorial integrity or political independence of Ukraine." The seizure of Crimea barefacedly defies the letter and spirit of the memorandum. It does the same with the 1997 friendship treaty, Article 2 of which upholds the territorial integrity and inviolable borders of the two countries. International law does not rule out secession, but holds that it should take place under constitutional procedures acceptable to the maternal state. No such procedures were abided by. Putin cited the separation of Kosovo from Serbia in 2008—an ill-advised action, to be sure, justified in the West by trespasses by a Belgrade regime (Milošević's) that went out of existence in 2000. Still, Russia deplored the recognition of Kosovo and never went back on it. No ex–Soviet republic other than the Baltic threesome has accepted Kosovo independence.

The United States and the EU excoriated Russia over Crimea, carnage in the Donbass, and the accidental shooting down of a Malaysian Airlines jetliner, with 298 passengers and crew, over Donetsk oblast in July 2014, by pistol-happy insurgents using Russian missiles. The United States froze the presidential commission set up in 2009 and all bilateral contacts judged nonessential. The non-Russian seven in the G8 shunned a Sochi summit and reshaped the G8 into the pre-1997 G7. Western countries voted for a resolution in the UN General Assembly describing the Crimea referendum as invalid; 100 nations voted for and 11 against; 58 abstained; 24 did not vote.

But the cudgel par excellence was economic sanctions. Visa bans and asset freezes were first slapped on Russian and pro-Russian policy makers and citizens. Successively more draconian penalties were then laid on businesses. Taking part were the United States, the EU, and nine non-EU countries (Albania, Australia, Canada, Iceland, Japan, Montenegro, Norway, New Zealand, and Switzerland). Russian banks' access to international financing was restricted, cooperation on oil exploration was hindered, and most purchasing in the defense sector stopped. As of mid-summer 2015, 160 persons were on no-admit lists. Among their number were Putin's chief of staff (Sergei Ivanov), the heads of almost every Russian security agency, the speakers of both houses of parliament, and a Soviet premier (Nikolai Ryzhkov, as a member of the Federation Council). Sanctions also homed in on businessmen said to be connected to Putin. On the lists were the aforementioned silovarchs Sergei Chemezov and Igor Sechin and, from the Ozero Dacha Cooperative, Yurii Kovalchuk, Arkadii Rotenberg, Gennadii Timchenko, and Vladimir Yakunin.

Moscow reciprocated with entry bans and in August 2014 with an embargo on food imports from the sanctioning countries. That Russians had to do without Norwegian salmon and French brie (but not French champagne—alcoholic beverages were exempted from the countersanctions) was the least of the government's worries. Crimea, which was the poorest region in Ukraine, will set back the budget tens of billions of dollars over the next decade. The federal purse has to pay pensioners and administrators at the Russian scale and update the infrastructure. The price tag for a twelve-mile road and rail bridge over the Kerch Strait, started in May 2015, could be $5–7 billion; the underwater power lines from Krasnodar completed in 2016 cost several billion; and fresh water will have to be found to replace the flow from the Dnieper into the North Crimean Canal, cut off by the Ukrainian government in April 2014. There will be extra transfusions for Russian special forces in the Donbass and for refugee aid. Foreign firms will be skittish about investing in Crimea, given sanctions and the likelihood of litigation. The long-estranged Crimean Tatars will not easily adapt. Mustafa Dzhemilev, Refat Chubarov, and some other Tatar elders opposed the annexation and have been refused entry to the peninsula by Russian border guards. Turkey has expressed support for the Tatars, though it did not join in Western sanctions over Crimea.

Worse yet for Russia was that these events coincided with an economic body blow. Caught in the pincers of weak demand and rising supply from US shale fields, crude oil on world markets cheapened from $111.87 per barrel in June 2014 (Brent monthly index) to less than $50 in January of 2015 and less than $40 in December. The depreciation of Russia's pot of gold combined with sanctions to produce a run on the ruble. From trading at 36 to the dollar in August 2014, the currency swooned to 56 to the dollar in December 2014, over 80 by January 2016, and 65 in the spring of 2016.

The crisis did not introduce any new notes to the music of Russian domestic politics but did give impetus to notes that had been there since 2000. Eighty percent of Russians agreed in polls with policy on Crimea; they were ready to support the Donbass rebels but not to take Donetsk and Luhansk into the federation. Putin convinced most citizens that the sanctions were an insult to Russian self-worth. His approval ratings, already head and shoulders above every other politician's, skyrocketed to 85 percent. Those who thought Russia was pointed in the right direction took wing from 38 percent in December 2011 to 64 percent in 2014–15, and those who took pride in their country from 53 percent to 71 percent (Levada Center), with Russia's natural wealth, history, and armed forces being the top sources of satisfaction.

This fabulous popularity, counterintuitively, was an excuse for narrow-mindedness and not for a political opening. Never in a generation has Russian leadership tried so assiduously to transform the political sphere into a security-related action site, basically by linking conformity to the government's will with allegiance to the nation. Putin's March 2014 public address on Crimea did not mince words, wafting out two trenchant phrases—"fifth column" (*pyataya kolonna*) and "traitors to the nation" (*natsional-predateli*)—that every adult in Russia knows how to parse. "Some Western politicians," he said, "pressurize us not only with sanctions but with the prospect of serious problems on our domestic front. I would like to know what they have in mind. Are they talking about some sort of fifth column, a motley bunch of traitors to the nation, or do they hope to put us in a deteriorating social and economic situation and make the public disgruntled? We consider such statements irresponsible and aggressive and will respond to them accordingly."

Are Russia and the West heading into a new Cold War?

Historical analogies have their uses. They can also be trite and misleading, and do strategists no favors. For Russia nowadays, as Andrew Monaghan of Chatham House, London, argues, we have been subjected to "a repetitive plethora of absurdly simplified explanatory images in which Russian actions are associated with, though rarely rigorously compared to," the European powers in 1914, Nazi Germany, and Brezhnev's USSR. Russian policy is "being compared to any number of indistinct events, usually the first that come to mind, cherry-picked from the last two centuries regardless of context, the role of the individuals involved, and the passing of time."

Cold War imagery prevails thus far. And, were we to judge solely by the outpouring of rhetoric, parallels can readily be found. Putin is nothing like the sharpest-beaked of Russian hawks, but his warming to hard-edged nationalism and anti-Westernism has been amply documented in this book. President Obama, addressing the UN General Assembly in September 2014, made out Russia's misbehavior in Ukraine to be the second scourge of our time, a notch less insidious than the Ebola virus and a notch more insidious than the barbarians in the Islamic State in Iraq and Syria (ISIS). Likewise reminiscent of the Cold War is animosity at the mass level. The Gallup organization found in February 2015 that Americans consider Russia enemy number one, edging out North Korea, China, and Iran. Seventy percent had an unfavorable rating of Russia in 2015; 44 percent did in 2011. In a January 2015 national survey by the Levada Center, 81 percent of Russians thought poorly or very poorly of the United States and 71 percent had a like attitude toward the EU.

And then there is the saber rattling. Not a day goes by without it. Putin mentions that he contemplated a high alert for his nuclear forces when drawing up the Crimean campaign. Russia escalates submarine patrols by 50 percent. Its supersonic jets buzz American warships and NATO planes, and disrupt civil aviation with "noncooperative" flights, transponders turned off. Iskander-M tactical ballistic missiles, nuclear-capable, are deployed to Kaliningrad oblast, in between NATO members Poland and Lithuania, and Backfire strategic bombers to Crimean airfields. Putin swaggers to an audience of the younger generation that the world should twig that "it's best not to mess with us." Russians hack the Warsaw Stock Exchange, a German steel plant, and the *New York Times*. The Kremlin publicizes drawings of a "Status-6" underwater drone for delivering dirty nuclear bombs that would douse an adversary's ports and coastline in radioactive spray.

Conversely, the United States mounts Operation Atlantic Resolve—war games against a "fictional enemy" in the Baltic states, Romania, Bulgaria, and (non-NATO) Georgia. The Pentagon prepares to preposition battle tanks and artillery for five thousand GIs in the Baltic countries and Eastern Europe. NATO's annual Saber Guardian drill, emphasizing interoperability of forces, goes through the motions in western Ukraine. The alliance plans to triple the NATO Response Force to forty thousand troops and set up small local staffs in Estonia, Latvia, Lithuania, Poland, Bulgaria, and Romania.

Beyond the bravado, the Cold War analogy gives us only so much purchase on the current scene. Twenty-first-century Russia is bereft of a universalist and transformative ideology such as lay behind Soviet behavior. It does not pose an existential threat to the United States. Its foreign policy has melded great-powerism, reactive and particularistic conservatism, and opportunistic partnership building. Much smaller in population (absolutely) and economic assets (relatively) than the USSR in its time, and without satellite states or reliable political kinsmen, the newest Russia does not have the wherewithal or the missionary spirit to carry on a worldwide struggle or to align the international system around it. It is in no position to be anyone's great Other. The mantra of the Foreign Policy Concept of 2000 was multipolarity, not the bipolarity of the Cold War. Moreover, it is an objective fact—with the rise of China and of regional powers (like India, Brazil, and Nigeria), the crisis of the euro, pandemonium in the Middle East, and the intensification of transborder issues such as global warming and migration—that our world is becoming terrifically more complicated. It outgrew bipolarity a generation ago and is now outgrowing unipolarity.

While Russia likes to see itself as a global actor, much of its attention will be grabbed by happenings in its backyard. The myriad rivalries in Eurasia—entrapping Russia, one or several former Soviet republics, and an outside party—differ from the Cold War altercations over out-of-the-way Vietnam or Angola. They are harder to deal with psychologically because they are within shouting distance, producing, so to say, geopolitical claustrophobia. "I found myself reminding our American friends," Putin said of the fireworks over Ukraine's association agreement with the EU, "how they always, directly or from behind the scenes, exert influence on our relations with our neighbors. At times you don't even know whether it is better to talk with the governments of some of these states or with their American protectors and sponsors."

From the clash over Ukraine, the fallout continues. The best to be hoped in the near future may be that the second Minsk accord, of February 2015, will hold—no party has implemented it—and the seesaw will subside into a deadlock over Crimea, with a legal war of attrition bringing lawsuits and property seizures on the side, and a gently unfreezing conflict in the Donbass, one degree Fahrenheit at a time. The darkest fear is that fighting will spread and outside powers will get directly involved.

Even if a veneer of calm sticks, loose ends will remain. Is Ukraine really to be a candidate for admission to NATO, crossing a red line for Russia? Was the Crimea landgrab a never-to-be-repeated act or the first installment of systematic irredentism (reoccupying lost chunks of the homeland)? Does the fracas in the Donbass, a region Putin says Russia does not covet, presage a policy of pan-nationalism (asserting the right to protect conationals in other states)? If so, would the conationals be ethnic Russians only or the more expansive category of Russophones, who are not necessarily ethnic Russians?

And what countries would be in the crosshairs of a more belligerent Russia? Presuming that ethnic Russians are the concern, the bullseyes, beyond Ukraine, would be Kazakhstan (3.7 million Russians, 22 percent of the population) and Belarus (780,000 Russians, 8 percent). But these are the CIS states friendliest to Moscow and the last it should want to offend. In Kazakhstan the Russian population is concentrated in the north and east, abutting southern Siberia; in Belarus it is weakly territorialized. A million Russians live in the Baltic republics, chiefly in Latvia (520,000, 26 percent) and Estonia (330,000, 24 percent). Here again, the Russians are scattered, with almost half in the capital cities of Riga and Tallinn. A strategy for playing on the emotions of Russians in Belarus and the Baltic would have to be very different from the tack taken in Ukraine in 2014.

Estonia, Latvia, and Lithuania are members of NATO, which brings up Western countermeasures and some phantasmagoric screenplays for conflict. The alliance would be duty-bound by Article 5 of the North Atlantic Treaty of 1949 to rally to the Balts' defense if they came under armed onslaught. A neocontainment paradigm would be a preventative against such an attack if one was imminent. It would not fit so well with some of the mischief Russia might cook up if it throws caution and common sense overboard and probes Western defenses or tries recklessly to destabilize adjacent states. Iran-level economic sanctions could be implemented, effectively shutting the Russian Federation out of the global financial system, but these would push it deeper into a shell and lessen Western influence for the future.

Russia also has choices about its future place in the world that are not first and foremost about its erstwhile empire. Putin used to speak glowingly about a Greater Europe, or Union of Europe, promoting economic cooperation from the Atlantic to the Urals—without convergence on values. Medvedev as president raved over "a unified Europe without dividing lines" and a new security treaty as its footing. The EU's enlargement and its Eastern Partnership, seeded in 2009 as outreach to the post-Soviet republics lying between it and Russia, were in the eyes of the Moscow power structure one-sided intrusions into Russia's comfort zone, and there was discordance over EU antimonopoly laws in the energy sector. Ukraine then put Russia and the EU wildly out of sync. Putin's cancellation in December 2014 of the South Stream pipeline (under the Black Sea and through the Balkans) has slammed the door on expansion of energy sales to Europe and on Russian Europeanism.

Souring on the West piqued Russian enthusiasm for looking farther out to the east, past the EEU. Rapprochement with the emerging though flawed goliath, China, began in the security sphere with Russian participation in the Shanghai Cooperation Organization, a Beijing franchise, in 2001. The two began holding joint military exercises in 2005. By now, however, the nub of the relationship is money. What might have appeared like a Russian feint or juggling act against Europe looks like a change of grand strategy in geoeconomics. The signs are plentiful: a thirty-year gas deal for several hundred billion dollars in May 2014, albeit at discounted prices; permission for Chinese companies to lease Siberian farmland; Chinese investment in railroads, seaports, and Arctic shipping; negotiations to link the EEU and China's Silk Road Economic Belt, a road corridor to Europe; an agreement to produce a wide-body passenger jet together; and chatter of a Greater Eurasia "from Shanghai to St. Petersburg."

China is also privy to multilateral frameworks where Russia is sinking effort and prestige. Most noteworthy is the BRICS interstate group. Russia was the moving spirit for BRIC (Brazil, Russia, India, and China) in 2006 and accommodated the founding confab, in Yekaterinburg, in 2009; South Africa, as S, came on board in 2010. The BRICS countries represent 43 percent of the world's population and 30 percent of its economy at purchasing power parity (20 percent in nominal dollar value). They promote trade and investment within the quintet but also "a fairer world order." Russia now references itself to this Global South group rather than to the Global North G7, which unceremoniously ejected it in 2014. There are differences country by country, but the BRICS partners have been as one in calling for reforms to the IMF and international finances. At their 2015 talks in Ufa, Bashkortostan, they resolved to support Brazil, India, and South Africa for seats on the UN Security Council. The Ufa meeting, and creation of a New Development Bank with startup capital of $100 billion, to be headquartered in Shanghai, mark "the transformation of the BRICS club into a nascent non-Western concert of major powers that focuses on their priorities, not those of Washington or Brussels."

What is the significance of the Russian intervention in Syria?

Putin's intervention in the Syrian civil war lacks the concussive quality of his behavior in Ukraine. It is nevertheless a telltale departure, as the first use of Russian military might outside Eurasia since 1991.

The campaign began with airstrikes on September 30, 2015. Jets lifted off from a Syrian base at Humaymin, near Latakia, on the Mediterranean coast, secretively filled with Russian equipment and personnel. The announced objective was to go after the ISIS (Islamic State) formation that controls eastern Syria and western Iraq, and "other terrorist groups." Five thousand Russians dug in at Humaymin, at a deep-water naval depot in Tartus, and at several other locations, bringing with them artillery and about eighty fixed-wing aircraft and attack helicopters. Long-range bombers from airfields in southern Russia, and cruise missiles from warships in the Caspian Sea and submarines in the Mediterranean, also saw action. The air force conducted nine thousand sorties between September 2015 and March 14, 2016, when Putin began a partial pullout.

Russian interest in the Middle East dates back to the 1700s. The emperor staked a right of guardianship over the Orthodox Christian subjects of the Ottomans, and their holy sites. A quarrel over the Church of the Nativity in Bethlehem was the trigger of the Crimean War. During the Cold War, Hafez al-Assad, the father of the current president (who spent a year in the USSR training as a pilot), gave Moscow access to Tartus, a twenty-year friendship treaty, and weapons contracts for his army. But the relationship had its ups and downs, with divergences over trade and the Arab–Israeli impasse. Bashar al-Assad, the ophthalmologist who took over from his father in 2000, got Russia to write off three-quarters of the Soviet-period debt and drifted its way as he grew more isolated after the eruption of the civil war in 2011. Russia armed the beleaguered Assad and, with China, blocked UN Security Council resolutions that would have condemned or sanctioned him.

Putin has been less than candid about the motivations behind the operation. Early on, he insisted that the central aim was to take on Russian jihadists in Syria, predominantly from the North Caucasus republics, and prevent them from returning home. This is debatable, since denial of readmission to the Russian Federation would assuredly be much easier than locating and destroying these roving warriors on foreign soil. The same applies to fighters from CIS countries in Central Asia, whose citizens can enter Russia visa-free but are subject to tracking.

Reading between the lines of presidential rhetoric, and taking Russian military actions as given, there is no question that the primary goal was to stave off the fall of the Assad government, fighting for its life through the most merciless of methods, and thereby to act out Putin's declarative doctrine of multipolarity. It came to pass that the other "terrorists" in the sights of the Sukhoi fighters and bombers were any armed outfit opposed to the Syrian regime. Assad was to be kept alive and in the presidential palace, and an end put to erosion of his administration's physical control over land and people (three-quarters of Syria's territory and one-third of its population were out of its grasp when the Russian planes arrived). If and when there was an endgame for the war, Moscow meant to be in on the process, be it in negotiations over a transitional government or in partition of the country.

Several subsidiary objectives were also in play. One was to draw the Western alliance into strategic cooperation and to deflect attention from the row over Ukraine, although this logic would not have led inevitably to the Syrian theater. Another was to demonstrate Russia's credibility as a power that stands by partners in need. And Putin wanted to flaunt the capabilities of his new-look armed forces, in front of geopolitical rivals and potential purchasers of Russian hardware.

Russia has achieved no small measure of success in Syria. Bashar al-Assad and his army stopped retreating within weeks of the first Russian strikes and racked up a series of victories, with several thousand square miles of territory back under their control. Contrary to Barack Obama's prediction in October 2015, the Russian military has not been "stuck in a quagmire" in Syria. The blitzkrieg is better likened to the American campaign in Afghanistan in 2001–2—"quick, effective, and strategically transformational." A fragile "cessation of hostilities" brokered by Russian Foreign Minister Sergei Lavrov and US Secretary of State John Kerry took effect on February 27, 2016. Peace talks mediated by a UN envoy began in Geneva several weeks later.

Russia also made progress on its collateral objectives. The United States and other Western countries have bargained with it and through it to bring about the ceasefire and preliminary negotiations over a settlement. Assad has obligingly attested to the Russians' reliability. They are, he says, "principled" and have been "sincere and transparent in their relationship with us," unlike the deceitful United States, which "abandons its allies, abandons its friends." No less gratifying to Moscow, the Russian military, compared to the Georgia war, "appears to have made great strides in increasing operational tempo and improving inter-service integration." "It has also made significant advances in its ability to carry out expeditionary operations," and has showcased precision-guided munitions, nighttime combat, surveillance drones, jamming equipment, land-attack cruise missiles, and its airborne early warning and control system. Six weeks into the campaign, Russian television displayed Putin and Defense Minister Shoigu being briefed in a spanking new National Defense Management Center in Moscow, seated in a three-tiered amphitheater that looked like a set from a James Bond movie.

The complications and risks are manifold. In Russia, popular support for the intervention has never been more than lukewarm. In the field, Russia is subject to the vagaries of war, and of a conflict in which the boundaries, strategies, and weapons of customary interstate warfare do not apply. On October 31, 2015, a homemade bomb, set by an ISIS-affiliated group, tore to shreds a Russian charter jet over the Sinai Peninsula. Two hundred and twenty-four passengers (mostly vacationers at an Egyptian resort) and the crew were killed, in the goriest act of terror against Russia since Beslan in 2004. Other terrorist strikes are apt to follow, and to overflow the lines between the domestic political arena and the international.

Furthermore, Russia must navigate treacherous waters in its dealings with fellow players. Rallying to Assad's side, it has made common cause with a major Middle East state, Iran, and with the nonstate, Lebanese-based Hezbollah movement. Both champion a neotraditional and belligerent version of the Shia branch of Islam, from which the Alawite sect of the current Syrian leadership is a sideshoot. The present Shia-dominated government of Iraq is also part of the coalition for some purposes. Arrayed against them are the Sunni Arab extremists in ISIS and more temperate Sunni groups; ethnic Kurds (some of whom have been willing to cooperate with Russia) and Turkmen tribesmen; Turkey; Arab League countries with Sunni majorities; and the United States, France, and Britain. It is not lost on Kremlin strategists that 95 percent of Russian Muslims are adherents of Sunni Islam and only 5 percent of Shia Islam. In the Middle East setting, particularly worrisome is the tense relationship with Sunni Muslim Turkey. Russia is Turkey's second-ranking trade partner and has hoped to route a future Black Sea gas pipeline through Anatolia to the

European market. The downing of a Russian fighter jet that strayed into Turkish airspace on November 23, 2015, was indicative of the dangers that await. Moscow's response was to strike out economically at Ankara and position at Humaymin an S-400 surface-to-air missile system—a cutting-edge Anti-Access/Area Denial (A2/AD) technology—whose range encompasses most of Syria and half of Israeli airspace.

A question mark continues to hang over cooperation between Russia and the West on Syria. The bad blood between them since 2012 pushes against any meeting of the minds. But revulsion at the tactics of ISIS, and at the bedlam it is making in the Levant, North Africa, and Europe, pushes the other way. In 1941 the United States and Britain elected to go into battle against Nazi Germany in coalition with the Soviet Union, as the lesser evil. Collaboration with Russia and, obliquely, with a Syrian president who has used chemical weapons and barrel bombs against his people, has emerged as necessary in order to overcome the greater evils of war without end and the Islamic State.

Can Russia's economy be modernized?

The economic perfect storm set off in 2014 and the recession that followed through 2016 left the Russian government with its hands full. Economic indicators went downhill across the board, with auto sales, for example, off 40 percent from their 2012 high; inflation was up and investment down; 40 percent fewer Russians vacationed abroad in 2015 than in 2014. President Putin, Prime Minister Medvedev and his ministers, and the Russian Central Bank have kept the crisis in check through budgetary austerity, a free float of the ruble (maintaining foreign exchange reserves), recapitalization of insolvent financial houses, and substitution of domestic production for imports in industry and agriculture.

If the political dust over Ukraine settles, Western sanctions may be lifted or watered down. But world oil prices will not rebound apace. The Russian economy was struggling even before 2014. Growth after the 2008–9 downturn had been sluggish, falling from 4 percent in 2010 to 0.6 percent in 2014. The stats testify to an outdated economic model—a conceptual cul-de-sac of the regime's own making—and to recalcitrant structural problems.

Economic and political systems are interlaced. So is economic modernization inconceivable without a political metamorphosis? One fine day, in the best of all worlds or in a post-Putin Russia, a grand reform coalition could set out to modernize the economy and open up the political system all at once. But there is no hard and fast link. Undemocratic governments have latitude to adjust economic policy and performance.

Putin has reserved a role in his administration and entourage for the so-called in-system liberals. Their roots go back to the glory days of the 1990s, and they are regulars at the World Economic Forum in Davos, Switzerland. Illustrative figures are Alexei Kudrin (former finance minister), German Gref (head of Sberbank), and Arkadii Dvorkovich (deputy premier for energy). The in-system liberals are pragmatic about working within the political arrangements such as they are and focus on economic advancement, reasoning that development and a solid middle class will be a good base for political change. Reformist papers come nonstop out of state institutions like the Higher School of Economics (where the dean of Russian economists, Yevgenii Yasin, holds court in his eighties) and the Presidential Academy of the National Economy and Public Administration, and independent think tanks like Kudrin's Civic Initiatives Committee, the Gaidar Institute for Economic Policy (named after Yegor Gaidar, who died young in 2009), and INSOR (the Institute of Contemporary Development) under Igor Yurgens.

Putin's administration also shelters a forceful mercantilist and protectionist group keyed to the public sector and defense industry. Its highest-profile members are Dmitrii Rogozin, the deputy premier for the military–industrial complex, and presidential aide Sergei Glazyev. Many siloviks and extreme rightists who do not make economic policy empathize with their point of view. A leading NGO of this persuasion is the Izborsk Club, chaired by ultranationalist writer Alexander Prokhanov. It counts among its members controversialists Mikhail Leontyev and Natalya Narochnitskaya, Archimandrite Tikhon Shevkunov (the abbot of a Moscow monastery and reputedly Putin's father-confessor), and Minister of Culture Vladimir Medinskii. A more restrained and economics-centered group is the Stolypin Club (of "realistic free-marketeers") to which Glazyev and Boris Titov, the head of Business Russia, belong.

It is well within Putin's power to invest a Kudrin, Gref, or Dvorkovich as head of a government that would grasp the nettle of a 2010s round of neoliberal reform. Why might he want to? His interests pull him in contradictory directions. The control freak in him wants to take a pass on reform; the realist, nationalist, and geopolitical gladiator in him would be tempted to take a crack at it. The dismal economic statistics pre-Crimea do not lie. No amount of patriotic chest thumping will alter the cold facts.

An in-system reform thrust would be about resumption of progress toward an intensive development model. Labor costs preclude the Chinese strategy of competing in low-wage manufacturing for global supply chains. Russia needs to diversify away from hydrocarbon and mineral exports and toward the knowledge economy while still cashing in on its bounteous resource endowment.

A moderate reform strategy would keep prudent fiscal management and system-neutral initiatives like expanding trade with China. Well-chosen plans to overhaul the transportation and communications infrastructure should have a place. An ambitious undertaking on rule-of-law problems would be unavoidable (see the discussion below). Property rights sorely need the formal bulwark they currently lack—a proposition repeated ad nauseam by Russian reformers. As Stanislav

Markus's analysis shows, these rights are prone to abridgment less by the state principal in Moscow than by unscrupulous lower-tier agents—piranhas, not sharks. "Acting with impunity, they are voracious mini-beasts, as lethal in groups as the shark ... [which] never coordinate their attacks and habitually attack creatures larger than themselves."

The legal measures most utilized by the piranhas are licensing rules, fire and sanitation procedures, tax laws, and the criminal code's Chapter 21 (Crimes against Property) and 22 (Crimes in the Realm of Economic Activity). Procedural amendments adopted under Medvedev in 2010, after the death of Sergei Magnitsky, were too lackadaisical to be effective. Businessmen are blackmailed or arrested under these provisions in dumbfounding quantity, in many cases held hostage until assets have been extorted. None other than the leader of the country put numbers on these practices in a speech in December 2015. In the year 2014, Putin said, nigh on two hundred thousand Russian entrepreneurs had been investigated for economic offenses. Fifteen percent had been convicted in court, but 83 percent had been dispossessed of their assets, all or in part. "That is, they were squeezed, shaken down, and let go.... This wrecks the business climate." The most the president could bring himself to do was commiserate with the fleeced capitalists and admonish detectives and prosecutors pro forma to do the right thing.

High on a reform agenda would be initiatives to reduce internal obstructions to trade. Russia's labyrinthine regulations nurse corruption; the special staff required to keep regulators at bay is most costly to business startups and small fry. This is the one area where Putin has intervened. Upon his third inauguration in 2012, he issued a decree ordering officialdom to do what it takes to raise Russia in the World Bank's Ease of Doing Business Index (EBDI) from 120th place to 20th, and to do it by 2018. The bureaucracy, under the gun, began to streamline anachronistic procedures. The results were positive if uneven, as Russia leapt to a world EBDI ranking of 51st in 2015, scoring as high as 5th for enforcing contracts and as low as 170th for transborder trade.

One takeaway from EBDI is that economic modernization in Russia is not mission impossible. Another is that, given political realities, progress will not come without backing at the apex of the system. Yet another is that reforms will work best if domestic initiatives are in lockstep with international forces. Putin shows no signs of wanting to apply this last point more broadly. The more Russia heads for isolationism, the more doubtful even narrowly conceived reforms will be.

How serious are Russia's demographic problems?

They are quite serious. The Russian bear is not on its deathbed, but it has been ailing for a generation. President Putin acknowledged this in 2006 when he spoke about a "demographic crisis" and about troublesome tendencies that picked up momentum after 1991. Population fell from 148.5 million in 1992 to 143 million in 2006. In 1986 the RSFSR, with 17.2 births per 1,000 and 10.4 deaths, had a natural increase of 6.9 per 1,000 people (the maximum figure post-World War II was the 17.6 recorded in 1954). The Russian birth rate fell to a low of 8.3 in 1999, and the death rate climbed to a high of 16.4 in 2003; from 1992 the Russian Federation endured a natural decrease, which reached a maximum of negative 6.5 per 1,000 in 2000 and 2001 (in those two years the absolute natural decrease totaled 1.9 million people). Only a positive net migration rate kept the population from dropping precipitously.

Lurking in the background was the acute discomfort produced by a conversion of political and economic systems. Childbearing often drops in parlous times, as it has in previous periods of Russian history. It is on the mortality side that research brings out several atypical factors.

One abnormality is the blatant disparity between the sexes. Internationally, women on average live to be about five years older than men. Russia's male–female gap, high to begin with, yawned to fifteen years in 1995, when men had a life expectancy of fifty-eight. A second peculiarity is the role of alcohol. On the word of the World Health Organization, Russians in 2010 consumed 15.1 liters of pure alcohol on average, fourth highest in the world. Men drink three times more than women, and half is in the form of spirits, more often than not taken in binges. Public health experts estimate that every third or fourth death is linked to overconsumption of spirits. A study of fifty thousand deaths in three cities, published in *The Lancet* in 2009, found "a marked excess of heavy vodka use" in Russians whose death was attributed to external causes (accident, suicide, homicide, and alcohol poisoning) or to eight disease groupings (liver disease, tuberculosis, acute pancreatitis, and the like). "Sharp fluctuations in Russian mortality rates from these causes during the 1990s were the main reason for the sudden large fluctuations in premature mortality in women and, particularly, men."

Information like this fed sensationalist reportage about Russia's "depopulation bomb," "downward health spiral," and "ethnic self-cleansing." Meanwhile, changes in policy and behavior were underway that made the situation less bleak.

The Kremlin unveiled a collection of pronatalist and mortality-reduction programs in 2006. Women who had a second or third child by birth or adoption were to get "maternity capital" of 250,000 rubles, about $10,000. The lump sum, since increased, was to go to purchase housing or for several other delimited needs. Seven million mothers have received these payments since 2007. Other laws lengthened parental leave and gave tax breaks to large families, supported adoptions and foster parenting, and funded in vitro fertilization. In terms of mortality, the initiatives have been investment in hospitals and campaigns against immoderate drinking, tobacco, and reckless driving. Russia has introduced minimum prices for vodka, tripled the excise tax on beer, and banned the sale of alcohol from street arcades or at nighttime. In 2013–14 smoking was illegalized at workplaces, in restaurants and bars, and in the stairwells of apartment houses, and display of cigarettes at stores was forbidden.

The demographic picture has plainly improved, to some extent because of governmental action. Births edged up from 10.2 per 1,000 in 2005 to 12.0 in 2008 and 13.3 in 2015, which is above the EU average. The death rate slid from 16.1 per 1,000 in 2005 to 14.5 in 2008 and 13.1 in 2015, and slid fastest among working-age males, the most imperiled group. General life expectancy for Russians hit a record-high seventy-one in 2013, the first year going all the way back to 1991 in which Russia experienced a natural increase in population (of twenty-four thousand people). There were other infinitesimal increases in 2014 (thirty thousand) and 2015 (thirty-three thousand).

Russia is hardly out of the woods, as there will be a "demographic echo" of the wilt in fertility of the 1990s. The cohort of women in their twenties, who in this part of the world account for two-thirds of births, will be almost one-half smaller a decade from now. Female mortality draws near the norm for Russia's level of development, with a life expectancy at birth in 2015 of seventy-seven years. For Russian men, a life expectancy of sixty-six in round numbers equals India, Laos, and Bolivia.

A recent report by the Presidential Academy pencils in a range of demographic futures. If inertia holds, there would be a contraction to 139 million people by 2020 and 122 million by 2040. An intermediate approach, whereby family policy spending is raised from 1.5 percent to 3 percent of GDP, would restrain the decrease, to 134 million by 2040. The way to stabilize the population and grow it after 2040 would be to combine fertility support with policies to eliminate excess mortality. Post-Communist Estonia, Poland, and the Czech Republic have had good results from healthcare spending, antialcohol and antitobacco policies, and better auto safety. Russian health advocates recommend restoration of the state monopoly on production and distribution of alcohol—which private distillers and brewers will fight tooth and nail.

One additional tool for cushioning the demographic echo in the labor force would be to induce workers to stay on the job later in life. The statutory retirement age in Russia is the same as in the Soviet Union, sixty for men and fifty-five for women; the mean for developed economies is sixty-four for men and sixty-three for women. Thirty percent of Russians give up work early for one reason or another, making the average age of exit from the labor market fifty-six for men and fifty-three for women. Standardization would be economically advantageous but politically contentious, since most Russian citizens look on pensions in their fifties as a birthright. In polls, about 65 percent want the status quo and 25 percent want even earlier retirement.

A second handle is migration policy. The World Bank's *Migration and Remittances Factbook* records that 12.3 million permanent residents of the Russian Federation in 2010 had immigrated from other countries, exceeded by only the United States. Four hundred and eighty-two thousand permanent immigrants and 2.9 million seasonal migrants were admitted in 2013; undocumented migrants were several million more. Eighty-five to 90 percent of these people come from the Caucasus and Central Asia, Russia's southern underbelly. Remittances from itinerant workers in Russia comprise a third to a half of the GDP of impecunious countries like Tajikistan and Kyrgyzstan. Russia could turn up the faucet by procedural changes, by providing social services to seasonal workers, and by showing more regard for their cultural and religious needs. The fly in the ointment is that, while officeholders and the business elite are positive toward the influx, Russian public sentiment is negative. Government policy in future may emphasize sub rosa accommodation of migrant behavior rather than rule making.

What are the prospects for rule of law?

Putin, like Lenin, Gorbachev, and Medvedev, has a law diploma and is well versed in how to use legal instruments, down to the last comma, in a piece of legislation or decree. Call this rule by law. Rule of law, not by law, is about constraints and not about instruments. The World Justice Project (WJP), a well-thought-of nonprofit, pegs a helpful definition of rule of law to four principles: (1) The government and its agents are accountable under the law; (2) the laws are clear, stable, and just and protect fundamental rights; (3) the laws are enacted and enforced accessibly, fairly, and efficiently; and (4) justice is delivered by competent, independent, ethical, and well-resourced adjudicators.

The record is awash in anecdotal evidence of Russian government scoffing at one or more of these principles. Among national political institutions, the courts get the lowest approval ratings, trusted by only 15 to 20 percent of the population. When it suits the high and mighty, justice is politicized. Few Russians would see anything remarkable in the prosecution of the ex-premier Mikhail Kasyanov, now outspokenly anti-Putin, in 2005 (for breaking the rules on privatization of the state dacha that once housed Mikhail Suslov), or the legal harassment of Alexei Navalnyi, an anticorruption blogger who skewered United Russia as "the party of swindlers and thieves." Yukos's oil fields, refineries, gasoline stations, and real estate were in all but words stolen in 2007 by Rosneft, majority-owned by the government, with judicial connivance. The restrictions on street meetings flout the constitutional right to peaceful assembly. There have been flagrant failures to protect liberal oppositionists—for instance, the leader of the Democratic Russia party, Galina Starovoitova (killed in 1998), investigative journalist Anna Politkovskaya (2006), and one-time first deputy premier Boris Nemtsov, viewed as a possible heir to Boris Yeltsin in the 1990s (2015).

Lamentable as these incidents of "legal nihilism" (a venerable watchword, recirculated by Medvedev) may be, it is not yet true that they have given rise to blunt repression or a neo-totalitarian Russia. Kasyanov gave back the dacha and paid a fine, and Navalnyi has stayed at liberty. Nothing will bring

Starovoitova, Politkovskaya, or Nemtsov back to life, but the government has tried reasonably hard to identify political assassins and bring them to justice. Mikhail Khodorkovsky was pardoned in 2013 and lives contentedly in London on a nest egg of several hundred million dollars. A retroactive charge of commissioning the mob-style murder of a Siberian mayor in 1998, lodged in December 2015, is a preventative against lawsuits over Yukos and not a serious judicial process, and Khodorkovsky will be safe from it.

Putin seems to delight in the Janus-like role Russians call "destroyer-saver" (*gubitel-vyzvolitel*). The destroyer-saver, as Gleb Pavlovsky summarizes it, puts in motion a terrifying process that he then counters by acting as an ombudsman against himself."

Nor is it true that developments on each and every score have been deleterious to individual rights. Reforms have been made to the criminal procedure code, and jury trials have been instituted for some offenses. Businesses resort to the courts to resolve economic disputes more than in the 1990s. Russia has a reformed legal profession, a human rights community, and a Presidential Council for Civil Society and Human Rights, a member of which is the octogenarian Lyudmila Alekseyeva, the matriarch of civil rights in Russia. The council regularly questions state decisions and in August 2015 scored a victory when it persuaded the government to proceed with a plan (the one given Medvedev's imprimatur in 2011 without follow-up) to build a national monument to the victims of Stalinism. Russian court judgments can be referred to the European Court of Human Rights. Russia has outnumbered all others on the ECHR docket (in 2014 the court handed down 129 judgments against Russian institutions), and it ordinarily pays penalties as ordered.

The thorough research of the WJP lets us put the Russian Federation into perspective. It scores and ranks countries, 102 of them in its report for 2015, relying on surveys of households, legal practitioners, and academics. An aggregate Rule

of Law Index (RLI) pulls together soundings for eight factors: checks on government powers, clean government, open
government, fundamental rights, order and security, regulatory enforcement, civil justice, and criminal justice. National
scores run from 0 to 1, where 1 indicates the most evenhanded
observance of rule of law.

An RLI score of 0.47 in 2015 positioned Russia near the
midpoint of the scale. By a Russian historical touchstone, this
is good performance. By modern-day international specifica-
tions, it is bad. Russia's global ranking for rule of law in 2015 is
a wan 75th out of 102. Of the eight factors captured in the RLI
index, its best rank, 60th, is for civil justice. The lowest, 90th, is
for constraints on government powers (which refers to checks
on the executive by parliament, the judiciary, independent
auditors, and the media and civil society). The second worst
reading is for fundamental rights (to life and security, due process, free expression, assembly, and labor protection), where
Russia in Putin's second decade finds itself 80th in the world.

Russia fares dismally on rule of law versus almost any comparison group. It is now a World Bank high-income country.
Of thirty-one high-income nations in the 2015 WJP, Russia is
dead last, and last on seven of the eight factors (it sneaks by the
United Arab Emirates on open government). If compared to
the upper-middle-income group it exited in 2013, Russia does
a bit better, finishing lower on the RLI ladder than twenty-six
of thirty-one units. If compared to lower-middle-income countries, it comes in behind fifteen out of twenty-five. Only against
low-income countries, where its RLI rating is better than
twelve out of fifteen, does Russia beat out the group average.
The two countries in the study still controlled by Communist
parties, Vietnam and China, are more law-governed than
Russia, if not by much. Of twenty-one post-Communist countries in the ranking, Russia stands second-to-last, outclassing
only Uzbekistan (ranked eighty-first) and miles to the rear of
countries like Estonia (fifteenth), the Czech Republic (twentieth), and Georgia (twenty-ninth).

The methodical WJP goes back only a few years and does not let us track change. On one factor, corruption, we do have available scorecards spanning two decades. The NGO Transparency International first scrutinized Russia in its Corruption Perceptions Index in 1996. Russia ranked forty-seventh out of fifty-four countries covered (more countries were fitted into the survey later), putting it at the eighty-seventh percentile. In Putin's first term, Russia's relative standing improved from the ninety-first to the sixty-second percentile; it declined to the eighty-second percentile in his second term and to the seventy-eighth in 2014, only to tick up to the seventy-first percentile in 2015. The Gestalt is one of underwhelming performance, with several turns for the better and several for the worse but no net change. The control-of-corruption statistic in the World Bank's Worldwide Governance Indicators follows much the same curve, putting Russia in the eighty-third percentile in 2013, indistinguishable from the eighty-fourth percentile it sat in in 1996.

What does all of this bode for time to come? The question is somewhat of a red herring. We normally measure achievement against aspiration. As a matter of fact, it is not that Russian governments have missed the mark in their attempts to produce disinterested rule of law, it is that they have not in any consistent way tried to produce it. Russia's record on rule of law is like America's on gun control—nothing ventured, nothing gained. There can be movement only if a political leadership, in all probability a post-Putin leadership, espouses it unequivocally and prepares to incur the costs of bringing it about.

Russian leaders bristle at the example of post-Soviet Estonia. Harder still to accept are successes in Georgia, which, under the same Mikhail Saakashvili who ordered the foolhardy offensive against Tskhinvali in 2008, implemented a heavy-handed campaign against domestic petty corruption. In 1999, under Eduard Shevardnadze, Georgia was in the eighty-fifth percentile on the Transparency International metric; by 2008, with Saakashvili as president, in the thirty-seventh percentile; in 2013, the year he left office, in the thirty-first. Officials indicted for corruption were interrogated live on national television, "asked to repay the allegedly stolen amounts ... [and] then released without standing trial." One of Saakashvili's more audacious decisions, in 2005, was to lay off Georgia's sixteen thousand traffic officers, a notoriously corrupt group, and hire beginners. A citizens' hotline and one-stop service centers for issuing licenses and inspecting vehicles rounded out the initiative. Dmitrii Medvedev as president disparaged all this as "nonsense" that was not for Russia, thanks to its innate ungovernability—shades of Catherine the Great. "Any attempt to throw all the bureaucrats in prison or dissolve the police force and pick a new one, like some of our neighbors did, will not work here," he said in 2011. "We can't do it, the country is just too big."

If Russia is ever to go in a healthy direction on rule of law, it would have to deal head on with attitudes on the ground floor of the power vertical. For most Russians, corruption has become run-of-the-mill. The Kremlin's own surveys indicate that half of all citizens are prepared to offer a bribe to a government official if one is demanded; the readiness to pay up ranges from 30 percent for protection from uniformed patrolmen to 40 percent for authorization to buy a plot of land, 55 percent for getting a son or daughter into a university, and 70 percent for vehicle inspections. Underhand behavior is ingrained in the popular culture as much as in the bureaucratic repertoire.

What are the prospects for civil society?

The rebirth of civil society, the "third sector," was a laudable result of the change of political regime in Russia. Yeltsin curried favor with the new volunteer associations when in opposition; in government, his stance was benign detachment. Putin took more of an interest. In November 2001, his administration hosted a Civic Forum with four thousand attendees. Russian civil society, he told them in a hospitable speech, had to grow "its own root system." Cooperation with government was in the interests of both: "There can be no strong state, and no . . . thriving society, without relations of real partnership between the state and society. What we need here is a dialogue on equal terms." Vladislav Surkov, who took the lead in setting up the forum, hankered to institutionalize the partnership in an umbrella structure of some kind. NGO activists were suspicious of anything that conjured up a "ministry of civil society."

The legal framework for civil society activity in Russia is baroque in its complexity. Twenty-odd types of nonprofit organizations, or NKOs, are recognized. They may have governmental or municipal stakeholders and not, strictly speaking, be Western-style NGOs. Several hundred thousand nonprofits are registered with the Ministry of Justice, but scads of them are inactive hollow shells or Kremlin-made fakes. Around half are trade unions, religious organizations, clubs, and foundations, and half are "socially oriented" NGOs working on social services, the environment, historical preservation, and human rights.

In 2004–5, during the course correction following Beslan and the Orange Revolution, the Kremlin waded into the associational market by sponsoring what we would call "government-organized nongovernmental organizations" or GONGOs. The best known was Nashi (Ours), a patriotic movement for young adults seventeen to twenty-five which organized summer camps (at which Putin bantered with the adoring crowd), flag-waving marches, and Internet forums. The government also followed through on the proposal broached at the 2001 forum of an institutional gateway for NGOs. The Public Chamber of the Russian Federation, a quasi-congress for monitoring state bodies and giving a "zero reading" to draft parliamentary bills (before they get a first reading in the Duma), began work in 2006. Its 126 members are selected by nonprofits and the presidential administration. One of its duties is to oversee another Putin initiative, provision of state grants to NGOs in a juried application cycle. Budgetary expenditures on NGOs (and GONGOs) came to 10 billion rubles, or about $300 million, in 2013. The final adjustment in policy was toward more stringent bureaucratic regulation of NGOs. The 1996 enabling law was altered in 2006 to give government departments extra authority to audit and require reports from nonprofits.

The GONGOs, which some Russians call "Potyomkin NKOs," had little effect on the situation, and official interest has waned. The puppet-on-a-string Nashi never had more than 120,000 members—the Soviet Komsomol had more than 20 million in the RSFSR in 1985—and in 2012 was turned into a do-nothing political party named Clever Russia. The Public Chamber and its secretary, business lobbyist Alexander Brechalov, are part of the subliminal hum in Moscow, not of the action; every now and then they nitpick about government policy. Financial support for NGOs has been well received by most grantees; some of the NGOs do cavil at possible co-optation.

The side of the reforms most censured in the West was the strengthening of state supervision. That paperwork for Russian NGOs was made more burdensome is obvious enough. Less obvious is whether this constituted a crackdown on civil society. Debra Javeline and Sarah Lindemann-Komarova rebut morning-after commentary that they say inflated the negative effects and overlooked the positives. The costs for most nonprofits were manageable, and "organizations receiving a clean bill of financial health [from government minders] can attract more funding, proceed more effectively with their activities, and facilitate the general effectiveness of Russian civil society." Data on organizational numbers corroborate Javeline and Lindemann-Komarova. The community did not roll over and die after the law was revised in 2006. Registered NGOs decreased a tad from 146,000 in 2006 to 142,000 in 2007, zoomed to 204,000 in 2008, stood still in the lee of the Great Recession, and moved up to 220,000 in 2013 and 227,000 in 2015. Rosstat, the state's statistical bureau, estimates that the net income of

Russian NGOs expanded from 255 billion rubles in 2005 to 603 billion rubles in 2013 ($19 billion at the going rate of exchange).

The latest turn of the control crank came during Putin's reactionary and besieged-fortress phase post-2011. It explicitly took aim at external funding, which he had fingered as a problem since the 2001 Civic Forum. In July 2012 a new statute obliged nonprofits to register as "performing the functions of a foreign agent [*inostrannyi agent*]" if they take part in vaguely delineated "political activity" and receive any income (as a donation, grant, contract, or even prize) from outside Russia. Russia is one of many countries (forty-five between 1993 and 2012) to adopt laws and regulations restricting foreign-funded NGO. Recent examples would be Egypt (2011), India (2015), and China (2016).

Russian nonprofits could have been required to post a list of funders on websites or file this information with government clerks; the method chosen, bringing to mind cloak-and-dagger espionage, was designed to intimidate. The Ministry of Justice was in 2014 empowered to make the designation itself, almost nobody having volunteered. In December 2015 its register listed 88 associations it had tarred as agents; 7 had had this status removed and 10 had shut down; Human Rights Watch counts 116 as mixed up in litigation or administrative hearings and 12 that have ceased operations sooner than work under the stigma. Affected have been well-known groups such as Golos (an election watcher), Memorial (historical memory and human rights), the Committee Against Torture, and Transparency International–Russia. Another law, from June 2015, allows the peremptory expulsion of any foreign organization the government deems "a threat to the foundations of the constitutional order of the Russian Federation, the country's defense capability, or the security of the state." The first to pull up stakes, in anticipation of eviction, was the John D. and Catherine T. MacArthur Foundation, which had distributed $175 million in grants to Russians over twenty-three years.

Neither foreign funding nor a focus on democracy promotion and rights is typical of Russian civil society en bloc. In 2013 some 2,700 NGOs (1 percent of the total) received foreign monies, to the tune of 36 billion rubles (6 percent of the total). Nonprofits for legal, rights, and political–procedural questions represented 4 percent of the set of 227,000. The vast majority of NGOs have not fallen under the hex of the 2012 law.

So what difference might the Russian third sector make going forward? One point is that civil society should produce beneficial political effects whether or not the activity is expressly political. As Robert D. Putnam has argued, associational life is consequential for "social capital"—feelings of trust and connectedness—no matter what the shared activity consists of.

A second point is that Russian civil society has shown it can be a squeaky wheel in within-system politics, raising and inflaming issues to which the leadership may well respond. Exemplars would be the "grannies' revolt" of early 2005, marches by pensioners against an attempt to monetize and sap social benefits previously provided in kind; horn-honking demonstrations by Siberian car owners that summer over an attempt, instigated by domestic automakers, to ban imports of Japanese-made vehicles; ire in St. Petersburg over a Gazprom skyscraper that would have cast the historic cityscape into shade; the movement to protect Khimki Forest, near Moscow, from an express highway; and the traffic-obstructing tactics of long-haul truckers up in arms in 2015 over an electronic road-toll system. In all these cases, the plans were modified or shelved.

The Runet has made it easier to coordinate protests and to crowdfund some activist platforms, but most events continue to be low-tech and parochial in scope. Mikhail Dmitriev and his New Economic Growth consultancy counted thirty-four thousand protest events in 2010, large and small, or ninety-three per day. The average demonstration was not over the self-realization goals pursued by the Moscow marchers in 2011 but over banal, bread-and-butter problems like back wages, corruption, and tensions between ethnic groups. "Oftentimes, grievances were addressed to local authorities rather than to the central government. Political demands were rare and, if anything, took a back seat. Most protests occurred in small and midsize cities." Future flareups in the hinterland may not point in a liberal or democratic direction. "A combination of survival mentality, hostility toward ethnic minorities, and anti-Western attitudes could tinge protest activities in the populist, leftist, and nationalist hues typical of many Latin American countries."

How creative a country is present-day Russia?

Creativity has no fatherland. Human freedom is its oxygen, but how many molecules are needed is not knowable with finality. Russia, which will never be misread as the freest of places, can lay claim to having been a creative place. In spite of everything, it has been home to the wizardry of Pushkin, Mendeleev, Prokofiev, and Chief Designer Korolyov.

For artistic freedom, the rendering asunder of the Soviet order was a bonus. Censorship, socialist realism, and manda-tory membership in official organizations had been cast off. But other factors militated against works of imagination. Value quandaries and conflicts swirled, balkanizing the intelligentsia to such an extent as to pose for some the question of whether it had died out as a social estate.

Economics and popular taste also unsettled the Russian cultural establishment to its core. In the literary world, for example, the USSR Union of Writers had provided apart-ments and dachas, royalties were princely, and periodicals and publishing houses were on the state's books. That went by the boards under shock therapy, as the official union was succeeded by penniless NGOs and publications had to shift for themselves in the fickle marketplace. New book titles went down by 25 percent between 1990 and 1992. Alexander

Solzhenitsyn had written in his novel *The First Circle* that in a dictatorship a great writer is "a second government in his country." After dictatorship, the suit no longer fit. A literature of disorientation sidestepped politics and the grand questions of the pre-1914 and Soviet canon. New voices like Viktor Pelevin and Vladimir Sorokin were postmodern and absurdist in style; pulp fantasy, romance, and detective stories blossomed.

Hard times and escapism were correspondingly the order of the day in the performing arts. The twenty-eight feature films made in 1995 were four times fewer than a decade before. Imports swamped the market: domestically produced features had 65 percent of the box office in 1986 but 8 percent in 1994. Russian movies of the "Black Wave" (*chernukha*) were preoccupied with community and family squalor—"socialist realism with a minus sign," as Nancy Condee calls it. The Bolshoi and Mariinskii ballet companies relied on foreign tours to make ends meet and saw stars abscond to the West. Russian sport went into a tailspin. Soviet-built facilities were allowed to decay; coaching and training of young competitors were neglected; the Russian Federation was an also-ran in sports (rowing, sprinting, soccer) at which the USSR had excelled. Gifted athletes moved away in search of higher salaries and better conditions, with their home clubs and federations skimming off transfer fees. In ice hockey, for example, 274 Russian players were recruited by National Hockey League teams between 1989 and 2015.

Things were worse yet in science and technology. Government funding for the Russian Academy of Sciences was slashed. Research and development was shortchanged by myopic private owners; patent applications declined 60 percent between 1992 and 1997. Scientists emigrated and took nonscience jobs, and the cadre of researchers aged.

With economic growth and fiscal health, there was recuperation in art, sport, and science. The book industry was solvent again by the late 1990s, with almost all production in commercial publishing houses. New titles surged to 125,000 by 2010, fourth after the United States, Britain, and China and triple the late Soviet years. In highbrow fiction, a "new realism" took center stage. Alexander Karasev, Zakhar Prilepin, and Olga Slavnikova write in direct prose about mundane social and personal problems, without the mysticism of the 1990s. The Bolshoi Theater was refurbished at stunning expense between 2005 and 2011, and the Mariinskii acquired a state-of-the-art concert hall. Ballet now shares the market with modern-dance troupes. Whereas in the 1990s they imitated European and American modes, today they "have their own style, characterized by an unusual choreographic lexicon and interesting stage designs."

The film industry also turned around, although foreign-made pictures are still the draw on the big screen. The federal government made development funds available to producers starting in 2002 and subsidized construction of new cinemas. Openings of Russian-made films rose to 67 in 2003, 99 in 2007, and 140 in 2011. At the front of the parade were historical blockbusters—Fyodor Bondarchuk's *The Ninth Company* (2005, about the Soviets in Afghanistan) and *Stalingrad* (2013, a love story set in the Battle of Stalingrad and the top-grossing Russian film), Andrei Kravchuk's *Admiral* (2008, about Alexander Kolchak, a White leader during the Civil War), Pavel Lungin's *Tsar* (2009, about Ivan the Terrible), and Vladimir Bortko's *Taras Bulba* (2009, about Russians, Ukrainians, and Poles in the seventeenth century, on the basis of a Gogol story), to reference a few. The fecund filmmaker Nikita Mikhalkov (*Burnt by the Sun, The Barber of Siberia, Sunstroke*) takes an elegiac approach to late Imperial and early Soviet Russia, "providing a spectacle simultaneously distinct from the West yet recognizably European in its cultural environment, retaining certain archaic ways of being, such as a leisured pastoral enchantment, that the West has putatively lost." Mikhalkov, son of the lyricist of the Soviet and Russian national anthems, is a fervid apologist for Putin.

Russian sport, too, put the worst of the 1990s behind it. Putin, a judo black belt for whom physical fitness is a point of pride, saw mileage for his government in the issue. "Victories in sport," he stated in August 2000, "do more to cement the nation than a hundred political jingles." A federal Ministry of Sport built stadiums, hockey arenas, and swimming pools and provided stipends to individual competitors. Team sponsorships were put forward as a corporate responsibility of Russian businesses and a new generation of coaches trained. When the premier Kontinental Hockey League, formed in 2008 (with twenty-two Russian members as well as teams in Belarus, Croatia, Finland, Kazakhstan, Latvia, and Slovakia), began to pay competitive salaries, the outflow of players slowed to a dribble, with a mere two Russian rookies in the NHL in 2015–16. And, since Russia began competing in its post-Soviet confines in 1994, it has taken 488 total medals in the Olympics (169 of them gold), second only to the United States' 631 medals (237 gold). It is a not unflattering result for a country with half of the American population, though it is severely stained by the doping scandal that resulted in many Russian athletes being banned from the 2016 Summer Olympics in Rio de Janeiro.

In higher education, Russia in 2007 restructured university curricula into the two-stage bachelor's-master's model of the Bologna Process, replacing specialized five-year degrees. The civil code's sections on intellectual property were revised in 2008 and in 2009 Russia joined the Patent Law Treaty; applications for patents increased twofold between 1997 and 2012. Reform of the sclerotic Russian Academy of Sciences has been limited, but in higher education, which is separate from the academy, the government in 2009 chartered twelve institutions as "national research universities" and doubled their budgets. Putin in 2012 committed Russia to placing five universities in the ranks of the world's top hundred by 2020 and to doubling R&D expenditures to 2.5 percent of GDP. These will be arduous targets to meet under conditions of a no-growth or shrinking economy.

A handy yardstick is the Global Creativity Index (GCI) worked up by Richard Florida out of the University of Toronto. For 2015 it rates and ranks 139 countries, using markers in three areas: technology (financial and human resources devoted to R&D and patents granted per capita); talent (educational attainment and size of the creative class); and tolerance (respondents in the Gallup World Poll who believe their locality is a good place for ethnic and racial minorities, and gay and lesbian people, to live), on the reasoning that "new ideas are generated most efficiently in places where different cognitive styles are tolerated." Australia comes in first and the United States second; Ghana and Iraq are second-last and last. The Russian Federation places thirty-eighth in the GCI ranking, or in the twenty-seventh percentile, which is better than twenty-two post-Communist countries but inferior to five (Slovenia, Hungary, Estonia, the Czech Republic, and Belarus). This was an advance over the preceding GCI, in 2011, which ranked Russia thirty-first out of eighty-two countries, or in the thirty-eighth percentile.

Illuminating is that Russia shows divergent results across the three components of the 2015 GCI. It is 22nd globally in technology (twelfth percentile) and 15th in talent (eighth percentile). In tolerance, it is a derisory 123rd (sixty-fifth percentile). These data sound an alarm. The mother lode of some forms of small-mindedness in Russia is the national government, with its shrill fearmongering about quislings and sexual minorities.

More than 1 million Russian citizens emigrated in the 1990s; the numbers dwindled to several tens of thousands annually by 2010. Will prejudices and stark domestic conditions now lead to a brain drain that will cramp innovation? Official statistics are in various ways unreliable. Sociologists who closely study population movement report no change over the last several years, and that interest in emigration has fallen off. All the same, there are reasons for concern. Most emigrants in the 1990s were low-skilled workers or retirees. Those who now show an interest in leaving are more likely to be in the creative class and in the prime of life. Experience shows that Russians can be creative outside of Russian borders—a gain for them and the world, a loss for Russia. Five Russian writers earned the Nobel Prize for literature in the twentieth century: Ivan Bunin (1933), Boris Pasternak (1958), Mikhail Sholokhov (1965), Alexander Solzhenitsyn (1970), and Joseph Brodsky (1987). Bunin was in exile in France when he won the award, Brodsky (expelled from the USSR for "social parasitism") lived in the United States, Solzhenitsyn was on the eve of eviction, and Pasternak died two years after he renounced his prize on charges of selling out to foreigners.

The months since the political crisis of 2011–12 have seen conspicuous individual leave-takings—for instance, of Sergei Guriyev and Konstantin Sonin (top-drawer economists), Andrei Kozyrev (Yeltsin's first foreign minister), Sergei Aleksashenko (former first deputy governor of the Russian Central Bank), Pavel Durov (founder of VKontakte), Boris Akunin (writer and organizer of protests in 2011), Yevgeniya Chirikova (environmentalist, Movement to Defend Khimki Forest), Masha Gessen (journalist), Garry Kasparov (former world chess titleholder), Marat Gelman (art curator), Leonid Bershidskii (founding editor of the newspaper *Vedomosti*), and Maria Gaidar (prodemocracy activist and daughter of Yegor Gaidar, now an official in Odessa, Ukraine). Russia can ill afford to lose so many of its best and brightest.

Roadblocks to artistic and technological originality are aggravated by Russia's rule-of-law deficit. Piracy of intellectual property is unchecked. Ninety percent of the e-books consumed are downloaded illegally; it may be almost as bad for music, film videos, and software. The United States trade representative, looking out for American interests, puts the Russian Federation third on its watch list. The damage is as severe to domestic innovation. Promising antipiracy legislation in 2013 and 2015 gives the government the power to close sites judged to be bootlegging media online. On the other hand, amendments to the civil code and lax enforcement provide breathing room for the brigands.

Where is identity politics taking Russia?

Interest politics is about what you want. Identity politics is about who you are. Russia watchers postulated after 1991 that interest politics would need some time to take hold, inasmuch as prerequisites like private property were in their infancy. Identity politics would be preponderate for now and would slowly fade.

A politics of material interest revolving around resource allocation did surface. It did not crowd out the politics of identity, which is alive and kicking all these years later. Identities in Russia break along crosscutting ethnonational, linguistic, and religious axes. They have generated and will generate a robust politics of three types: prosystem, within-system, and antisystem.

The keystones of the prosystem game, which is about propping up the legitimacy of the regime, will continue to be civic nationalism, valorization of World War II, sovereign resistance to foreign meddling, and antiglobalism. The big change lately has been apropos religion. Seventy to 75 percent of Russians in polls claim loyalty to the Russian Orthodox Church (attendance at services is much lower). Under a new primate, Patriarch Kirill (elected by the bishops in 2009), the church has gone to new lengths in pro-Kremlin identity formation and activation. At a televised all-faiths meeting with Putin during the 2012 election campaign, Kirill practically endorsed his presidential candidacy and thanked him for his role "in correcting this crooked twist of our history" after 1985. Putin applauds the church's "formative role in preserving our rich cultural and historical heritage and in reviving eternal moral values."

Courtship of the other traditional faiths will need to accompany the intimate relationship with the Orthodox. Putin has done this to a not inconsiderable extent through authorized leaderships—two for Russia's 16 million Muslims (the Central Spiritual Board of Russian Muslims and the Russian Council of Muftis), one for the seven hundred thousand Buddhists (the Buddhist Traditional Sangha of Russia), and one for the two hundred thousand Jews (the Federation of Jewish Communities of Russia, which mostly subs for Chabad Hasidic congregations). The Muslim community is anchored in the Volga basin, the Urals, and the North Caucasus; the Buddhist in the republics of Buryatiya, Kalmykiya, and Tuva; and the Jewish in Moscow and St. Petersburg.

Within-system politics ranges far and wide. Concerning ethnicity and the minority homelands, the equilibrium is that republic leaders negotiate over cultural issues like historical interpretation and language lessons and, otherwise, an economic calculus prevails. Concerning religion, the most successful claimant at the national level has been the Russian Orthodox hierarchy. It has lobbied the return of historic buildings and landholdings, grants for erection of parish churches, a working group with the Foreign Ministry, and, in 2009, appointment of chaplains in army units and prisons. The national church, mind you, is not always pleased with government behavior—it has taken a cool tone toward the intervention in Ukraine, where it has millions of followers and hundreds of parishes. And the church can overplay its hand. It tried for years to have instruction on "foundations of Orthodox culture" inserted into the elementary-school curriculum. Muslim muftis and the leaders of the eight republics with Islamic titulars were incensed; secular scientists called it unconstitutional "clericalization." Putin and the Ministry of Education and Science decided to go for the middle ground. When after some experimentation classes were implemented for fourth-graders in 2012, Orthodoxy was only one of six selections, the others being Islam, Buddhism, Judaism, world religions, and secular ethics. To the dismay of the patriarch, the most popular course with parents was secular ethics (46 percent), with Orthodoxy in second place (31 percent) and world religions in third (19 percent).

Latitudinarianism, at least so far as the traditional confessions are concerned, has also been written into the policy on chaplains: Islam, Buddhism, and Judaism, and not just Orthodoxy, are represented. And the other religions are not bashful about pushing projects of their design: new mosques, an Islamic TV channel, Sharia-compliant financial transactions, Russian membership in the Organization of Islamic Cooperation, and assistance with the Hajj pilgrimage to Mecca for the Muslims; for the Buddhists, temples, learning centers, and entry visas for the Dalai Lama (opposed by China); for the Jews, new and reopened synagogues, a Jewish museum in Moscow (to which Putin donated a month's salary), and denunciation of anti-Semitism.

The antisystem challenge of the 1990s, separatism, was contained by the reconquest of Chechnya, centralized federalism, and some accommodation of local interests. But several new identity-based threats have materialized.

One comes from the swerve at governmental level to high-octane Russocentric nationalism with a civilizational subtext. Putin sacralized the absorption of Crimea by pointing out that Khersones, the Greek colony now an archaeological site in Sevastopol's city limits, was where Vladimir I of Kievan Rus, the long-ago antecedent of the Russian Federation, was baptized in the tenth century. Crimea, he said, was as hallowed for Russians as the Temple Mount in Jerusalem for Jews. Taking the hint, a government commission in 2015 decided to run up what will be a fifty-foot bronze statue of Grand Prince Vladimir at the Borovitskii Gate of the Kremlin.

Presidential verbiage has punctured the distinction between civic and ethnic nationalism. It has rehabilitated the word *natsionalist* (nationalist), which in Soviet phraseology had only negative overtones, unlike *patriot* (patriot), which has always had positive overtones. "The biggest nationalist in Russia is me," Putin said to the Valdai Club in 2014. He granted in the speech that strident ethnonationalism on the part of the majority could be hazardous in a society with multiple identity communities: "If nationalism comes to mean intolerance of others or chauvinism, this would destroy our country, which has always been a multinational and multiconfessional state. This would lead us not only into a dead end but also to self-destruction." Time will tell if he takes his own advice.

If Putin can be absolved of bigotry, the same, unfortunately, cannot be said about all his countrymen. The most frequent outgroup is guest workers from the CIS countries. A 2014 Levada survey revealed that 76 percent of citizens supported moves to "limit the flow of migrants" (that figure was 45 percent in 2002); 64 percent wanted illegal immigrants deported, and only 19 percent favored legalization and assimilation. A paltry 12 percent felt respect or sympathy for arrivals to their communities; 42 percent felt dislike or fear, and 55 percent had no reaction. Eighteen percent agreed to the hilt with, and 36 percent gave qualified approval to, the slogan "Russia for the [Ethnic] Russians" (*Rossiya dlya russkikh*), doubling the 27 percent who opposed it as "real fascism."

Hate crimes against individual migrants increased after 2005 but declined in 2009–10 when arrests and prosecutions were intensified. A raft of associations and movements pursue ultraright causes; some are surreptitiously organized, some are inchoate, and most all by now use social media sites. The most xenophobic have been banned by the courts—for instance, the Slavic Union (2010), the Movement Against Illegal Immigration (2011), and the skinheads group Russkiye (2015). Anomic street pogroms will often begin with a gang fight over a dignity dispute and result in one or two deaths and demolition of private property and police vehicles. Few Russians—24 percent in the 2014 Levada poll—actually think that mass, nationality-based violence is in the stars at the level of the country as a whole, and fewer still, 13 percent, think it will happen where they live.

Other warning signs concern Russia's second religion. As in most of the world, Islam in Russia is a multijointed belief system. The Sunni–Shia divide has been a secondary issue, as the relatively few Shias in the federation are principally migrants from post-Soviet Azerbaijan. As a rule, Sunnis in the empire and the USSR were followers of traditional teachings—those of the Hanafi school for central Russia and of the Shafi school and Sufi brotherhoods in the North Caucasus. Nontraditional approaches made inroads in the 1990s, pushed by foreign Muslim charities, migrants from Central Asia, and younger imams, often trained in Saudi Arabia or Egypt. The new outlook can broadly be termed Islamist or fundamentalist; the Salafi strain has been especially attractive to converts.

Nontraditional Islam took a furious turn in the North Caucasus during the Second Chechen War. The rebels in the back country were Salafists, as were the terrorists at the Dubrovka Theater and Beslan and Doku Umarov, the desperado who, until Russian agents killed him in 2013, campaigned through bombings and online propaganda for a "Caucasus Emirate." The most blood was spilt in Dagestan and Ingushetiya.

Moscow since 2010 has gained has the upper hand, with insurgency-related deaths in the region dropping from 750 in 2010 to 340 in 2014 and 209 in 2015 (19 of the 209 civilians). Russian frontline tactics have become more ruthless, lockdowns in advance of the 2014 Winter Olympics (Sochi is just west of the North Caucasus republics) had an effect, and deals have been struck with moderate Salafist preachers. The area has also been the recipient of financial carrots from Moscow. In six of the seven North Caucasus republics in 2013, federal subsidies stood at more than 50 percent of the unit's budget (Adygeya barely missed, at 47 percent); in Chechnya, Dagestan, Ingushetiya, and Karachayevo-Cherkessiya, the level of subsidy topped 65 percent.

Perhaps most important, several thousand Caucasus fighters have departed to take on infidels in Syria. No one can say what will happen in the event that battle-hardened jihadists return in numbers. ISIS in June 2015 announced it had set up a Dagestan Governorate of the Islamic State, to enlist warriors for Syria and eventually spread its hand into the Caucasus area, and heaped vitriol on Russia: "We will take this land away from you.... We will kill you....You will try on our orange robes and taste the heat of our swords." ISIS has since then taken responsibility for several attacks on police officers and tourists.

A potential growth area for Islamic extremism is the middle Volga, the Urals, and western Siberia, far removed from the Caucasus. In July 2012 an attempt was made on the life of the mufti of Tatarstan, and his deputy was assassinated; an FSB drive against subversives ensued. An oil refinery in the Tatar city of Nizhnekamsk was shelled in November 2013 with Qassam rockets developed by, and fired into Israel by, the military arm of Hamas. Sunni traditionalists, in the estimation of Alexei Malashenko, a knowledgeable student of Russian Islam, are losing out with Muslim youth. "They have few charismatic and professionally educated clergymen and have been tarnished by collaboration with the secular authorities, to whom they remain loyal. The young people are seeking something new in Islam.... The traditionalists ... are unable to provide satisfactory answers. Salafists and radicals, for their part, are often capable of offering answers."

When is Putin going to step down?

We do not know when. We do not even know whether he will ever step down. If Putin has made up his mind, he would not tell us. Chances are that he cannot yet give an answer himself.

We do know the timetable set forth by the constitution. An amendment to Article 81 secured by Dmitrii Medvedev in December 2008, without explanation, lengthened presidential terms to six years from four. Consequently, Putin's current, third term goes until May 2018. If he runs for reelection, he will be the crushing favorite to win and will be eligible to serve until 2024, when he turns seventy-two and will have been king of the hill for six years longer than Brezhnev and only five years shorter than Stalin. To continue, he would need either to have the constitution tweaked or to duck out and return after an intermission.

Putin has flat-out denied that he yearns to be a lifetime president—it would be "harmful for the country, and I don't need it," in his usage. But he glosses over what would be harmful and is more than a little disingenuous. A broad reading would be that he is concerned about the social costs of one person ruling ad infinitum. A narrow reading, and a more reasonable one, would be that he opposes a legal provision to give him a life term, as Julius Caesar and Napoleon had in their day. A line in the constitution to let him serve until death is not his métier and would invite international ridicule.

Putin has everything it takes to be president for life by completing the terms given him and tweaking the rules to buy time. In Eurasia, his ally Nursultan Nazarbayev of Kazakhstan has shown how longevity can be achieved with a docile legislative branch and approval ratings in the stratosphere, which Putin still has. The CPSU first secretary appointed by Gorbachev in 1989, Nazarbayev was elected president of the republic in 1990, had his term elongated by plebiscite in 1995 and term limits lifted in 2007, and was voted in again in 1999, 2005, and 2015, when he gathered 98 percent of the official ballots.

Putin is well advised to put on the scales the chances of wearing out his welcome, as did once-unassailable strongmen like Suharto of Indonesia (who stepped down under fire in 1998 after thirty-one years) and Hosni Mubarak of Egypt (hounded from office in 2011 after thirty years). If he were to die in office, he could not select a successor from the grave, and would take a chance on his policies being undone, and his memory sullied, soon after he is gone.

In 2007–8 Putin arranged a half-succession. In future, his trepidation about loss of control may be as great. Yeltsin's person was respected after 1999–2000, but his program for Russia was not. A dynastic solution—seeing to it that a family member inherits the commanding position—has clicked in

North Korea and in Azerbaijan, where President Heydar Aliyev, in failing health, transferred power to his son Ilham in 2003. It is not to be had by Putin. He has two daughters, now in their thirties and married: Maria (born in 1985) and Yekaterina (1986). They live behind a privacy wall, have not sat for an interview since they were teenagers, and have shown no interest in politics. Even if either of them did, Russia has not had a female leader since Catherine the Great's death in 1796 and is not ready for one now.

The odds of Putin calling it a day in 2018 are better than many pundits make them out to be—circa 50/50. Leading candidates to succeed him would be in order of age Foreign Minister Sergei Lavrov (b. 1950); Defense Minister Sergei Shoigu (b. 1955); Moscow Mayor Sergei Sobyanin (b. 1958); and Putin's 2008–12 proxy and trustworthy prime minister, Dmitrii Medvedev (b. 1965). In order of political position, they range from Medvedev as the most liberal, through centrists Lavrov and Sobyanin, to the conservative Shoigu.

If he is on the lookout for a multistage, error-proof exit, Putin could do worse than to learn from a duo of Asian nations with Confucian traditions. In China from the late 1970s to the mid-1990s, the canny visionary Deng Xiaoping was a godfather or "paramount leader," vetting decisions through a group of "eight elders" from his generation. He contrived a formulary for a line of succession for subsequent generations: A boss governs as president and party general secretary for two five-year terms; in the second term, the heir favored by the selectorate serves an apprenticeship to the outbound leader. This would be most practicable in a Leninist polity with a single, disciplined party. Putin could not import it without making changes to the personalist and patronage-oriented United Russia. The single lofty office Deng held was as chairman of the Communist Party of China's Central Military Commission. A Russian analogue might be commander-in-chief of the armed forces, which ought to be more attractive to Putin in the twilight of his career than prime minister. It could be legally separated from the presidency only by constitutional amendment.

A formula a cut above Deng's in terms of eagerness to let go might be found in Singapore. Lee Kuan Yew was the city-state's political father, sitting as prime minister from 1959 to 1990 and leading his People's Action Party to victory in seven general elections. Leaving the premiership at the peak of his powers, Lee took a tutelary title—"senior minister" until 2004 and "minister mentor" from 2004 until 2011 (he died in 2015). He attended some cabinet meetings but held no executive position. Some variation on this model may appeal to Putin. United Russia is more like the People's Action Party than it is like the Chinese Communist Party; Russia has no Confucian heritage, but it has a patrimonial, father-knows-best heritage of its making. It is far from certain that Putin would be able to live with seeing his influence grow faint.

Is a second perestroika in the cards?

Take the long view, and time is the friend of regime change in Russia. The reason for positivity is the correlation between governance and economic development set down by the political sociologist Seymour Martin Lipset. "The more well-to-do a nation," Lipset wrote in 1959, "the greater the chances it will sustain democracy." Social scientists debate why the association holds, but it is as strong as in the 1950s—with inconvenient exceptions. When the World Bank sited Russia in its high-income category in 2013, 82 percent of countries in that bracket were democratically governed (free in Freedom House terms), 46 percent of upper-middle-income countries, 30 percent of lower-middle-income countries, and only 8 percent of low-income countries. Russia is one of eight nondemocratic outliers in the high-income group. All of the others are petrostates, addicted to oil and gas revenues that amplify the state's coercive abilities and autonomy from society. And six of the seven are hereditary monarchies; the seventh is Equatorial Guinea, the former Spanish colony in West

Africa where Teodoro Obiang Nguema Mbasogo has ruled since taking over in a coup in 1979. Russia has an incomparably more diverse economy than the other nations in this category, with large manufacturing and service sectors; fossil fuels account for 16 percent of Russian GDP but 40 percent in Saudi Arabia and 83 percent in Equatorial Guinea.

A perestroika v2.0 is not about to happen. Perestroika v1.0 originated with a dreamer of a general secretary responding to pent-up demand for change and given room to operate by a disunited and demoralized elite. It spiraled out of control when he ripped to pieces the institutional machinery on which his and the regime's power depended. Some of Dmitrii Medvedev's "Go, Russia!" soundtrack resonated with the early Gorbachev, but here the congruence ends. The Bolotnaya protests at the end of his term, revisiting the language of perestroika and glasnost, were neutralized by the following summer.

It goes without saying that Putin will not be the prime mover in any root-and-branch restructuring. Decisions such as the creation in April 2016 of a National Guard subordinate to the president and commanded by a Putin loyalist, Viktor Zolotov, point in the opposite direction. This praetorian unit's four hundred thousand troops will be taken from the MVD and trained in crowd control and counterinsurgency.

Most Russians are with Putin in looking back at the stormy years 1985 to 1999 with distaste. Polls find that a majority believe Gorbachev's perestroika did more harm than good, that the demise of the USSR had been a tragedy, and that the 1990s were a decade of disarray and debility. Nostalgia for the good old days of Communism—and in particular for features such as guaranteed employment, interethnic peace, stability, and income equality—is still widespread.

Russian preferences for regime type are always ambivalent in tone. In the World Values Survey of 2011, 67 percent agreed that democracy was a very good or fairly good way of governing Russia; the exact same percentage wanted Russia to have "a strong leader who does not have to bother with parliament and elections." The median voter, it seems, would let the national government rule unfettered, but wants to choose it in the voting booth. Asked how important is was to them personally "to live in a country that is governed democratically," 71 percent gave positive answers. About Russia in 2011, the survey asked people to locate it on a ten-point democracy scale, with scores ranging from completely democratic to completely undemocratic. Sixty-two percent placed their country toward the undemocratic end of the scale and just 27 percent toward the democratic end. This negation of the ideal by the actual suggests latent demand for reforms.

Also, majority support exists for a number of the building blocks of democracy. For example, Levada data from 2015 give 58 percent agreeing political opposition is necessary for Russia and 22 percent saying it is not (in 2011 those numbers were 72 percent and 26 percent). The top reason given was accountability—"to keep the authorities under the control of society." Survey respondents were asked to pick between two interpretations of the right of assembly: that mass demonstrations and rallies are "a normal democratic means for citizens to achieve their aims, and the authorities have no right to prohibit them"; or that "if street rallies and demonstrations interfere with others, or lead to disturbances or destabilization, then the authorities should forbid them." The second, Putinesque interpretation was approved by 34 percent; the first, lenient interpretation was approved by 54 percent. When respondents were shown a list of demands put forward by Russian demonstrators, 32 percent agreed with "legislation against the illicit enrichment of officials" and 30 percent agreed with "ensuring fair elections."

In world practice, it has been only a matter of time before the tide of elation after a winning war, one way to understand the Russian appropriation of Crimea, recedes. Winston Churchill lost a British general election two months after V-E Day in 1945; George H. W. Bush had a trust rating of 89 percent after the Gulf War of 1991 but fell to Bill Clinton in 1992. Putin has a far more unrelenting grip over his political system than would have been possible for Churchill or Bush. But the close call of the 2011 parliamentary election, and the flash-in-the-pan protests over electoral falsification, show he does not have an impermeable Teflon coating against revolt from below. Resentment and anger can always bubble up afresh when the conditions are right. The most likely focal point is semicompetitive elections in which incumbents are suspected of fraud. Parliamentary elections are less important than presidential; they are also harder to control, and in future the bar will be set higher for cheating. Losses in a parliamentary election could force Putin to accept a prime minister from outside the United Russia juggernaut and a coalition cabinet.

Putin himself has repeatedly spoken of the reversals of fortune to which he has been an eyewitness. In the *From the First Person* interviews, he referred to being blindsided by the Soviet implosion a decade beforehand. "Often there are things that seem to us impossible and unachievable," he told his interlocutors, "but then all of a sudden—bang! This is the way it was with the Soviet Union. Who could have imagined that it would have up and collapsed? Even in your worst nightmares no one could have foretold this."

Contextual changes—a prolonged economic slump, a military cataclysm in the Black Sea area or Syria, a color revolution in Belarus or Kazakhstan, or some such—might cue a crisis. Much will depend on Putin's health, personal plans, and resilience in the ratings. Eventually he will quit the stage, at which point all bets are off.

One qualification as we peer into the crystal ball is that far from every popular uprising in the name of democracy produces a democratic outcome. In the Arab Spring of 2011–12, for example, despots were pushed from power in Egypt, Libya, Tunisia, and Yemen and there were mass rebellions in Bahrain and Syria. Only in Tunisia is there now a semifunctioning democracy; a new dictatorship under Abdel Fatah el-Sisi has come to Egypt and the Bahraini king has put down the rebellion; Libya and Yemen are failed states; and Syria, of course, was engulfed in its madhouse war of all against all. In Russia, should the present system become enfeebled or crumble, left-wing socialists and right-wing nationalists will be as well placed to benefit as liberals. Almost any government that breaks with Putin and Putinism will be attentive to much the same conservatizing moral he drew from perestroika v1.0 and the sequel under Yeltsin—it is imperative that change not incapacitate the state.

Who would provide the leadership for a new direction in Russian politics? The opposition parties that have sprouted since the reform of 2012 are with few omissions esoteric clubs, and years of marginalization have eaten away at public interest in parties in general. Of seventy-eight certified parties, only twenty-nine raised or disbursed funds in the third quarter of 2013. Thirty-five had zero balances in their bank accounts, and only fifteen parties had cash on hand or income of 1 million rubles (about $30,000).

Everyman politicians who can raise issues that resound with citizens, and connect with them through up-to-the-minute technologies, are only now appearing. The avatar for the time being is Alexei Navalnyi, a forty-year-old lawyer who made a splash in the blogosphere and as a protest organizer. He has twice been convicted and given suspended sentences on specious criminal charges, and his Progress Party has been refused registration. In September 2013 he was allowed to run for mayor of Moscow against the incumbent, Sergei Sobyanin, and took a surprisingly healthy 27 percent of the vote. A liberal on rights issues, Navalnyi also accepts the reincorporation of Crimea and calls for visa requirements for Central Asian migrant workers. He is too maximalist for most Russians in the present atmosphere but someone to watch for the future.

A more plausible scenario would pivot on a power struggle or loss of cohesion within the ruling stratum—if Putin dies unexpectedly, fumbles an effort to anoint a successor, or loses control under conditions of dire domestic or international crisis. Lucan Way speaks persuasively about "pluralism by default" in precarious post-Communist states such as Moldova and Ukraine, arguing that the same factors that have impeded conclusive democratization have impeded the construction of strong authoritarian regimes. Way treats Russia as a clear-cut autocracy, but this is an oversimplification— aspects of hybridity of the regime, and points of vulnerability, do remain. While Putin has outdone Moldovan and Ukrainian leaders in propping up the state, its political core, and ancillary structures like United Russia, some factors are present that might in due course make for pluralism by default, as a next-best solution for leaders who cannot agree on an affirmative outcome. Possible facilitators include factions and cliques within the elite, weak institutions other than the presidency and the security bloc, the growth of the creative class and of a bourgeoisie that would jump at the chance to bolster property rights against confiscation by state-based piranhas, high and rising levels of education in the population at large, openness to international influences, and the Internet.

If Putin were to develop an interest in building a regime halfway house—a monstrously big "if"—the experience of Asian countries like Singapore could again be relevant. Governance in Singapore is more competitive than in China, yet not so competitive as to be out of reach for Russia, should the will for controlled change exist. In the 1990s, when Lee Kuan Yew took up his emeritus position, Singapore's Freedom House score was 5, the same as Russia's in 2000. Singapore has made it to a score of 4, which is comparable to Russia in Yeltsin's second term and to Malaysia in 2014, Taiwan in the late 1980s, and India and Mexico in the mid-1990s.

Is Russia the prisoner of its history?

No, but in the grand scheme of things Russia is the upshot of its history, and a checkered history it is. It has supplied beauties, beasts, and everything in between. It is *The Firebird* and the Gulag, globalization and insularity, crackups and crackdowns, cascades of change and lifespans lost in the doldrums. Russia is "martyred, stubborn, extravagant, zany, irresponsible, adored," with a penchant for "splendid, and disastrous, and unpredictable adventures"—Yurii Zhivago's directory of superlatives, not mine, and not necessarily the lengthiest there exists.

Regularities and rhythms in the Russian trajectory have long since acquired a life of their own. But for key choices—adventures and misadventures among them—the taproot has time and again been purposive effort by flesh-and-blood human beings. This applies to farming in frigid climes, settling and colonizing an awesome swathe of land, warding off intruders, slinging a metal capsule and a man into the cosmos before anyone else, creating a socialist economy from scratch, and starting all over again with capitalism.

In politics and in the workings of its phoenix state, which has trumped all else, Russia has been steered at critical and semicritical junctures, if not invariably by Pasternak's frenzied revolutionaries, then by leaders who fit the rest of his job description— "men of action with one-track minds, geniuses at confining themselves to a limited field." They have assembled, disassembled, and reassembled nations, empires, and systems of control and allocation, nine times out of ten listening to society's voice as little as they can get away with. Russia's ultimate strength and its ultimate weakness continue to be, as Johann Kohl scribbled succinctly in the 1840s, that the ordinary people "adapt ... with wonderful suppleness to the prevailing mode" set by those who hold power. All too often, Russians end up being made small by rulers who are engrossed in making Russia great.

About the future, the test will be to discover a formula for development and governance that engages the talents of all and builds on the best of Russia's past and present. Its governments close their eyes to this challenge at their peril. But into what will Russia be remodeled in this iteration? It is a fallacy, as Putin rightly says, to think that it will any time soon become a second edition of America or Britain. What Russia can and must become is a better edition of itself.

NOTES

Excerpts from the rhetoric of Russian leaders and political actors are with the odd exception translations by the author from the original text.

Chapter 1

p. 5 *"a screen on which Americans projected"*: David S. Foglesong, *The American Mission and the Evil Empire* (Cambridge: Cambridge University Press, 2007), 62.

p. 5 *"the great Other"* and *"represented the socialist antithesis"*: Martin Malia, *Russia under Western Eyes: From the Bronze Horseman to the Lenin Mausoleum* (Cambridge, Mass.: Harvard University Press, 1999), 3.

p. 9 *"lonely power"*: Lilia Shevtsova, *Lonely Power: Why Russia Has Failed to Become the West and the West Is Weary of Russia* (Washington: Carnegie Endowment for International Peace, 2010).

p. 11 *"shared ... both the sense of wonder"*: "General Introduction," in Lloyd E. Berry and Robert O. Crummey, eds., *Rude and Barbarous Kingdom: Russia in the Accounts of Sixteenth-Century English Voyagers* (Madison: University of Wisconsin Press, 1968), xvii.

p. 11 *"the most singular state"*: as given in Marquis de Custine, *Empire of the Czar: A Journey through Eternal Russia* (New York: Doubleday, 1989), 15.

p. 11 *"So remarkable and peculiar a people"*: J. G. Kohl, *Russia: St. Petersburg, Moscow, Kharkoff, Riga, Odessa, the German Provinces on the Baltic, the Steppes, the Crimea, and the Interior of the Empire* (London: Chapman and Hall, 1844), 145.

p. 11 *"Shreds of information"*: Heinz-Dietrich Fischer, ed., *The Pulitzer Prize Archive* (Munich: K. G. Saur, 1987), 1:163.

Chapter 2

p. 14 *"There is nothing but distance"*: Custine, *Empire of the Czar*, 366.

p. 17 *"A calf born at the foot of the Great Chinese Wall"*: Kohl, *Russia*, 198.

p. 19 *"the amount of health continually sacrificed"*: ibid., 402.

p. 20 *"Born in Lisbon"*: Andreas Kappeler, *The Russian Empire: A Multiethnic History* (Abingdon: Routledge, 2001), 152.

p. 21 *"The Russian Empire grew by settlement"*: Orlando Figes, *Natasha's Dance: A Cultural History of Russia* (New York: Metropolitan Books, 2002), 381.

p. 23 *"In Russia, where there are few persons"*: Kohl, *Russia*, 386.

p. 25 *"In Russian administration"*: Custine, *Empire of the Czar*, 83.

p. 26 *"were prepared to acclaim the Russian novelists"*: Malia, *Russia under Western Eyes*, 194.

p. 26 *"a prime source"*: ibid., 196.

p. 26 *"was transformed into the symbol"*: Figes, *Natasha's Dance*, 276.

Chapter 3

p. 36 *"littered with bundles"*: Frank Alfred Golder and Lincoln Hutchinson, *On the Trail of the Russian Famine* (Stanford: Stanford University Press, 1927), 71.

p. 36 *"made up a shadow nation"*: Figes, *Natasha's Dance*, 528.

p. 37 *"cloaked nonconsensual control"*: Mark R. Beissinger, "Rethinking Empire in the Wake of Soviet Collapse," in Zoltan Barany and Robert Moser, eds., *Ethnic Politics after Communism* (Ithaca: Cornell University Press, 2005), 29.

p. 38 *"the Soviet Union's awkward nationality"*: Terry Martin, *The Affirmative Action Empire: Nations and Nationalism in the Soviet Union, 1923–1939* (Ithaca: Cornell University Press, 2001), 395.

p. 44 *"circular flow of power"*: Robert V. Daniels, "Soviet Politics since Khrushchev," in John W. Strong, ed., *The Soviet Union under Brezhnev and Khrushchev* (New York: Van Nostrand-Reinhold, 1971), 20.

p. 45 *"supremacy-insecurity dyad"*: Stephen Kotkin, *Stalin: Paradoxes of Power, 1878–1928* (New York: Penguin, 2015), 530.

p. 47 *"consisting of an official body of doctrine"*: Carl J. Friedrich and Zbigniew K. Brzezinski, *Totalitarian Dictatorship and Autocracy* (Cambridge, Mass.: Harvard University Press, 1956), 22–23.

p. 59 *"In the absence of terror"*: William Zimmerman, *Ruling Russia: Authoritarianism from the Revolution to Putin* (Princeton: Princeton University Press, 2014), 147.

p. 62 *"the visible tip of the iceberg"*: Vladimir Kozlov, *Mass Uprisings in the USSR: Protest and Rebellion in the Post-Stalin Years*, trans. Elaine MacKinnon (Armonk, N.Y.: M.E. Sharp. 2002), 177–78.

p. 68 *"Acts of contention"*: Mark R. Beissinger, *Nationalist Mobilization and the Collapse of the Soviet State* (Cambridge: Cambridge University Press, 2002), 72.

p. 68 *"Brezhnev's inability to function"*: Chernyayev diary for 1975 in English translation, at http://nsarchive.gwu.edu/NSAEBB/ NSAEBB516-Anatoly-Chernyaev-Diary-1975-Uncertainty-Detente-Brezhnev/.

p. 72 *"all thumbs, no fingers"*: Charles E. Lindblom, *Politics and Markets: The World's Political-Economic Systems* (New York: Basic Books, 1977).

p. 73 *"authorities . . . carried out continual and often economically unfounded increases"*: Kozlov, *Mass Uprisings*, 308.

p. 74 *"assume[d] that bad and seemingly unfair outcomes"*: Valerie Bunce, *Subversive Institutions: The Design and the Destruction of Socialism and the State* (Cambridge: Cambridge University Press, 1999), 30.

p. 76 *"the dislike and even hatred"*: Chernyayev diary for 1972 in English translation, at http://nsarchive.gwu.edu/NSAEBB/NSAEBB379/.

p. 80 *"I came here"*: references to Gorbachev's memoirs are the author's translations from the Russian original, *Zhizn i reformy* (Life and Reforms), 2 vols. (Moscow: Novosti, 1995); available in English as *Memoirs* (New York: Doubleday, 1996).

p. 82 *Moscow Spring*: William and Jane A. Taubman, *Moscow Spring* (New York: Summit Books, 1989).

p. 83 *"alienated youth with their protest rock"*: Vida Johnson and Elena Stishova, "Perestroika and Post-Soviet Cinema 1985–2000s," in Rimgaila Salys, ed., *The Russian Cinema Reader: The Thaw to the Present* (Boston: Academic Studies Press, 2013), 194.

Chapter 4

p. 90 *"god, tsar, and master"*: author's translation from the Russian original, *Ispoved na zadannuyu temu* (Confession on an Assigned Theme) (Moscow: PIK, 1990); available in English as *Against the Grain* (New York: Simon & Schuster, 1990).

p. 92 *"the Achilles' heel of Soviet federalism"*: Henry E. Hale, "Making and Breaking Ethnofederal States: Why Russia Survives Where the USSR Fell," *Perspectives on Politics* 3 (March 2005), 55–70.

p. 95 *"would start building its own ark"*: Serhii Plokhy, *The Last Empire: The Final Days of the Soviet Union* (New York: Basic Books, 2014), 218–19.

p. 99 *"A united empire"*: references to the second volume of Yeltsin's memoirs are the author's translations from the Russian original, *Zapiski prezidenta* (Notes of a President) (Moscow: Ogonyok, 1994); available in English as *The Struggle for Russia* (New York: Crown, 1994).

p. 104 *"rebuilding a ship on the open sea"*: Jon Elster et al., *Institutional Design in Post-Communist Societies: Rebuilding the Ship at Sea* (Cambridge: Cambridge University Press, 1998).

p. 109 *"more like the competition of viziers"*: Andrei Soldatov and Irina Borogan, *The Red Web: The Struggle between Russia's Digital Dictators and the New Online Revolutionaries* (New York: PublicAffairs, 2015), 53.

p. 118 *"more than 80 percent of the former Soviet nomenklatura"*: Stephen White, "Soviet Nostalgia and Russian Politics," *Journal of Eurasian Studies* 1 (January 2010), 2.

p. 121 *"been downgraded from a great power"*: Strobe Talbott, *The Russia Hand: A Memoir of Presidential Diplomacy* (New York: Random House, 2002), 157.

p. 121 *"galloped through the agenda"*: ibid., 67.

p. 127 *"I never liked and I do not like"*: references to the third volume of Yeltsin's memoirs are the author's translations from the Russian original, *Prezidentskii marafon* (Presidential Marathon) (Moscow: AST, 2000); available in English as *Midnight Diaries* (New York: PublicAffairs, 2000).

Chapter 5

p. 134 *"petty kitchen squabbles"*: references to these revealing interviews are the author's translations from the Russian original, *Ot pervogo litsa: razgovory s Vladimirom Putinym* (From the First Person: Conversations with Vladimir Putin) (Moscow: VAGRIUS, 2000); available in English as *First Person: An Astonishingly Frank Self-Portrait by Russia's President* (New York: PublicAffairs, 2000).

p. 136 *"made himself indispensable"*: Steven Lee Myers, *The New Tsar: The Rise and Reign of Vladimir Putin* (New York: Knopf, 2015), 62.

p. 137 *"working with people"*: Fiona Hill and Clifford G. Gaddy, *Mr. Putin: Operative in the Kremlin* (Washington: Brookings Institution Press, 2013), 185.

p. 141 *"one of those who were passively waiting"*: Gleb Pavlovsky, "Putin's World Outlook," interview by Tom Parfitt in *New Left Review* (July–August 2014); at http://newleftreview.org/II/88/gleb-pavlovsky-putin-s-world-outlook.

p. 141 *"Millennium Manifesto"*: author's translation from the original Russian; available in English at http://pages.uoregon.edu/kimball/Putin.htm.

p. 147 *"One moment Surkov would fund"*: Peter Pomerantsev, *Nothing Is True and Everything Is Possible: The Surreal Heart of the New Russia* (New York: PublicAffairs, 2014), 67.

p. 147 *"a viable and charismatic candidate"*: Karen Dawisha, *Putin's Kleptocracy: Who Owns Russia?* (New York: Simon & Schuster, 2014), 250–51.

p. 153 *"are afraid to ask for clarifications"*: Yevgeny Gontmakher, "Russian Federalism: Reality or Myth?" in Leon Aron, ed., *Putin's Russia: How It Rose, How It Is Maintained, and How It Might End* (Washington: American Enterprise Institute, 2015), 43.

p. 153 *"a new political triangle"*: Elena Chebankova, "Adaptive Federalism and Federation in Putin's Russia," *Europe-Asia Studies* 60 (August 2008), 997–98.

p. 153 *"clientelistic exchange"*: Grigorii V. Golosov, "Machine Politics: The Concept and Its Implications for Post-Soviet Studies," *Demokratizatsiya/Democratization* 21 (Fall 2013), 459–80.

p. 158 *"intimately, obsessively, involved"*: Myers, *New Tsar*, 435.

p. 161 *"a personal creed"*: Thane Gustafson, *Wheel of Fortune: The Battle for Oil and Power in Russia* (Cambridge, Mass.: Harvard University Press, 2012), 280.

p. 161 *"In one flash"*: ibid., 293.

p. 162 *"silovarch"*: Daniel Treisman, "Putin's Silovarchs," *Orbis* 51 (January 2007), 141–53.

p. 162 *"our own class of capitalists"*: Pavlovsky, "Putin's World Outlook."

p. 163 *"a defining element was machismo"*: Helena Goscilo, ed., *Putin as Celebrity and Cultural Icon* (Abingdon: Routledge, 2013); Valerie Sperling, *Sex, Politics, and Putin: Political Legitimacy in Russia* (Oxford: Oxford University Press, 2014); Elizabeth Wood, "Hypermasculinity as a Scenario of Power: Vladimir Putin's Iconic Rule, 1999–2008," forthcoming in *International Feminist Journal of Politics*.

p. 167 *"What was for most Western capitals"*: William H. Hill, *Russia, the Near Abroad, and the West: Lessons from the Moldova-Transdniestria Conflict* (Washington: Woodrow Wilson Center Press, 2012), xii.

p. 170 *"quiet military revolution"*: Gustav Gressel, "Russia's Quiet Military Revolution and What It Means for Europe" (Berlin: European Council on Foreign Relations, October 2015); at http://www.ecfr.eu/publications/summary/russias_quiet_military_revolution_and_what_it_means_for_europe4045.

p. 173 *"the country needs change"*: Pavlovsky, "Putin's World Outlook."

p. 173 *"talked of what his speechwriters thought to call"*: Masha Gessen, *The Man without a Face: The Unlikely Rise of Vladimir Putin* (New York: Riverhead Books, 2012), 264.

p. 174 *"When Medvedev told a group"*: ibid.

p. 177 *"a general loss of faith"*: Daniel Treisman, "Putin's Popularity: Why Did Support for the Kremlin Plunge, Then Stabilize?" unpublished paper, February 2014; at http://www.sscnet.ucla.edu/polisci/faculty/treisman/PAPERS_NEW/Putins%20popularity%20draft%20Jan%202014%203.pdf.

Chapter 6

p. 183 *"the issue that first sensitized them"*: Bohdan Nahaylo and Victor Swoboda, *Soviet Disunion: A History of the Nationalities Problem in the USSR* (New York: Free Press, 1990), 161.

p. 194 *"a repetitive plethora"*: Andrew Monaghan, "A 'New Cold War'? Abusing History, Misunderstanding Russia" (London: Chatham House, May 2015); at https://www.chathamhouse.org/sites/files/chathamhouse/field/field_document/20150522ColdWarRussiaMonaghan.pdf.

p. 199 *"the transformation of the BRICS club"*: Cynthia Roberts, "Are the BRICS Building a Non-Western Concert of Powers?" July 2015; at http://nationalinterest.org/feature/are-the-brics-building-non-western-concert-powers-13280.

p. 201 *"quick, effective, and strategically transformational"*: Robert Fry, "Putin's Syria Success Puts Western Military Strategy to Shame," March 24, 2016; at http://www.prospectmagazine.co.uk/world/putins-syria-success-puts-western-foreign-policy-to-shame.

p. 201 *"appears to have made great strides"*: Dmitry Gorenburg, "Russia's Syria Operation Reveals Significant Improvement in Military Capability," November 2015; at http://www.lowyinterpreter.org/post/2015/11/13/Russias-Syria-operation-reveals-significant-improvement-in-military-capability.aspx.

p. 206 *"Acting with impunity"*: Stanislav Markus, *Property, Predation, and Protection: Piranha Capitalism in Russia and Ukraine* (Cambridge: Cambridge University Press, 2015), 11.

p. 208 *"Sharp fluctuations in Russian mortality rates"*: David Zaridze et al., "Alcohol and Cause-Specific Mortality in Russia: A Retrospective Case-Control Study of 48,557 Adult Deaths," June 2009; at http://www.ncbi.nlm.nih.gov/pmc/articles/PMC2715218/.

p. 209 *"A recent report"*: English version is Vladimir Arkhangelsky et al., *Demographic Policies of the Russian Federation: Challenges and Scenarios* (Moscow: Russian Presidential Academy of the National Economy and Public Administration, 2015).

p. 212 *"an ombudsman against himself"*: Gleb Pavlovsky, *Sistema RF v voine 2014 goda* (The Russian Federation's System in the War of 2014) (Moscow: Yevropa, 2014), 55.

p. 215 *"asked to repay the allegedly stolen amounts"*: Alina Mungiu-Pippidi, *The Quest for Good Governance: How Societies Develop Control of Corruption* (Cambridge: Cambridge University Press, 2015), 154.

p. 217 *"organizations receiving a clean bill of financial health"*: Debra Javeline and Sarah Lindemann-Komarova, "A Balanced Assessment of Russian Civil Society," *Journal of International Affairs* 63 (Spring/Summer 2010), 175.

p. 219 *"As Robert D. Putnam has argued"*: Robert D. Putnam, *Making Democracy Work: Civic Traditions in Modern Italy* (Princeton: Princeton University Press, 1994).

p. 220 *"Oftentimes, grievances were addressed to"* and *"A combination of survival mentality"*: Mikhail Dmitriev, "Evolution of Values and Political Sentiment in Moscow and the Provinces," in Aron, *Putin's Russia*, 74, 81.

p. 221 *"socialist realism with a minus sign"*: Nancy Condee, *The Imperial Trace: Recent Russian Cinema* (Oxford: Oxford University Press, 2009), 62.

p. 222 *"have their own style"*: Tatiana Smorodinskaia, Karen Evans-Romaine, and Helena Goscilo, eds., *Encyclopedia of Contemporary Russian Culture* (Abingdon: Routledge, 2007), 61.

p. 222 *"providing a spectacle"*: Condee, *Imperial Trace*, 85.

p. 231 *"They have few charismatic and professionally educated clergymen"*: Alexei Malashenko, "The Dynamics of Russian Islam" (Moscow: Moscow Carnegie Center, February 2013); at http://carnegieendowment.org/files/Article_Malashenko_Moscow_English.pdf.

p. 234 *"The more well-to-do a nation"*: Seymour Martin Lipset, "Some Social Requisites of Democracy: Economic Development and Political Legitimacy," *American Political Science Review* 53 (March 1959), 75.

p. 238 *"pluralism by default"*: Lucan Way, *Pluralism by Default: Weak Autocrats and the Rise of Competitive Politics* (Baltimore: Johns Hopkins University Press, 2015).

INDEX